# interactive art and embodiment

## THE IMPLICIT BODY AS PERFORMANCE

Nathaniel Stern

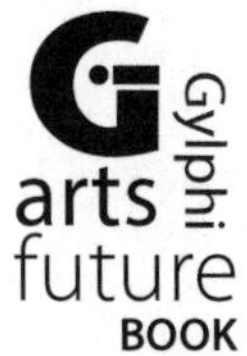

A *Gylphi Limited* Book

First published in Great Britain in 2013
by Gylphi Limited



A CIP catalogue record for this book is available from the British Library.

ISBN 978-1-78024-009-1 (pbk)
ISBN 978-1-78024-010-7 (Kindle)
ISBN 978-1-78024-011-4 (EPUB)

Cover image: *undertoe* | a proposal by Greg Shakar and Nathaniel Stern | rendering by Tana Green | *undertoe* is discussed in the book's companion chapter at http://stern.networkedbook.org. Cover design and typesetting by Gylphi Limited. Printed in the UK by imprintdigital.com, Exeter.

Gylphi Limited
PO Box 993
Canterbury CT1 9EP
UK

Small portions of this book have appeared, as partial/earlier drafts, in the *Leonardo* journal Vol. 44 No. 3 (2011, MIT Press, © ISAST), and *Cyberculture and New Media* (2009, Rodopi) – the latter in collaboration with Nicole Ridgway. Some of its preliminary ideas first appeared in *Consciousness, Theatre, Literature and the Arts 2007* (Cambridge Scholars Publishing), *Perspectives: International Postgraduate Journal of Philosophy* (2008, UCD), and on *Rhizome.org*.

*with Nicole and Sidonie*
*'my girls'*

**Partners and Associates**

- The Center for 21st Century Studies, an interdisciplinary research institute at the University of Wisconsin-Milwaukee, USA.
- HUMlab, Umeå University, Sweden, a dedicated laboratory for research into the digital humanities.
- Jussi Parikka, Reader in Media and Design, Winchester School of Art, University of Southampton.
- PhD2Published an organization offering academic book publishing advice to early career academics while investigating technical developments in systems for distributing academic research.
- if:book a think and do tank exploring the future of the book in the digital age.
- Proboscis, an organization developing online tools and offline models that challenge the physical format of the book including bookleteer.com and StoryCubes.
- Open Mute/Progressive Publishing Service, an organization supporting cultural practice in the information age, building knowledge architectures and new publishing tools for cross-platform content.

# Contents

# List of Figures

# Acknowledgments

First and foremost, I would like to thank my inspiration, best friend, collaborator, editor, and life partner over what have been the best years of my life, Nicole Ridgway, as well as our amazing daughter, Sidonie Ridgway Stern. Your guidance, support, and love have made all things possible. Thank you also to my parents, Jeanette and Phil, my aunt Harriet, my sister Samantha and her family, and my dearly departed uncle, Dan – you are always with me. Special thanks go to the Arts Future Book series editor and my now good friend, Charlotte Frost, for her insights and occasional drink runs during the review and editing process.

I am extremely grateful to The Center for 21st-Century Studies (and all my fellow fellows) at the University of Wisconsin–Milwaukee (UWM), most specifically Richard Grusin and John Blum, as well as to my other colleagues at UWM who read various texts along the way, especially Kennan Ferguson and Peter Paik. Many thanks go to my former PhD supervisor, telecommunications engineer Linda Doyle, for her ongoing encouragement, counsel, and trust, as well as her convictions around the vitality of art and technology at large. Thank you, too, to Sven Anderson, Martin McCabe, and Monica Pearl for their invaluable feedback on the nascent text.

Thank you to my colleagues in the Department of Art and Design, and Peck School of the Arts, especially my mentor, Denis Sargent; and my students who help me embody and practice what I teach. My various studio assistants – Bryan Cera, Jesse Egan, D. Kent Watson, Joseph Grennier, Chris Butzen, Foster Stilp, Garrett Gharibeh, Angela McFarlane, Wyatt Tinder, Andrew McConville, Neetu Katiyar, and Rhianna Lynn Andrews – have been remarkable in helping my art and writing come alive. This book would not have been possible without the support I received from Trinity College Dublin, the UWM Graduate School, UWM Office of Undergraduate Research, and UWM Research Growth Initiative.

The book could also not have happened without my ongoing practice as an artist. To my UWM collaborators Jessica Meuninck-Ganger, Yevgeniya Kaganovich, Jennifer Johung, Mike Lovell, Brian Thompson, and Ilya Avdeev: I am indebted to your strength and inspiration. The Milwaukee art scene gets props, with special mention for their support: Mary Louise Schumacher and the Art City gang, Lynne Shumow at the Haggerty Museum, Graeme Reid,

Polly Morris, Elaine Erickson, Jeff Ganger, and Brad Lichtenstein; as does my man in Chicago, Patrick Lichty, and my online / distance collaborator, Scott Kildall. *Furtherfield.org* (Ruth Catlow, Marc Garrett, Alessandra Scapin, and others) and Michael Szpakowski: I am grateful for your inspired work and feedback over the years. Many thanks to the parties that guided my thinking and making back at the Interactive Telecommunications Program – most of all, Marianne Petit (also of Greylock Arts), Dan O'Sullivan, Danny Rozin, Tom Igoe, David Schwarz, Greg Shakar, and Red Burns – as well as in South Africa – in particular Alet Vorster, Wilhelm van Rensburg, Christo Doherty, Tegan Bristow, Marcus Neustetter, Sean Slemon, Franci Cronje, Clive Kellner, William Kentridge, Jillian Ross, Colleen Alborough, João Orecchia, and David Krut. Jo-Anne Green and Helen Thorington of *Turbulence.org* deserve infinite praise for their support of thousands of artists worldwide, including me. Erin Manning, Brian Massumi, Christoph Brunner, Troy Rhoades, and all the cats at The Sense Lab: the world is a better place with you in it – as are my life and work; thank you for your ongoing inspiration, stimulation, friendship, and belief in what we do and make, together.

I feel exceptionally privileged to work with all of these wonderful people – who continue to inspire me as producer, academic, and thinker – and so many more not mentioned.

## About the Author

**Nathaniel Stern** is an Associate Professor of Art and Design in Peck School of the Arts at the University of Wisconsin–Milwaukee, and a Research Associate at the Research Centre, Faculty of Art, Design, and Architecture, University of Johannesburg.

# Series Foreword

## Butterflies Unpinned

> Considering that, in the domain of art and of the spirit's very spontaneous inclinations, things have freshness and virtue only as long as they are left unnamed, the cultural club, in its eagerness to heavy-handedly name and endorse, fills a function comparable to that of the butterfly catcher. Culture cannot stand butterflies that fly. It knows no rest until it has immobilized and labelled them. (Jean Dubuffet, *Asphyxiating Culture and Other Writings,* New York, Four Walls Eight Windows, 1986, p. 46)

I was accepted in 2005 to produce a poster presentation at 'Refresh!', the 'First International Conference on the Histories of Media Art, Science and Technology' held in Banff, Canada. For some reason, despite being an art historian (and sometimes maker), the idea of presenting my work on a poster seemed wrong. Somehow it felt too much like making a page out of a book and I felt anxious about certain contradictions between the subject of my studies and print media. Or, to put it another way, I was becoming increasingly interested in the relations between the form and content of art history, criticism and theory. In the end I opted for a rather tongue-in-cheek format which I felt would literally demonstrate these concerns as well as share my research.

My poster presentation was on email discussion list culture and its relationship to art history, and consisted of a number of pages of writing (printed in Courier New) attached with an excessive amount of pins to my allocated boards. These pages were then studded with butterfly-shaped acetate prints of Internet artworks with their wings bent so they stood away from the surface. As the first visitors arrived for the poster session (and I panicked over the jarringly low-fi aesthetics of my poster presentation alongside all the other glossy, professional-looking panels), I whipped out a handheld fan and pointed it at my board so that it was a ripple of flickering pages and flapping butterfly wings. Here was a display on a highly mobile art historical archive, incongruously represented in print and clumsily reanimated by an art historian holding a fan, which raised important questions about the correct 'habitat' within which to stage such analyses.

The Arts Future Book series represents a substantial effort in answering some of the questions about how and where we should encounter the history, criticism and theorization of emerging – and often technology-rich – artforms. The series fosters new scholarship in the arts, and publishes unique works that rethink contemporary visual culture and establish new systems for considering art. It highlights aspects of the impact of digital technologies on contemporary culture and indicates the ways in which technology informs our knowledge of the arts. The series additionally exploits recent technological advances in publishing to better disseminate such bodies of arts knowledge and develop wider readership and new reader experiences. Its premise is the notion that ideas are formed in dialogue with the media that represent them and that authors can actively forge the future of disciplines by recreating their core media. Each project within the series respects established academic standards, while redefining what an academic text might be and how it might be used. In short, if you thought you knew what an art history / criticism / theory book was, think again!

Charlotte Frost
Series Editor, Arts Future Book

# Introduction

## Art Philosophy

More than a decade before I write these words, I was in Dan O'Sullivan's 'Physical Computing' class at the Interactive Telecommunications Program (ITP), New York University. It was still the dotcom boom and so the world was flush; the streets around Broadway and Waverly seemed abuzz with coffee, Radio Shacks, startups, and geek speak; 'interactive' – not that we agreed on a definition for the word – was all the rage, and ITP was blazing ahead with computer vision technologies, creative microcontrolling, networked art, and more. The next generation of researching makers was figuring out what we could do with all this technological *stuff*, whether it had value, and where that value lay.[1]

So there I was, shifting as I stood, waving my hands around as I spoke, exuberantly explaining to my peers what I hoped to produce for *enter*, my first, large-scale, interactive installation (Figure 1).[2] My most basic goal when I began designing the installation was to invite participants to experience and practice meaning-making and bodiliness as relationally emergent activities. The work's interactors, I explained as I performed by example, use their full bodies to grab animated words that constantly retreat from them on a large projection screen. If they touch any one, I said as I stretched my right arm while up on my tiptoes, it stops, turns red, and recites spoken word in the space. Words *run away* from us, as we *turn* on a phrase, or *reach* (for) the end of a sentence.

I gave a long and very energetic monologue to the class about what I was working on. Everyone noiselessly paused when I finished, intensifying the dampened sounds of city traffic, four floors below us. Out of breath and a little anxious, I tried to figure out whether the silence was because of an interested thoughtfulness around such an interaction, distaste for the situation it set up, or wariness around its feasibility given the technologies of the day. After a short while, my professor said something along the lines of, 'It'd be great if you could get people to move the way you do when you talk.'

It was an astonishing thought, and one I've been engaging with on some level ever since. I do not believe Dan O, as his students and colleagues call him, was asking me to elicit a specific, semiotic gesture or classifiable behavior from my viewers; rather, he meant for me – and them – to think off the screen and outside the interface. And this became my core intention with the work. *enter* is neither about looking at or reading projected text; and nor is it simply a choreographed direction in front of an image. It is a *situation* that accents embodiment and signification as on the same plane of existence. It *frames* how we *move–think–feel* with and as an active body, with and as an articulation of meaning. Moving and thinking and feeling, I am arguing, are all a part of the same process, and interactive artworks such as *enter* stage a *rehearsal* of some of their possibilities.

When we move and think and feel, we are, of course, a body. This body is constantly changing, in and through its ongoing relationships. This body is a dynamic form, full of potential. It is not 'a body,' as thing, but *embodiment* as incipient activity. Embodiment is a continuously emergent and active relation. It is our materialization and articulation, both as they occur, and about to occur. Embodiment is moving–thinking–feeling, it is the body's potential to vary, it is the body's relations to the outside. And embodiment, I contend, is what is staged in the best interactive art.

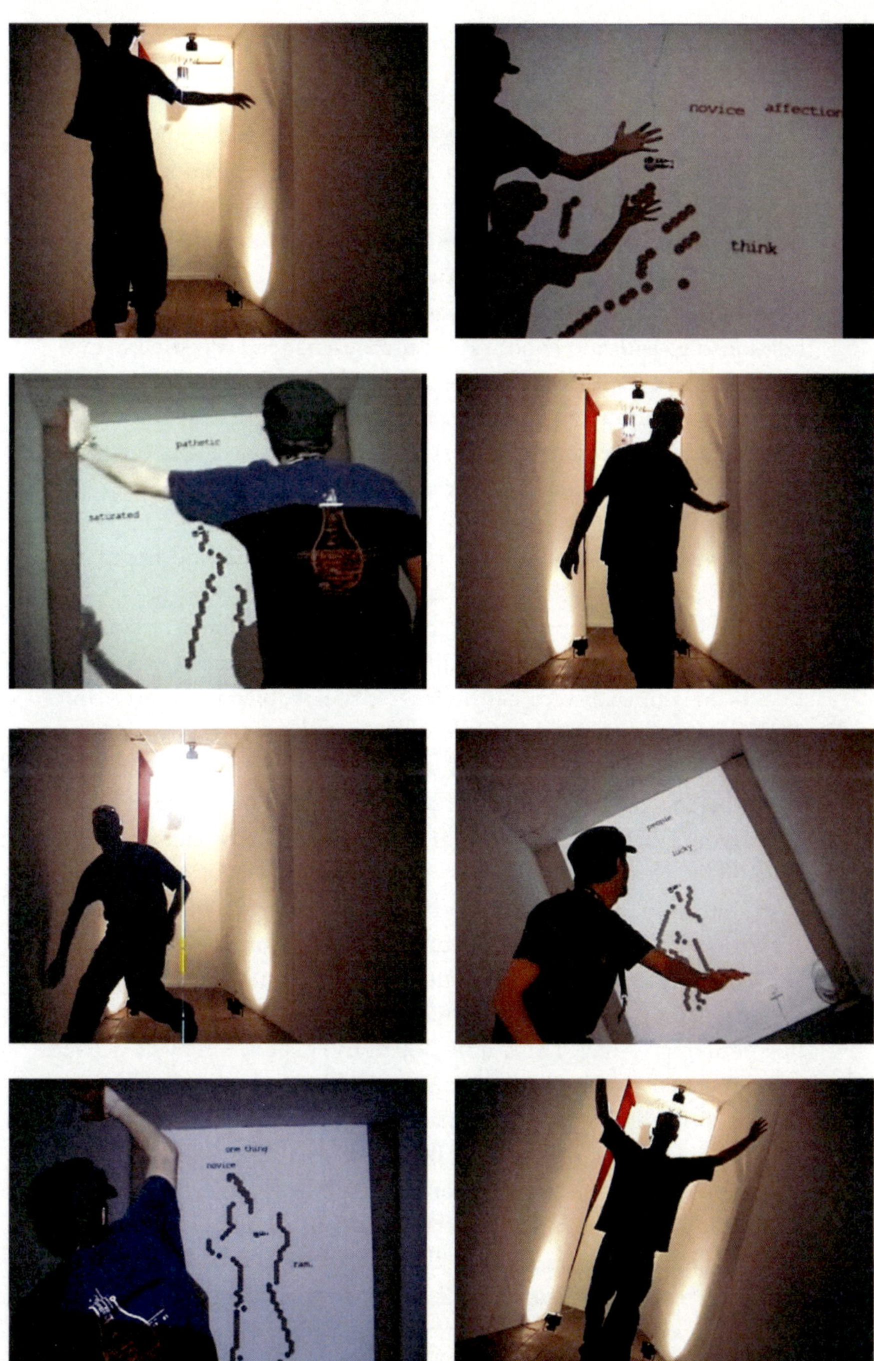


Figure 1. Nathaniel Stern, *enter*, 2000–2013

Interactive art frames moving–thinking–feeling *as* embodiment; here 'the body' is addressed as it is formed, and in relation. Interactive installations amplify how the body's inscriptions, meanings, and matters unfold out, while the world's sensations, concepts, and matters enfold in. The work creates situations that enhance, disrupt, and alter experience and action in ways that call attention to our varied relationships *with* and *as* both structure and matter. I suggest that new media has the ability to intervene in, and challenge, not only the construction of bodies and identities, but also the ongoing and emergent processes of embodiment, as they happen. My main focus throughout this text is a framework for the critical experience, practice, and analysis of contemporary art. I ask, 'How might the body – as process and event – and its potential disruption or resistance, be attendant, provoked, and contextualized in interactive art?'

What you hold in your hands is an *art philosophical* book. It is about how we might move–think–feel different philosophies, in (art's) practice. It does not advance aesthetics – a philosophy about art – but rather understands art and philosophy as potential *practices* of one another. It is about rehearsing the possibilities of what and how we might be, through what and how we perform. Art and philosophy, in other words, have the ability to create, transform, and mobilize each other.[3]

As philosopher and writer Brian Massumi tells us, 'philosophy and art bookend science,' and where philosophy is 'thought-sensed,' art is 'sensationally performed' (Massumi, 2002: 252). More simply, philosophy is thought (and felt), while art is felt (and thought). In each, our 'thinking-feeling' (Massumi, 2002: 135) is continuously active, changing, *moving*. This moving is virtual and actual: we move and are moved. Both philosophy and art present what I go on to call moving–thinking–feeling (or affect), but do so in different modes. Art is 'actually expressed'. It presents, or re-presents, affect in context. It is with us in the room: not an object per se, but a limitation, a contextual framing that invites moving–thinking–feeling. Philosophy is 'virtually expressed' (Massumi, 2002: 252). It opens and has us move–think–feel connections; it contains the potential for action. Art provokes affection, philosophy invokes reflection, and the two work together, in practice. Philosophy tells us the stakes, art brings those stakes to the table – usually as material form. With *enter,* for example, we move–think–feel the making of bodies and meaning, together. We see and feel how they manifest: as a practice, in the practice, and with the practice, of each other – what Karen Barad calls a discursive practice. We rehearse how and why bodies and meaning come to matter. Interactive artworks like *enter,* I am arguing, set a stage for such mutually emergent practices. They frame our practice for us. We are *there,* moving and thinking and feeling, affecting and reflecting and becoming. Interactive installations give us situations where we might develop and produce a *sense* of philosophy.

But what is interactive art? Is this a genre? A medium? An art movement? Must a work be physically active to be classified as such, or do we interact when we sense and make sense? Is a switch-throw or link-click enough – I do *this,* and *that* happens – or must subjects and objects be confused over time? Is interaction multiple in its engagements (relational), or a one-to-one reaction (programmed)? Are interactive designs somehow more democratic and individualized than others, or is that merely a commercial strategy to sell products and ideas?

When I began writing this book, I tried to define interactive art as 'work' where 'the *work* of the art' is the movement of the viewer – and the affection and reflection thereabouts. But this is not really a definition of interactive art; it is, rather, a loose description of the framework with which I hope to approach interactive art. Such a definition also leads to problematic questions like, 'What is the "work" in a landscape painting, sculpture, or video?' The answers are contextual for each piece, rather than based on a medium or genre. My objective is to pose ways of placing emphasis on the potential of individual interactive artworks within its category, not to capture, define, or value it categorically. I begin and end with singular works in the gallery space, and am interested in creating a discrete critical framework for encountering interactive art.[4]

For the purposes of clarity, I define interactive art (and interactive installations) as including works of electronic and digital art that feature: various forms of sensors or cameras for input; computers, microcontrollers, simple electronic circuits, or other digital or analogical terminals for processing; and any form of sensory output – audiovisual, tactile, olfactory, mechanical, or otherwise; where all are placed together in a system that responds to the embodied participation of viewers, either in real-time, and/or over lengths of time. And in these circumstances, interactivity is understood as the required physical activity of a viewer–participant in order to fully realize a technology-generated and process-based work. I do not include performances such as happenings, relational, or Situationist art because these are very different in form, experience, and import. Neither do I include interactive technologies used by performers we, as spectators, watch – a very different experience from performing the piece oneself. I also avoid simple navigable or hypertext works, such as websites or DVDs, or goal-oriented and videogame-based art that uses gaming controllers and consoles directly. This is not to devalue any of the aforementioned categories of art on any level, or the forms of interactive art that pre-dated such work's dominance in the late 1990s to the present day. Rather, I recognize the need for a different kind of emphasis in understanding the potential of each.[5]

Although necessary for the sake of differentiation and thus critique, understanding interactive art in this way suggests a flawed priority: an emphasis on the computer, sensor or projection, on the tools we use rather than the situations they create. We focus not 'on the dynamic form of experience… It is the form of the technical object that is emphasized, for what it affords' (Massumi, 2011: 45–6). If we explain what interactive art *is* primarily through technology, then we will comprehend it as merely a technological object. We should, rather, approach what interactive art *does* – and what we do – when it frames our moving–thinking–feeling. And that is precisely the project of this book. I pose that we forget technology and remember the body. *Re-member*: Embody again. Art and media histories have frequently (mis)categorized both information and the body in technology as immaterial, while new media theory has often (mis)understood the act of looking as discrete and incorporeal rather than as cross-modal and embodied. I revisit perception, data, embodiment, and interactivity in the technological realm, and call for a material approach to digital art more broadly, one that does not focus on 'new media' itself (Chapter 1).

Art theorist and curator, Christiane Paul, describes digital art as work that uses any form of new media technology either as a tool for production – ending up, for example, as a digital print or fabricated sculpture – or as a real-time medium where the piece is stored and presented in a digital format. This includes interactive software that responds to users or the environment, Internet art we engage on a screen, or reactive and kinetic sculptures that use microcontrollers for processing (Paul, 2002: 471–2). Paul's shift from thinking about digital technologies solely as a production tool (or illusion machine) to additionally thinking about them as a medium facilitates an analysis of the networked and reactive interface as art with which we interact – what she calls the 'post-object' (Paul, 2002: 473) – and which, in turn, affects our understandings of ourselves. I continue Paul's trajectory of thinking, going from object to post-object and then to situation, from computer to interface and then to our embodied styles of relation within that situation. Interactive art, I maintain, is itself a situational framework for the experience and practice of being and becoming. It requires an art philosophy, a critical framework, that engages with that potential.

The materials used in, and for, this work can span anything from phones, laptops, or the software either contains, to transgenic art, tissue engineering, or body modification. Rather than trying to make all-inclusive and potentially exclusionary lists, digital arts curators like Sarah Cook and Beryl Graham prefer to problematize new media's novelty by referring to 'the artworks currently or formerly known as "new media art"' (Cook and Graham, 2010: 4). I tend to draw a very inclusive circle around new media, in this book mostly concentrating on digital art, computer art, and electronic art. I go between them in usage to avoid too much repetition, but they should not be read as precisely synonymous terms. While all computer art is digital on some level – utilizing zeroes and ones as data – digital works do not necessarily require a computer (they may use digital machines such as player pianos or musical jewelry boxes), and electronic art may be completely analogical (using only sensors and motors, sound equipment or tube televisions, without analog to digital conversion or processors).

The field of new media, then, refers to discourses surrounding technologies and media of the moment – the word 'new' is, after all, a relative term. Beyond the obvious fact that what gets to be labeled a new medium is 'continuously being reinvented, continually in a state of flux', media theorist Kelli Fuery argues that 'new' can be understood as previously unseen or unexperienced; as original; as viral – meaning something that induces agents, human or otherwise, to replicate it; as corruption; as interdisciplinary and polymorphic; or, as political investment. But mostly, we hear it in terms of 'consumerism, bias and trend' (Fuery, 2009: 1, 7, 11–22).

In Chapter 1, through the work of practitioners Theodore Watson, William Kentridge, Char Davies, Stelarc, and Janet Cardiff, I argue for an approach to digital and new media art that recognizes the potential to amplify *sensation*. Here sensation is understood as intensive: that which is felt (and thought). I go on to question the definition, benefits, and shortcomings of interactivity and affective bodies as they have been co-opted by commercial companies trying to sell digital products. I turn to the work of gamer artist Carlo Zanni and dancer Tero Saarinen as examples of digital art that forgo new media hype, to intervene in consumer culture narratives.

As Cook and Graham explain, each new medium passes through 'hype cycles' of technical discoveries, inflated expectations, disillusionment, enlightenment, and finally acceptance (Cook and Graham, 2010: 24). While new media are most often lumped together (rather than being separated into, for example, net art, virtual reality, robotics, and interactive art), each of these is not only at a different point on its own hype cycle, but traveling at a different speed across the slope. Only when 'the peak of inflated expectations' for each medium has passed can their long-term effects be understood (Cook and Graham, 2010: 284). I believe now is that time for interactive art. Rather than focus on interactivity as hyped up idea, we must study 'how things are done' (Cook and Graham, 2010: 12). I ask us to move–think–feel with interactive art as a space for doing, as a proscenium for the rehearsal of embodied relations.

Such a starting point for interactive art differs greatly from those offered by most media / culture texts, like Fuery's, which draw on 'poststructuralist thinkers... to explain cultural phenomena within the context of new media' (Brodsky, 2010: E22), and where new media is itself seen as a cultural phenomenon whose 'processes must always be tracked back to its sociocultural status and interventions' (Fuery, 2009: 1). In such texts, society and culture are understood through the language and images they produce and respond to. Approaches like this are ideal for understanding what is at stake in art that intervenes specifically in linguistic and visual significations. In Chapter 2, I look closely at 'explicit body' art as one example. But they are less than ideal as approaches for encountering interactive art, in practice.

Fuery states that interactions can be 'symbols for other cultural mechanisms, like ideology, subjectivity, and entropy' (Fuery, 2009: 25). Interaction, I would counter, is much more than a 'symbol.'[6] This is neither an attempt to undo the important work of poststructural theory, and its critiques of language and structure, nor to undo their readings of digital media. Not only do such critiques and readings continue to be vital to contemporary humanities discourses, but this book is in a productive dialog with them. My point of departure lies with my conviction that readings of interactive art completely embedded within language and structure occlude the potential of prelinguistic and non-representational moving–thinking–feeling. Here I align myself with affect theory and process philosophy in order to explore interactive art's potential, outside of signification alone.

The recent academic turns to embodiment and affect, process ontology and the new materialisms – which follow and interweave various trajectories of feminist studies, cultural studies, continental philosophy and more – are all attempts (at least on some level) to address the questions and potentialities around 'active, agential... self-differing and affective-affected matter,' to '"fluidify" the boundaries between nature / culture and matter / signification' (Parikka, 2010). Karen Barad, both a feminist theorist and particle physicist, highlights a stark contrast between poststructural and process-based approaches, broadly construed, when she says:

> Language has been granted too much power. The linguistic turn, the semiotic turn, the interpretative turn, the cultural turn: it seems that at every turn lately every 'thing' – even materiality – is turned into a matter of language or some other form of cultural representation. The ubiquitous puns on 'matter' do not, alas, mark a rethinking of the key concepts (materiality and signification) and the relationship between them. Rather, it seems to be symptomatic of the extent to which matters of 'fact' (so to speak) have been replaced with matters of signification (no scare quotes here). Language matters. Discourse matters. Culture matters. There is an important sense in which the only thing that does not seem to matter anymore is matter.... How did language come to be more trustworthy than matter? (Barad, 2003: 801)

Matter matters, at least as much as language and (its) structure. Matter matters, at least as much as its metaphorization and theorization. I follow in Barad's wake in examining interactivity as more than a symbol or theory. I investigate the matter of the body and its movement, its physical interaction with new media art (and new media's materials) simultaneously with the forces of culture and structure, language and images, on and with embodiment. As with philosophy and art, these are understood as potential practices of one another.

Interactive artist Daniel Rozin's series of mirrors, which are made of uncommon materials, provide a case in point. His *Wooden Mirror* (1999) reflects back at passersby as they cross the threshold into ITP on the fourth floor of 721 Broadway. Eight-hundred and thirty wood chips carved as squares with concave surfaces are on individual servo motors. Each one can quickly point up towards lights on the ceiling – making it very bright – down towards the floor so it is mostly in shadow, or at any one of over 200 positions of grayscale (we could call it woodgrainscale) in between. A small web camera in the center of the 'mirror' captures live video of everything directly in front of it, and converts black and white image data into wooden-pixel positioning: a live woodcut. Aside from the seemingly magical material that begs investigations into our understandings and experiences of dynamics and stasis, I have witnessed many interesting embodied performances in / with this piece. People hide from and seek for each other, the camera, and the wood; they slow and quicken their gestures, dance,

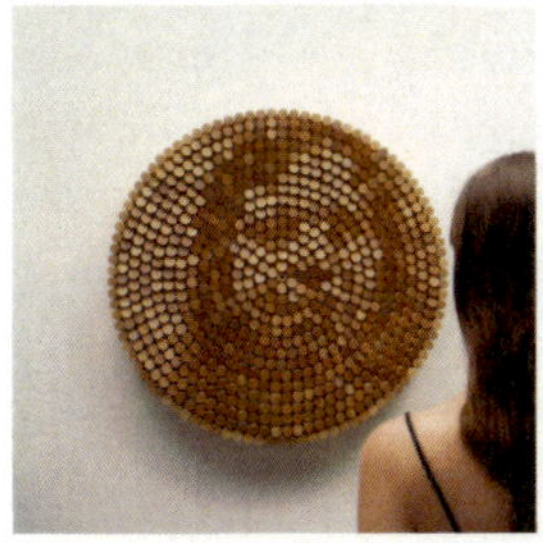
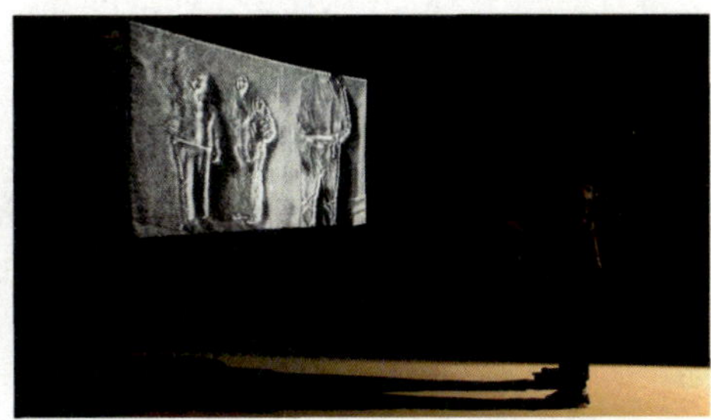

Figure 2. Daniel Rozin | Left: *Peg Mirror*, 2007 | 650 cylindrical wood pieces, motors, control electronics, custom software, microcontroller | diameter 41.75' / 106 cm, depth 8' / 20 cm | edition of 10 | Image courtesy Bitforms Gallery NYC | Right: *Snow Mirror*, 2006 | silk, projector, video camera, custom software, computer, black box environment | dimensions variable | edition of 6 | Installation view at the Chrysler Museum of Art | Photo by Ed Pollard | Image courtesy Bitforms Gallery NYC

and attempt to mirror the materials. They move in and around with their heads, fingers, mouths, or eyelids, which activate a single wood chip or move several in unison. They wave their arms or spin their full bodies to make the wood chips rustle like leaves in the wind. The sound of nearly a thousand click-clacks as each piece of wood flips up and down adds to how its contributors navigate the space of interaction. From anywhere and everywhere on the fourth floor, we are beckoned by a plethora of loud yet soothing and overlapping snaps of physical pixels, as the *Wooden Mirror* makes movement, and images, appear. Move, think, feel; sense, perform, do; body-mirror, wood-mirror, body-mirror; matter, body, matter.

Across the series, it is fascinating how performances change depending on the matter of matter. Rozin's *Shiny Balls Mirror* (2003, ball bearings moving forward and backward in tubes), *Circles Mirror* (2005, printed spirals and lines on disk-shaped cardboard), *Weave Mirror* (2007, literally interwoven prints that resemble a textile) and *Mirrors Mirror* (2008, individual mirrors that turn to make a reflective mosaic) each materialize differently: ever-changing images, bodies, performances, 'stuff'. In *Act/React*, an exhibition at the Milwaukee Art Museum, Rozin exhibited *Peg Mirror* (2007) and *Snow Mirror*

(2006) side by side to great effect (Figure 2). The former is a lower-resolution wooden mirror variation, with rotating and slanted pegs that reflect and direct light and shadow in their circular positioning. The latter is a video software projection, which slowly reveals our bodies in what looks like falling snow. The subtle temporal differences in these newer works bring possibilities for more affective and reflective feedback between bodies, media, matter, and culture. In *Peg Mirror*, for example, the very slow rotation of each individual pixel means that there is a lovely lag that trails off behind everything we do. It is less of a direct response, and more of a call and response with our reduced, or distilled, movement materials. *Snow Mirror* breaks direct mirroring by building an image, which is also not an image, over a kind of tangible time, with external forces – the snow constitutes us, as we produce it, in intensified movement and stasis. This is more than structural, cultural, or linguistic in its investigation, in that we are asked to remember our interactions and their lasting affects / effects across matter and its matters. It asks, 'What does movement do, change, make?' Here is a situational framework for practicing philosophy. It is an encounter with materialization in process. It is, as the title of this book brings together, *Interactive Art and Embodiment*.

A critical framework for interactive art necessitates that we revisit both the body and interactivity in depth (Chapter 2). This begins with the distinction between a semiotic and static reading of the body, and an emergent and relational embodiment; between a language- and image-based view of the body as an independent external thing, and an embodiment that is continuously constituted through its ongoing relations. This distinction is heuristic, rather than absolute; neither 'body' can exist without the other. The conception of a continuous embodiment, however, allows us to rethink bodies as formed through how we move in, and relate to, our surroundings. Embodiment, I contend, is not a *pre-formed* thing, but incipient and *per-formed*.

Performance studies scholars like Richard Schechner examine both art that *is* performance – theatre and dance for example – and human practices *as* performance, for example political and critical discourse (Schechner, 2002). Thinkers like Barad and Nicole Ridgway have more recently come to understand bodies, physicality, and materiality as performance, and I build on their research towards an art philosophy for interactive art. A distinction between terms can help: this time between the *interactivity* of digital media and the body's *relationality*. Relationality is continuous; it is embodiment's (or materality's) always-ongoing formation. Interaction is much more finite; while it is certainly responsive, it restricts the possible outcomes of what we perform. Interaction is a limitation – but it is also an amplification. At its limits, interactive art disrupts our relational embodiment, and thus attunes us to its potentials. Embodiment is per-formed in relation, and interactive art stages us, and our surroundings, so as to suspend, amplify, and intervene that very performance.[7]

Rebecca Schneider's book, *The Explicit Body in Performance,* proposes that feminist performance artworks, mostly from the 1980s, stage and question our understandings of women's bodiliness. Annie Sprinkle's *Public Cervix Announcement,* for example, invites audiences to study the artist's cervix with a speculum and flashlight. She makes explicit, using both shock and beauty, the symbols and structures, language and images, culturally inscribed on and attributed to the female body more generally. The Latin root of explication, Schneider reminds us, means to unfold. An explicit body unfolds the meanings behind a raced or classed or gendered body to reveal the sedimented layers of how we come to understand these classifications in the first place. Explicit bodies radically literalize, and thus deconstruct, how we experience and practice the body's supposedly static identification.

The explicit body deployed in such work is an exemplary intervention into what I call *static bodies* – into the image of the body as it is constructed in culture. Chapter 2 examines the work of Karen Finley, VALIE EXPORT, and The Guerrilla Girls as excellent examples of the explicit body in performance, where penis envy, sexual desire, and a male-dominated art world are challenged through literalization and irony. In parallel to Schneider's thinking, I argue that interactive art is uniquely positioned to intervene in a *continuous embodiment.* It has the potential to question process in addition to construction. Interactive art stages an *implicit body,* not *in* performance, but *as* performance. Here the Latin root of implication, to enfold, remembers our active relations with the world. Bodies, matter, and their matters, are implicated as always unfolding and enfolded with one another to make what *is*. We engage in activities that move us, literally and metaphorically, virtually and actually, as an investigation into how construction and constitution interrelate. When I write of virtual movement, I mean the potential for change – a movement that is not-yet, but still present as a force. Virtuality is the 'immanence of a thing to its still indeterminate variation,' an 'unfolding toward the registering of an event' (Massumi, 2002: 8). With interactive art, the potential of the body is felt as a continuous variation: always happening, always about to happen. The reaches and limits of bodies and meaning are explored, *together*, to better understand how they are formed, *together*.

Interactive artworks – I give Tegan Bristow and Brian Knep as two examples – situate embodiment as always per-formed, and fold other concepts and materials with/ in that ongoing formation. They interfere in, and thus highlight, the moving–thinking–feeling of relational emergence. These works reconfigure not only the relationship between artwork and participant, but also between affect and action. They frame and intensify bodiliness, how bodies relate to and *are* through their incipient activities, giving us a space to experience and practice 'styles of being and becoming' in and with the environment (Massumi, 2011: 52). Here we encounter the implicit, implicated, and implicating body. Exploring the body's reconfiguration, intensification, and relationships with digital art in this way, looking again at interactivity, will expand both practical affection and theoretical reflection surrounding embodiment, materiality, relationality, and beyond.

Digital art theorist and practitioner Anna Munster shows us that 'digital bodies can engage incorporeally with the informatics universe precisely because digital machines can replicate, amplify and split us from the immediacy of our sensory capacities' (Munster, 2006: 18). Like the baroque – which for Munster means bizarre or irregular – embodied engagements with technology dislocate habitual experience. Munster's information aesthetics understand new media art as an intervention into both technology and the body, making each strange, and inviting us to investigate how they affect one another.

Munster thus recognizes the power of technology to highlight and intervene in relational emergence. But where she engages with (digital) art and media as topics that support her aesthetic theory, my core subject matter is individual works of (interactive) art that create their own art philosophical formations – that is, experience and practice. Here interactive art is understood as a situation for encountering the performance of bodies, of matter, of culture, of philosophy.

From the late 1990s to the present, we have seen the rise of artist–researchers who are less interested in what we see, and more interested in how we move. Their installations are not objects to be perceived, but situations where we feel relations performed. Interactive art creates encounters with our ongoing and constitutive relations. It frames the moving–thinking–feeling of how relations matter, as matter. The play in and around all that technology accents how experience and affect, action and abstraction, implicitly and explicitly relate and emerge. It is not merely that interaction – as thing – is put on display for all to see. Rather, individual interactive artworks pose a challenge to how bodies are formed, mediated, re-mediated, and re-formed in contemporary culture, asking precisely what is at stake in the ways we perform our bodies, media, concepts, and materials. We are magnified as always and actively inchoate, and rehearse how we *are*: dispersed, enacted, entwined, interfered, differentiated, shared, and continuously embodied. In this way, interactive installations exceed extant models for understanding art.

And so I offer a new framework to move–think–feel with (Chapter 3). I turn to Zach Lieberman and Golan Levin's *Messa di Voce* to help propose a concentration on four key areas when examining a given piece: artistic inquiry and process; artwork description; interactivity; and, relationality. Traditional readings of digital art and new media most often stop after the first two areas of concentration, and I assert it is the latter two that recognize the radical possibilities with interactive installation. Most writing on interactive art will explain that a given piece *is interactive*, and *how it is interactive*, but not *how we inter-act* (with emphasis on the action). This is vital to understanding the *work* of the art: what it does, and what we do. We must get away from concentrating only on the signs and images on the screen or in the interface, away from privileging the technology and what it affords. We must engage with the quality and styles of movement that are rehearsed with interactive art.

With regards to the fourth area in my framework, namely relationality, I maintain that interactive art enables participants to experience and practice *conceptual–material* relationships. How, in our interactions, does the process of embodiment relate to, for example, meaning-making or spatialization? How does the ongoing formation of each influence and inaugurate the ongoing formation of the other? I argue for, and begin, an ongoing list of what I call implicit body thematics: relational couplings between embodiment and varying activity-based themes found in contemporary interactive art. Each implicit body thematic aims to highlight a specific art-philosophy relation. They encourage intensive explorations of embodied and embodying practices, through interaction.

While a framework that breaks into four areas of examination may seem somewhat prescriptive, this is intended as a guide for shifting emphasis on how we approach and understand interactive art. Like the distinction between static and continuous bodies, the implicit body framework and thematics help accent and analyze the ways interactive art intervenes in embodied and relational performance.

In encountering and rehearsing how we interact, there is potential for different ways of relating. How might we find alternative routes of making meaning through and with embodiment? What happens when we use our bodies to listen and communicate with more care? How can we better make space in and with and for the world, and others around us, through movement? Can we take account of and change how we move and think and feel in the everyday, and what are the implications and impacts of that change? These are not idle questions. Interactive art asks us, and shows us how, to move and become differently.

The approach I propose, like interactive art, is best used in practice. In Chapters 4, 5, and 6, the implicit body framework and several of its thematics are developed and utilized in a series of intensive case studies of interactive artists and artworks, each chosen because of their exemplary staging of an implicit body and their widely recognized contributions to the field of digital art at large. I put forward and concentrate on three thematics: body-language, social-anatomies, and flesh-space.

I examine interactive installations by Simon Penny and Camille Utterback as interventions into the relational feedback loops between text and activity. These help define the body-language thematic, which, I argue, frames the performance of what philosopher Jean-Luc Nancy calls 'exscription': where bodies and meaning make one another, through their making of one another. In Penny's work, we encounter possibilities for embodying philosophy and meaning, while in Utterback's we 'make sense' of art at large, through our active and intensified re-presentations of continuous bodies and images.

The Millefiore Effect's *Front* leads us into the social-anatomies thematic by highlighting how pluralities of bodies make and transform the social world we live in, just as that world makes and transforms the many bodies inhabiting it. The social-anatomies thematic is defined with the help of Nick Crossley's 'intercorporeality': participants rehearse the collaborative and embodied formation of societal rules, while simultaneously moving–thinking–feeling society's forces on embodiment. This chapter analyzes Mathieu Briand's perspective- and perception-swapping 'systems', which make the stakes for reciprocally constitutive bodies and societies strange and almost dangerous, and Scott Snibbe's participatory narratives, which encourage different modes for fleshly contributions to story and culture.

David Rokeby's *Very Nervous System* introduces the thematic of flesh-space, where I examine artworks that suspend and intensify the relation between embodiment and spatialization. Drawing on dance philosophy from José Gil and Erin Manning, I explore 'the space of the body' as both interior and exterior, as incipient and topological. Rafael Lozano-Hemmer provides work that gives us architectures, spaces, and bodies that are dynamically mapped, and Norah Zuniga Shaw's continual transformations open up potential and agency in interaction, and relational space.

There are likely an unlimited amount of implicit body thematics worth defining and exploring, and any given interactive artwork could be experienced, practiced, and analyzed with what any number of them frame. While I offer them here as part of the *implicit body approach* for encountering interactive art, thematics could also positively feed back into the fields of new media at large, and digital art more specifically.

Chapter 7 highlights a small number of contemporary digital artworks that are not interactive by my definition, but whose production and critique still gain from an understanding of matter and bodies as relationally per-formed. Dubbed *potentialized art,* this work is performed, or transformed, through some kind of technologically mediated process. Potentialized art 'promises more than can be delivered' (Simon, 2012), and we move-think-feel with and in its 'more-than.' Discussed in the chapter are the thematics of vestigial-vision, tangible-temporality, and virtual-performance, where I briefly investigate potentialized art by fifteen contemporary artists. I close with a recent artwork of my own, exemplifying how the implicit body framework might continue to be used in order to grow understandings of embodiment and relation beyond the confines of this text, in contemporary production, research, writing, critique, and criticism. That is, I extend the theories and practices this book offers for interactive art, to ask if we can learn to perform philosophies in and with other emergent art forms – in the work's making, in our encounters with them, and in how we understand what they do.

Along these lines, in my digital companion chapter I write at length about my own interactive work from the perspective of a producing artist. This text is about moving–thinking–feeling and making, in the studio. While only the introduction for 'In Production' is included at the very end of the printed edition, the entire chapter is within the e-book, and available for free online at http://stern.networkedbook.org. Part of *networked: a networked book about networked art,* and co-published with Internet art commissioning organization, *Turbulence.org* (2012), this text is an/other form of case study, which explores the understanding of interactive art through embodiment, and vice versa, within the production of media art itself. Here my own process of making interactive and digital work becomes a somewhat fictionalized but rigorous story about performance and relationality – (mostly) from the original perspective of an artist completing a humanities-based PhD in an engineering department, rather than a professor writing a book on the topic several years out. I spend the first half of the chapter arguing for arts production as research, and an experimental form of narrative inquiry as the best way to examine the implicit (and explicit) connections that are made in the studio. The second half uses affirmative methods of creative and scholarly writing to reveal the processes that led to the book's core ideas, and continue to inform, perform, and transform their articulations as texts and works of art. The online version allows new contributions, and I invite practicing artists, curators, and scholars to make their own additions – whether as artist writings/ narrative inquiries, curatorial or critical case studies, or broad theoretical texts – to continue to expand and explore, again in reference to my title, *The Implicit Body as Performance.*

## Notes

1 For more on ITP, see 'Technology is Not Enough: The Story of NYU's Interactive Telecommunications Program' (Huff, 2011) or 'ITP Launches Entrepreneurs, Dreamers' (Connor, 2012).

2 Fuller details on *enter* are in this book's digital companion chapter at http://stern.networkedbook.org, where I tie research and performance in the studio to research and performance in the gallery space and text.

3 Elizabeth Grosz (2006: 15–16) believes philosophy need not merely be for assessing art, but can address 'the same provocations or incitements to production as art,' and can 'work *with* art or perhaps as and alongside art'. From the other side, Erin Manning and Brian Massumi (2009), who run The Sense Lab in Montreal, consider philosophical 'research to be creation in germ, and creation to produce its own concepts for thought'. I build on these foundations, among others.

4 This is similar to Kate Mondloch's (2010) goals for what she calls 'screen-reliant art'.

5 New media arts writers such as Sarah Cook, Beryl Graham, and Régine Debatty, along with Barbara Glasner and Petra Schmidt, have called the work I define as '*inter*active' *re*active (Cook and Graham, 2010: 112; Debatty, 2010; Glasner and Schmidt, 2010). I do not dispute their arguments for this classification, but in the interest of clarity, rely on the contemporary colloquial definition of interactive art.

6 Fuery (2009: 26) goes on to differentiate between 'interactivity as a practice and interactivity as a theory', but throughout her book stays mostly in the realm of metaphor, and what it means to 'become interactive'.

7 Recent choreographic thinking can also add to this discussion. For example, Susan Broadhurst's many books – some with Josephine Machon – understand that digital technologies emphasize 'the corporeal in terms of both performance and perception' (Broadhurst, 2006: xvi), and ask for a greater concentration on the moving, sensory body, and its emotive and sometimes ludic relationship to interactive interfaces. And dancer / choreographer Susan Kozel (2008: 8) more specifically seeks 'new modalities of reflection' for computer systems and interfaces through a phenomenological study of her own arts practice. She even goes so far as to say, as I do, that we must think interactivity as 'experience and practice' (Kozel, 2008: 43). What we can take from practitioners of dance is their understanding of how technology might be used to engage with movement and affect. In their language, we explore with our bodies, unpattern habits, and intervene in embodied epistemologies. With interactive art we ask not only what constitutes a body, but also what emerges along with bodies, how matter and concepts and bodies shift and change each other, and what those relations imply.

# Chapter 1

## Digital is as Digital Does

### Forgetting Technology

To truly appreciate and study what new media do, we must first acknowledge that vision is more than an isolated sense, that data has materiality, that bodies are always present with the machine, and that technology and interactivity are not inherently and always good. To feel and produce complex movements and meanings in the situation of interactive art, we must forget the computer's input / output modes that might have us mistakenly understand ourselves as information machines, simply viewing and triggering content. Whether it is a PC playing audiovisuals in reaction to button-presses and mouse movements, or the interactive artwork that senses us as a point in space or pixels on a two-dimensional plane, technology reduces us to positioned fingers, eyes, ears: data – and very little of it. But we are always more than that which the computer detects. We must forget technology and rather study the encounters it creates, the quality of our movements with them, and the techniques we rehearse in and around them. We must look with, and feel, the body.

Vision is more than external data transmitted to our eyes: it is embodied and cross-modal. Even 'data' is more than what we think: it, too, has a body. Embodiment and materialization, in other words, are central to the affection and reflection we move–think–feel with a work of art. This argument is not meant to reinscribe the mostly untempered hype of the 1990s surrounding interactive media. I want to get away from the notion that interaction invariably adds quality, so that we may rather qualify individual interactive works of art. Here we must critique the idea that interactivity's supposed provision of choice means it is intrinsically more democratic (or freeing) than other media, and show that such language – as well as that of pliable bodies – has in fact been adopted by commercial companies trying to sell us digital products. Only then can we remember that new media art might pose questions of relation outside of, in parallel to, or as a challenge against, consumer culture.

## Vision is Seeing is Looking

First and foremost, all art – from painting and drawing to digital and interactive work – is much more than that which can be observed. While placing new media along and within art history helps to contextualize its movement with and departure from the conceptual and aesthetic trajectories that came before, understanding it as visual art qua visual, alone, devalues its other properties and potentials. Looking always involves the other senses, the potential for movement, and abstraction based on past experiences. Vision folds thinking and possibilities into what we are looking at, in order for us to see. And art and media open new possibilities in that experience.

In new media scholar Mark B. N. Hansen's examination of digital images as 'postphotography,' he maintains that the body 'has become the crucial mediator between information and form (image): the supplemental sensorimotor intervention it operates coincides with the process through which the image ... is created' (Hansen, 2001b: 79). Hansen says that new media artworks activate a seeing that is completely embodied, and that this, in turn, compels us to see both seeing and embodiment differently. What he calls haptic vision – where we feel and are touched by what we see – emerges through a cooperative effort.[1] Body and image mediate one another, and the locus of perception is between, and of, the two.

Central to Hansen's critique of seeing is its elevation as the pre-eminent sense, and more importantly as an essential source of knowledge and objectivity. In this elevation, what is seen is not subjective, but fact. This misapprehension of vision has also mistakenly led to the disarticulation (or disincarnation) of the eyes from the body: if looking is objective rather than subjective, then there must not be a subject (or body) who is looking. The disembodied eye is all knowing. As Hansen acknowledges, this critique has been extensively proffered elsewhere, and rather than revisit this terrain at length,[2] he argues instead for the ways in which digital images (postphotography) highlight a proactive experience of looking in which the co-operative effort between seer and seen creates what *is*. Hansen is basically saying that with digital images we remember that vision is less than fact, but more than what we are looking at. It is an extension of touch.

Media theorist Richard Grusin (2010: 101) expands this claim to say that the body's senses are not independent, but rather 'different manifestations of touch via different bodily organs'. In other words, 'seeing the world is touching it with one's eyes, or hearing the world is touching it with one's ears, so smelling it is touching it with one's nose, or tasting it is touching it with one's tongue' (Grusin, 2010: 101). Grusin does not want to privilege touching in the same way as Hansen and others claim we have elevated seeing. His larger point is rather to articulate that our distinctions between the senses are somewhat arbitrary. He and Hansen make it obvious that perception (if you will forgive the pun) is more than meets the eye – even with what we traditionally think of as vision.

More than haptics and touch, Brian Massumi understands sight as working through our potential for movement. 'Vision has gotten bad press,' he says in an interview with a representative from V2 – an interdisciplinary center for art and media technology in Rotterdam (Massumi, 2011: 55). This is in response to a question where V2 wants to differentiate visual from interactive art; the latter, they argue, accesses more of the body's dimensions. V2 takes a position that sight erroneously dominates all of art's discourses, including those of new media. Massumi rebuts that such a standpoint misunderstands what people mean when they say 'visual.' This is 'almost always a certain mode of what in perception studies is called cross-modal transfer – a certain way that different senses interoperate' (Massumi, 2011: 55). He asserts that seeing is 'a kind of action… without the actual action – with the action appearing in potential' (Massumi, 2011: 43). Seeing is never only seeing. When we look, we understand what we can do in and with what we see.

Artist and open source advocate and practitioner, Theodore Watson, provides an example of this extension, in the form of an interactive audio installation, where seeing is derived from the other senses, cross-modally. For *audio space* (2005–8), an installation in a large empty room, Watson equips his 'viewers' with a microphone and stereo earphones on a headset, and prompts them to leave sonic messages behind. They speak phrases from personal stories, vocalize or hum tunes in relation to their activities, or whisper commands as they move around the space. Each contributor's movements and activities – where they go and at what speed, and all the sounds they make as they do so – are recorded together. Any given collaborator leaves their aural contributions across exactly the paths they spoke them, and hears past sounds from around the room as if every participant is still present and active. In other words, if I say something while standing in the centre of the space, that message will have the highest volume in the headphones for future participants in the same spot. But this sound will also be heard at a distance, at lower and lower amplitudes as listeners move further from the point where I left it. If I crawl on the floor and whisper, sprint around the edges with hard breathing, or hum an eerie tune while squatting in a corner, these actions and their soundtracks are partnered with the space, as well as past and future contributions. Participants experience the aural and multidimensional performances that came before them, while also adding their own.[3]

Watson calls his system a sonic architecture where people sculpt the space with their voices. He began with the premise that sound is often 'thought of as a transitory medium,' yet 'has an immense power to move people' (Watson, 2005). Later, Watson became more interested in using *audio space* as a psycho-acoustical instrument, where people could experience sonic forms three dimensionally (Watson, 2008). This 'relational architecture' – to borrow a phrase from interactive artist Rafael Lozano-Hemmer (Chapter 6) – is both defined and perceived invisibly, through a history of sounds and movements that take on a density in their shared creation and experience. We are invited into a virtual and immersive, but imageless, 3D tracking system to explore the relationship between the creation of sound, the production of space, and the visualization of the two. We see it, in our minds. Here perception and visualization are one and the same, and speak across all the senses, despite that there is nothing to actually *see*. Our interactive looking and doing make past, present, and future movements and sounds affective and substantial. Vision is part of sensation as a whole.

Seeing always works this way, folding in the past, present, and possible futures of our actions, and additional modes of perception. When we look at objects in a room, we understand that we can move in, around, over, and under them. Through our past experiences and other senses, we know there is more than what we are seeing directly. This is a form of 'lived abstraction' (Massumi, 2011: 55). We see what we see, and we imagine what we do not see, and both are a part of vision. 'The perceived shape of an object is [an] abstract experience of volume ... We're seeing, in the form of the object, the potential our body holds to walk around it, take another look, extend a hand and touch' (Massumi, 2011: 42). We bring to vision all our present and past experiences of embodied sensemaking to abstract and understand what we are looking at. Vision wraps potential moving–thinking–feelings into itself; we see an object's *qualities*, even when they are not visible to us (Massumi, 2011: 43). In this way, vision is an active event.

When we take three-dimensional space and capture it on a two-dimensional plane – in two-dimensional art such as perspective painting – we suspend the potential for movement. We can no longer walk to the backside of a couch in the painting's frame, touch and feel the tactility of the represented lamps and chairs with our hands and skin.

But we still abstract the work in much the same way we abstract an actual space. We still imagine we could move around it, in order to understand what we are looking at. Massumi calls this a semblance. Artists compose lines, shape, and color, to craft the experience of time and space, without time or space. It 'takes the abstraction inherent to object perception and carries it to a higher power' (Massumi, 2011: 43). 'Suspending the potentials' in this way, holding them only to visual form, makes vision all the more potent. The movement and abstraction are no longer actual potential, but virtual potential, that 'actually appears' (Massumi, 2011: 16). Vision's potential is made apparent, 'can only appear and can only appear visually ... It's a kind of perception of the event of perception in the perception' (Massumi, 2011: 43-4). 'Visual' art, as it is actively and cross-modally seen, occurs in the event of experience / perception. It is active, potent, and in relation to us, and our past, present, and future occurrences of vision. Art is thus occurrent, it occurs as a moving–thinking–feeling, in this case in visual form (Massumi, 2011: 44).[4]

Taken together, neither Hansen, Grusin, nor Massumi (nor Watson nor I, for that matter) fall into the trap of privileging vision over the 'other' senses, but rather show us that vision is always an embodied, multisensory, and relational activity, a small and indivisible part of sensation as a whole. And art has the capacity to virtualize and thus magnify these qualities in how we view it. Here I propose that the work of contemporary arts pioneer William Kentridge provides a perfect example of art that we might 'look' at in this way. Kentridge is best known for his trace and erase method of charcoal animation, applied most famously in his series *9 Drawings for Projection* (1989–2003, Figure 3), which centers on South African historically-based fiction towards the end of apartheid rule. His stories and images emerge through a labor-intensive process, where he adds a mark of charcoal on paper, erases another, walks to his camera a few feet away and shoots a couple of frames, then walks back to his drawing to do some more mark-making and erasing before snapping a few more shots. He incorporates erasure and redrawing, walking, looking, and photographing into his ongoing moving, viewing, thinking, and making. Each narrative moment both shows and leaves behind traces of all that came before; each instant makes apparent the art and artist's gestures, ambiguity, contradictions, and movement. Kentridge's films are doubly potent and thus doubly political. First in how he views and sees and looks and makes, from camera to drawing, erasing to making, apartheid to post-apartheid; and second, in how *we* view and see and look and make. We move–think–feel visually, with the material, with the content, and with the artist, as the work occurs. His drawings only reveal so much, but we imagine that which is not there, yet could be – whether in the past of his narrative, in the present mode of affect, or in the future traces we know they will leave behind.

This doubling is made even more apparent in Kentridge's exhibition, *Seeing Double* (2007–8), which includes a series of anamorphic projections and stereoscopic drawings and photogravures, among other things. In several collaborations with South African photographer John Hodgkiss, Kentridge created what he calls 'stereoscopic light drawings' that are probably better understood as virtual light sculptures (Figure 4). Each 2D print dissolves into a 3D image when viewed through a stereopticon. In production, Kentridge uses a flash-

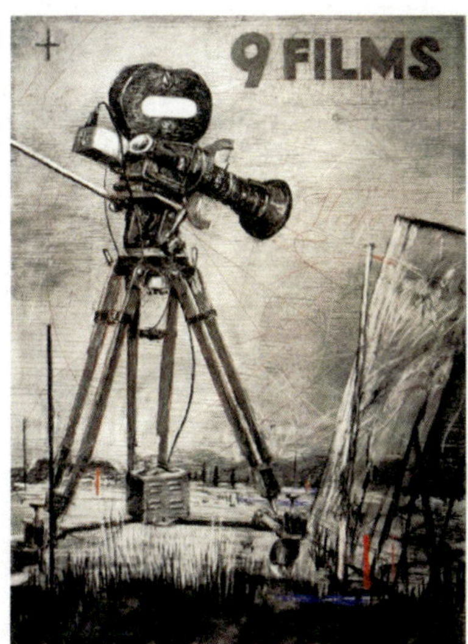


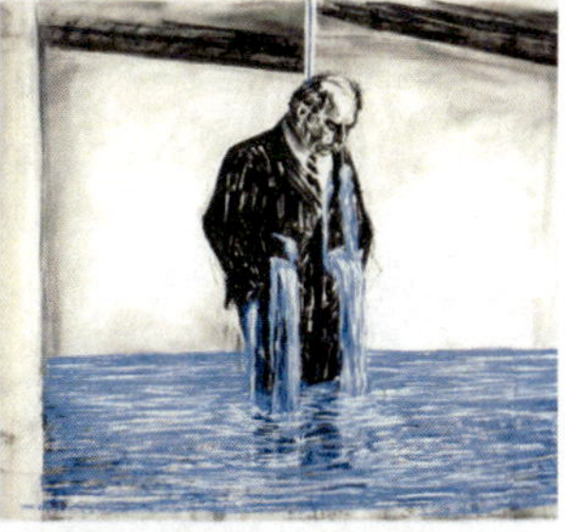

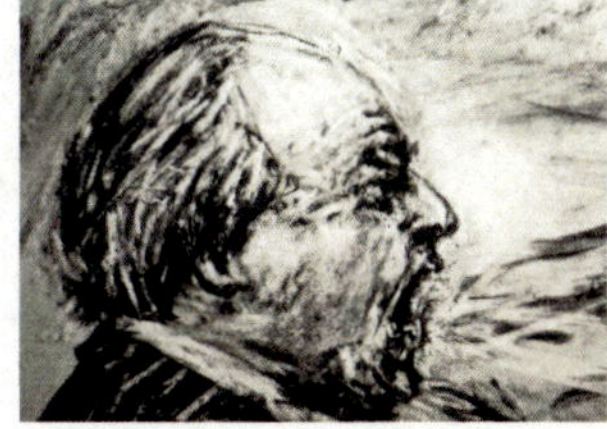

Figure 3. William Kentridge | *9 Drawings for Projection (stills)*, 1989–2003 | 9 videos, dimensions variable

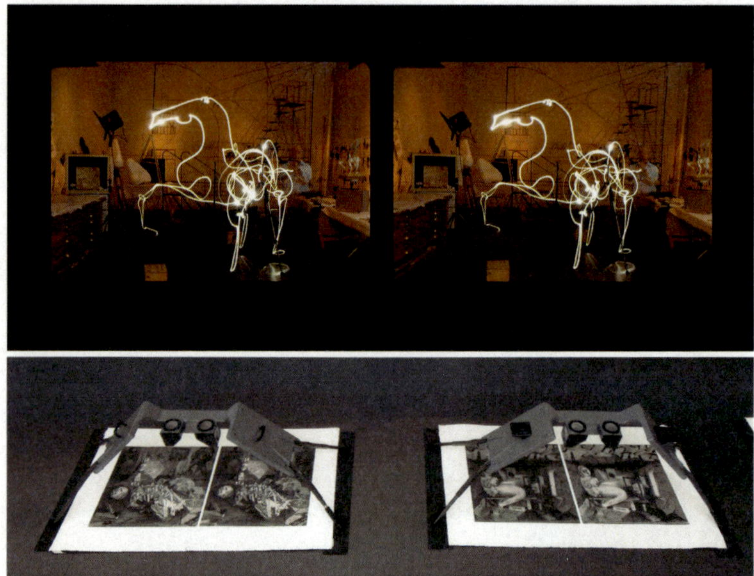

Figure 4. William Kentridge | Top: Untitled stereoscopic light drawing, later used for photogravure print, 2007 | Bottom: stereopticons and 3D prints at *Seeing Double* | Marion Goodman gallery, New York

light and his whole body's sweeping gestures to draw out large, three-dimensional sketches, while Hodgkiss captures two photos of Kentridge and the moving light over time, through a combination of flash and slow exposure. When placed side-by-side and viewed in one eye each, these photos re-produce the spatial effects of Kentridge's studio for the viewer, and a voluminous light sculpture – such as a horse – comes to vision. The artist turns 'dimension and duration' into 'time and space' (Gray, 2007b: 63), and they are given as a sculptural image: as a semblance of what occurred in his studio.

The works in *Seeing Double* emerge from the dynamic performances of Kentridge's moving and looking body. He draws out spatialized images through his active and reciprocal process of seeing and doing, perceiving and creating. And the works must themselves always be viewed by two embodied eyes, part of a whole fleshly thing that walks to the stereopticon, bends to its call, adjusts matter and mind until dimensionality takes hold, and sighs as their suspended potential appears. Our body, philosopher Henri Bergson reminds us, is not merely a mathematical point in space. It is active both virtually and actually: perception requires affection. As viewers we are always already a part of every image, within and among a field of relating and related imagery. Kentridge's stereoscopic drawings transform understandings of embodied looking and making by revealing just how interrelated looking and making are. They show us, quite literally, that seeing is active, embodied, and full of potential. The artist's imaging re-members that perception implicates, involves, and amplifies an expansive and continuously transforming field of matter, bodies, affects, effects, memories, and times. We move and are moved. When viewing his light sculptures, our virtual potential *for* movement meets Kentridge's actualized potential *of* movement.

In the, posthuman, perceptual regime brought about by technology, the lens or sensor does not 'see' for us – replacing the work of the body with data from a camera – but rather makes available different possibilities for the understandings of, and investment in, a given image. Vision is always already in relation to all of affect, action, and abstraction, in, of, and with the world: how we take account of our surroundings, and they take account of us. This is an Alfred North Whitehead reference: 'taking account' is when an event feels the influence of other events, and its trajectory of becoming shifts (Whitehead, 1938). Vision is one such shared event, which can change and / or be changed in process. Mediated images and artworks, then – digital or otherwise – suspend that potential for change, and may emphasize a reinvestment in looking. A processual or event-based understanding of seeing, doing, and occurrence, potential and virtualization, is vital to recognizing what is at stake in art, interactive or not. In this approach, art is understood as both a limitation and amplification of the forces and potentials, matter and concepts, with which we are always interacting and emerging.

## Data is not Immaterial (and neither are we)

In his analysis of how digital images enhance embodied relationships, Hansen is explicitly speaking back to one specific and dominant narrative within new media theory: disembodiment (whether it is seen as a crisis or something to be celebrated). His books have extensively critiqued studies of technology rooted in text and symbols alone. Media scholar Timothy Lenoir reminds us that in the digital age, the dominance of data and ocularcentrism – information and the all-knowing eyes – have been increasingly coupled with immateriality and disembodiment (Lenoir, 2004: xiii). Here neither intelligence nor perception need physical instantiation. In his book on 'visual truth,' the late William J. Mitchell asserts that a 'worldwide network of digital imaging systems is swiftly, silently constituting itself as the decentered subject's reconfigured eye' (Mitchell, 1992: 57). Vivian Sobchack writes on electronic space as 'a phenomenological structure of sensual and psychological experience that seems to belong to nobody' (Sobchack, 1994). Friedrich Kittler went so far as to contend that with digital convergence human perception is becoming obsolete.

This history of disembodiment in Western thinking can be traced from Plato, who argued we sense the world as a copy of an abstract reality, via Descartes, who asserted that knowledge is objective: it only begins when we remove ourselves from the senses (Bolter and Gromala, 2003: 118). Allucquére Rosanne Stone says that the retreat of the body in the West into text, and / or brute physicality, is being continued and refigured through the mediation of computing technology. Like many other critics, artists, and scholars in the field of new media, Stone contends that the 'discourse of visionary virtual world builders is rife with images of imaginal bodies, freed from the constraints that flesh imposes ... Forgetting about the body is an old Cartesian trick' (Stone, 2000: 525). In the work of Hans Moravec, disembodied brains think alongside artificial intelligences, while cyberpunks download themselves from network to hard drive and back again. The mythic power of bodiless humans grew with the creation of the World Wide Web, cyberspace, and simulated worlds, leading

John Perry Barlow to assert, 'Cyberspace ... is not where bodies live' (Barlow, 1996). Barlow and Moravec epitomize an ongoing drive to escape flesh's limitations. This escape, I argue along with N. Katherine Hayles, is pure fantasy.

The most influential treatise on, and critique of, our procedural disembodiment through the communication and information ages is Hayles' *How We Became Posthuman: Virtual Bodies in Cybernetics, Literature, and Informatics.* She begins by unequivocally asserting that in the computer age, we as a people have mis-equated 'intelligence' with the 'formal manipulation of symbols' (Hayles, 1999: xi).[5] In this avowedly ironically titled book, Hayles completely rejects Moravec's proposal that 'human identity is essentially an informational pattern' (Hayles, 1999: xi). She refutes the idea that how we input / change / output data – whether in computer code, or linguistic or visual in nature – is what makes us human, and alive. We need bodies to practice consciousness. Hayles couples the disembodiment of intelligence with the now conventionally (and practically) accepted logic that informational data can exist without material form. It is not only humans that require materiality, she maintains, but also information.

Hayles unearths and describes the histories of computer and information theory that led to human–computer interaction's dominant discourses of immaterial information and disembodiment. Here interwoven narratives about competing factions show that personalities and people with agendas argued for years before it was basically decided that data is devoid of matter, and humans are nothing more than data and computation. This was not a scientific conclusion, but a compromise. Hayles asserts that information lost its body around the time of the Macy Conferences, a series of interdisciplinary meetings held between 1946 and 1953, which spawned many breakthroughs in systems theory. She explains that it was electrical engineer Claude Shannon who first posited a theory of communication whereby information could exist in an immaterial form, and which merely needed a vessel to be transmitted.[6] His paper, 'A Mathematical Theory of Communication' (Shannon, 1948) introduced what is now called information theory, and it is considered by most thinkers in the field to be at the heart of the digital revolution – the microcontrollers and processors in our present-day technical gadgets owe a great debt to Shannon's work.

To borrow from media scholar Lev Manovich, as the language of new media has infected the cultural layer, so Shannon's model of immaterial information, contentious and yet agreed upon at the Macy Conferences, has become conventional wisdom. In this model, 'pattern is predominant over presence. From here it is a small step to perceiving information as more mobile, more important, more essential than material forms' (Hayles, 1999: 19). Hayles warns us that if information is seen as separate from, and more important than, materiality, then it can also be misconstrued as more fundamental. Many years after her publication, this distortion is indeed still pervasive and mainstream. For example, in the February 2007 issue of *WIRED* magazine, an article entitled 'What We Don't Know,' examines '40 of the biggest questions in science' today (Gleick, 2007). One of these asks, 'Is the universe actually made of information?' Using the foundations set forth by Shannon, alongside quantum physicist John Wheeler's work, James Gleick freely asserts that informational bits are likely to be the irreducible particles of existence.[7] The obvious question to ask Gleick is, how can something be both a particle and immaterial (information)? The two are mutually exclusive.

A person with no pen or paper cannot write a letter; without a cell phone and signal, he or she cannot make a call; with no computer and network cable, there is no email. There is no such thing as a message without a signal, and no signal without matter and form to carry it. Although 'it can be a shock to remember ... for information to exist, it must always be instantiated in a medium' (Hayles, 1999: 13). We think of data in much the same way we think of text as an abstract concept, rather than as something instantiated materially. But just as texts and translations do not exist without pages and ink (or someone to speak them aloud), neither does data without magnetic strips, hard drives, or air-bound radio waves.

At the same time that information was becoming immaterial, humans were becoming information tabulators. As computers become more and more complex, and we simplify our understandings of complex thinking in order to get computers to do work for us, we are equating humans and computers as no different from one another. Now humans are essentially seen as information processors, as intelligent machines. Put insubstantial data and human as information processor together, and we too wind up without matter. If data and computation – and thus intelligence – need no-body, why should we require one? In other words, after information lost its materiality, so did we. But data, like us, 'cannot exist apart from the embodiment that brings it into being as a material entity in the world, and embodiment is always instantiated, local, and specific' (Hayles, 1999: 49). Neither bodies nor information can exist without form and embodiment, and intelligence encompasses far more than informational processing. As Hayles reminds us, the stakes in remembering this are high: while data might be replicated or sometimes salvaged, embodiment and the material world cannot be replaced.

## Being Bodily

The discourse of disembodiment (and of immaterial information) that has been so pervasive in computational and new media theorizing is reinforced in discussions of digital arts in which the artworks are explored as instantiations of data observed by a disembodied eye. While it is certainly true that 'compared to the analogical arts – which are always instantiated in a fixed, Euclidean space – the digital arts seem abstract, ephemeral, without substance,' this sense of 'becoming immaterial' is contingent on two misrecognitions (Rodowick, 2001: 212). First, a misrecognition of the question of materiality and embodiment in relation to technology and, second, a misrecognition in which the unraveling of 'spatial coherence' is read as a 'desubstantialization' (Rodowick, 2001: 212–3). The 'challenge for new media art and theory in both making and thinking with digital technologies,' says Anna Munster, 'is to move beyond the twin premises of disembodiment and extension in space that continue to qualify both information and corporeality' (Munster, 2006: 178).

Digital art can challenge us to explore anew our embodied relations without returning to the narratives of disembodiment and immateriality. Writes performance and visual studies scholar Nicole Ridgway, far 'from eviscerating the real and occluding the body,' new media at its best 'invests in bodily affectivity. As such, it has the capacity to go beyond the aesthetic perception of the object' and have us encounter a 'non-representational experience' (Ridgway, forthcoming). Technologies affect what it means to be an embodied agent; they create spaces for experience and practice.

In Char Davies' *Osmose* (1995, Figure 5) minimal movements, breathing, and balancing, control images, sound, and text in a Virtual Reality environment. As with all images, our movement potential is suspended. The last section explained that although we cannot walk into the 'space' of everyday images, we still understand them as spaces that go beyond the surface and the frame of the image; we grasp that we could move in, around, under, and beyond their objects and borders, even if only virtually. Davies' sensors and interaction reinvest in such virtual movements – but in a way that turns our bodies and senses inward, as well as into the space of the image. This internal / external connection between a subtly moving body and subtly moving image intensifies occurrence, where relation and emergence can appear.

With *Osmose*, viewer–participants literally breathe generative, image-based life into Davies' 3D world, and navigate it using the simple angling of their torsos. They are strapped into a custom vest outfitted with motion and tilt sensors, and fitted with a standard VR head-mounted display. As they slowly exhale, their chest cavities emptying of air, trees and poetry sprawl out, in sculptural waves around them. They float or fall, turn and dive, using a combination of slow and fast gasps of air, and leaning into space with their bodies. *Osmose*, according to the artist, 'is a space for exploring the perceptual interplay between self and world, i.e. a place for facilitating awareness of one's own self as consciousness embodied in enveloping space' (Davies, 1995). This awkward combination of action and affect becomes a heightened sensitivity to and awareness of the complex embodied relationship between vision and looking, seeing and what is seen.

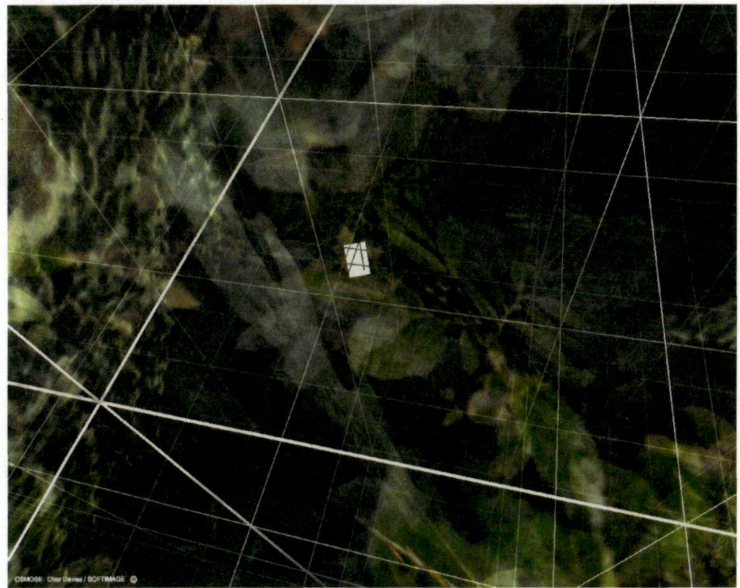

Figure 5. Char Davies | Forest Grid, *Osmose*, 1995 | Digital still captured in real-time through HMD (head-mounted display) during live performance of the immersive virtual environment *Osmose*

*Osmose* does not merely simulate perspectival space, but rather presents vision as a continuous, active, and fully embodied event. The artist relies neither on joysticks nor touch pads for her interaction, nor computer vision technology using cameras. She instead employs conscious movement, unconscious movement, and the potential for movement, towards growing and shifting the space around us. We move–think–feel our way through both the environment, and seeing that environment. It is an exchange, a taking account that while out of the ordinary in terms of habitual perception, is not extra-ordinary in its workings. Looking, Davies asks us to remember, always works this way. It always goes beyond our eyes, and that which is seen. Her work frames how we see, and look, as embodied agents in and of the world. *Osmose* is an artwork that magnifies our experience and practice of images as something felt in our bodies. Affect, in fact all of sensation, is amplified as relational and emergent.

Andrew Murphie reminds us that affect has an ongoing and sometimes contradictory list of definitions. 'Simply affecting or being affected. Affection. Emotion. Feeling. Background feeling ... Mood (which can be different to background feeling). Affective tone ... Motivation. Interest' (Murphie, 2010a). In short, affect is an autonomous, preconscious, embodied sense of the body. Here the body 'moves as it feels, and it feels itself moving' (Massumi, 2002: 1). Proprioception, on the other hand, folds the external senses of tactility into the body – what we sense from our skin, for example, and how that feels. Proprioception is still preconscious, but brings sensibilities from the outside in. Affect and proprioception, together, make up sensation. Where perception is about segmentation, is a 'qualified intensity' (Massumi, 2002: 28), sensation is an unqualified intensity that precedes perception. Perception is our conscious understanding of what we feel, our feelings. Sensation happens before we've given word or thought to what is sensed, before we make sense of it. It is the abstract pain in the hand we pull away from the stove, before we even realize that it 'hurts,' that it is 'burning.' We move before we 'know' this, we sense and move before the fire is fully perceived.

For Massumi, sensation is always an enfolding, an openness and bodiliness that is outside of conscious reflection on, or understanding of, the body. It is 'self-referential (intensive),' while perception is 'exoreferential (extensive)' (Massumi, 2002: 259). This does not mean that sensation is completely without thought. The two feed into one another, perception qualifying sensation and thus shifting how we sense, and as we sense, which in turn transforms that which we sense. And so using digital art to focus on sensation rather than perception does not mean retreating from thought, ideas, or concepts – as Ruth Leys' critique of the turn to affect would have us believe (Leys, 2011). It is about exploring the intensive in addition to the extensive. The arts, Elizabeth Grosz reminds us, 'produce and generate intensity,' create an affective 'system of dynamised and impacting forces rather than a system of unique images' (Grosz, 2006: 15). Affect, proprioception, and their sensibilities are the intensive part of moving–thinking–feeling bodies and matter, and art intensifies intensive experience.

To concretize what he calls the 'sensible concept' of the 'thinking body' (the body in sensation, in the intensive mode and in process), Massumi (2002: 89) turns to Australian performance artist, Stelarc. From his earlier works, where Stelarc suspended his body from gallery ceilings or outdoor cranes using steel cables and large hooks that pierced his skin, to his latest projects that incorporate electro-mechanical and / or biological prostheses, the artist sustains a ceaseless and critical examination of the body, embodiment, and their representation. He uses new technologies to blur the distinction 'between what an organism is and what a mechanism is' (Jones, 1995).

In Stelarc's art we encounter the 'physical experience of ideas' and the 'body as concept,' performing a 'joining [of] the body and thought' (Massumi, 2002: 89–90). It requires 'a willingness to revisit some of our basic notions of what a body is and does as an acting, perceiving, thinking, feeling thing' (Massumi, 2002: 90). Rather than impose an outside frame onto Stelarc's art, Massumi attempts to approach the works as 'manifested' only through his performances; like the body, they 'do not preexist their physical expression' (Massumi, 2002: 89–90). They are, literally, per-formed. Massumi mostly concentrates on Stelarc's *Suspensions* (1980 and ongoing) for his study of how the potentials of subject and object – and the body thereof – can be suspended. I turn to *Ping Body* (1996, Figure 6) as an example of where Stelarc conceptually senses his own body, an Internet data stream, and the relation between the two.

In *Ping Body,* Stelarc's embodied activities are merged with (supposedly) disembodied online relationships in such a way that each is materialized only through its connectivity and reciprocity with the other. Stelarc adorns his barely clothed body with a multitude of wires, at the end of which sit electrical-stimulation nodes. The flex and extend muscles across his arms, legs, shoulders, and thighs – the actions of all his natural appendages, and thus also his movement across space – are controlled by his hardware. This system was first used in *Split Body: Voltage In / Voltage Out,* where gallery goers could make Stelarc involuntarily move using a touch screen interface. In *Ping Body,* random 'pings' are sent from his location to 40 others – participants watching the performance on their computers – and the

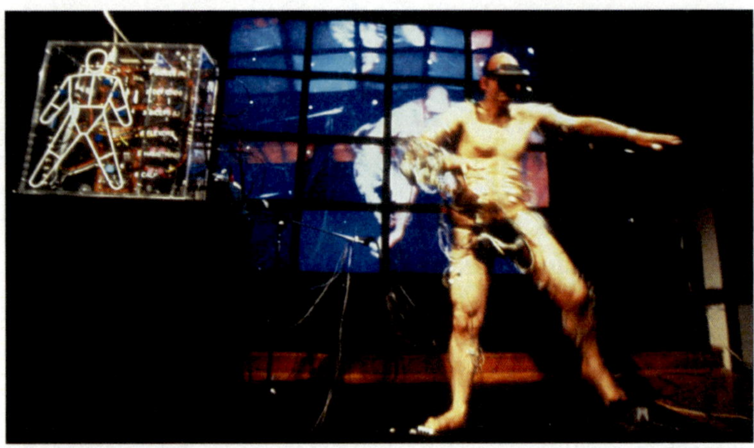

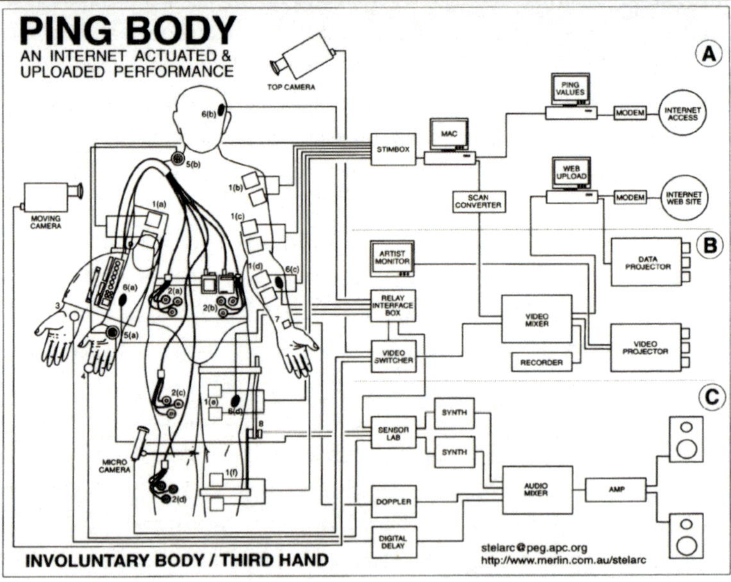


Figure 6. Stelarc | Top: *Split Body: Voltage-In / Voltage-Out* | Galerie Kapelica, Ljubljana 1996, photo by Igor Andjelic Stelarc | Bottom: *Ping Body* Digital Aesthetics | Artspace Sydney 1996, Diagram by Stelarc

system measures how long it takes for those pings to return to the site of Stelarc's performance. It then maps distance and transmission time to movement in the artist's body, where reverberating signals of Internet data trigger muscles, and drive movement. Viewers the world over can access, watch, and actuate Stelarc's limbs from a live website. His gestures are controlled through an uncoordinated public collaboration; he jumps and flails and kicks across the stage like an enfleshed marionette. As Stelarc involuntarily moves in response to electronic stimuli, he uploads real time photos of the performance, and his audience responds in kind, indirectly interacting by tweaking their clicks and browser refreshes, playing out networked media and embodied activities all at once.

In addition to this feedback loop between the body of the artist and a participating public, Stelarc adds an 'extra' appendage to the *Ping Body* performance: his *Third Hand*. This is a robotic arm that is controlled with sensors attached to the artist's abdomen; after years of practice, Stelarc can move each finger individually and direct it almost as if it were his own. In *Ping Body*, Stelarc's cyborg hand is the only part of his body that he can himself still control; this is what he uses to upload images to the Internet and otherwise collaborate with his viewers online.

Stelarc asks us to consider 'a body moving not to the promptings of another body in another place, but rather to Internet activity itself' (Stelarc, 1996). Here every movement is stimulated by the external waves and stillness of data flow, rather than internal bodily promptings. The Internet's time and space parameters 'choreograph and compose the performances' so that the 'Internet becomes not merely a mode of information transmission, but also a transducer, effecting physical action' (Stelarc, 1996). A wide net of external / extensive ideas and activities become internal / intensive sensation and action.

What Stelarc performs in *Ping Body* is a moving–thinking–feeling and becoming-together of body and information, materiality and thought, activity and relationality. Digital media, Stelarc shows us, has the potential to amplify bodiliness and materiality in a way that exceeds the frames of language and visuality, where we understand objects and bodies as independent things. He alternatively focuses us on materialization and abstraction, on affect and perception, on their relation and emergence. *Ping Body* intensifies the intensive embodied experience. This is not to privilege materiality over construction or discourse. Concepts and sensations, bodies and objects, emerge together: a networked performance as sensible concept. While undoubtedly material, embodiment is realized as event not thing: an unfolding actualization and enfolding potential of both sense and concept.

With Stelarc and Massumi, we think the body neither as naive realism nor subjectivism, neither as concrete materialism nor linguistic text, but rather as always in motion, and always in relation to its potential, both present and nonpresent. This body is 'only ever in passing', it is indeterminate in 'its openness to an elsewhere and otherwise than it is' (Massumi, 2002: 5).[8] Thinking the body in this way, says Massumi, means accepting that there is an incorporeal dimension to it. The corporeal and incorporeal, the matter and matterless (but no less real), are dimensions of the same reality: always accompanying one another to make 'the body.' Such a body is an incipient, relational agent whose movement, affect, and sensation in and with the world continuously redefine what and how we are. And new media, I argue, can create spaces in which we experience and practice this body, its agency, and how they might become.

## The Doings of Digital Art

The oft-heard promises declared by many new media advocates differ greatly from the possibilities for digital art that I present here. The world of commerce commonly espouses, for instance, that new media's individual activation, distinctive choice, unique preferences, and never-ending personalization are extremely desirable in our purchases. This language has dominated what digital and interactive products can and should provide, and what we as a consumer culture ostensibly want and even need. More specific to 'interactivity,' this ill-defined term has become a 'catch-all phrase that is used to sell many new media technologies as an added bonus, or special element' (Fuery, 2009: 27). Here simple button clicks on toys and finite menus in our DVD or MP3 players are sold as more choices and thus more democratic and thus freer and inherently better, when in reality what many techno-gadgets have to offer is often less than underwhelming, and tied to proprietary media formats. And consumer-based interaction between ubiquitous technologies with social media platforms has been marketed as all but compulsory in the most powerful markets of youth culture. *Interact or Die!* as the 2007 edited collection on networked behavior is called (Brouwer and Mulder, 2007). As time goes on, it is rarer and rarer to hear the surprised question, 'You're not on Facebook?' – and sites like Facebook are the perfect place to advertise the aforementioned techno-gadgets.

Theories surrounding the body's openness, too, have been coopted as a point of valuable exploitation for profiteers. Many current scholars are arguing that the body's very mutability has become a key resource for contemporary forms of capitalism, especially in the domains of creative industries and digital culture. The works of Maurizio Lazzarato (2002), Tiziana Terranova (2010), and Nigel Thrift (2008) show how the contemporary discourses of creativity and innovation, especially in the entertainment industry and its production of surplus value, relies on and hails a body that is pliable, relational, and capable of new contacts and sensations – and subsequently, experiences/ideas. Thus, a body's relation to dominant social forces is an ambivalent matter, one that must be approached with more care by media artists than that which is seen in the model used to sell mobile phones, tablets, and games. This has not always been, and is still often not, the case.

As writer and film critic Chris Darke points out, '"Interactivity" was the buzzword, the promise ... for a certain techno-euphoria taking shape in the early and mid-90s. The false promises of "democratizing" art that were attached to the term are slightly embarrassing to recall' (Darke, 2003: 1, cited in Cook and Graham, 2010: 112). Critiquing that very discourse, Massumi (2011: 48) argues that it is simply not enough to champion interactivity itself. This is 'something that mainstream informational capitalism' is already doing, 'ever so profitably' (Massumi, 2011: 57). Further, the notion that 'interactive' (art or otherwise) offers more choice and possibilities, is intrinsically democratic and thus superior, is both counter-productive and false. We almost never find a product that actually does all the things and plays all the files we want it to, and the first investigation of any given digital artwork is usually to find out how it works, technically (Where is the sensor? What does it do?), and how we can circumvent its inner-workings. This is expanded on in the following chapter, where I argue that it is not interactive art's openness, but its limitations that make it a powerful space for rehearsing embodied agency.

My purpose in this section is to unpack what different types of digital encounters can enable in the gallery space, before asking that we *forget* the technologies used to create those encounters in our experience and practice with media art. Cook and Graham warn that contemporary art curators tend to use words which signal interactivity and connection 'with the vague sense that they are "good things," but without any clear idea of the levels of engagement involved in each' (Cook and Graham, 2010: 112). The following paragraphs will briefly define levels of engagement. They first expand an understanding of digital images, and then explain activation, navigation, reaction, interaction, participation, and collaboration.

Lev Manovich's main argument in *The Language of New Media* is that digital media are like film, the difference being in the construction of images beneath their surface. Unlike Paul's broad approach to practice, Manovich has been justifiably criticized for having too narrow a focus: explicitly starting with language and film makes for a largely semiotic reading, rather than recognizing a vast field of cooperative and material agents. Inke Arns sums up Manovich's text most succinctly when she says 'the book should have been called "The Language of New Visual Media"' (Arns, 2002). While I have argued that vision is never vision alone, Manovich concentrates mostly on the computer as a tool for image production, on how digital art is made, on the technology behind the images. But much can be gained, I am asserting, if we add Manovich's analyses to an understanding of the feedback loops between sensation and perception in the age of new media.

What Manovich teaches us mostly centers on his five core 'principles' that he claims are 'essential' (and even unique, when presented jointly) to new media (and by extension, digital art). They also gesture towards possibilities beyond static images, opening up spaces for generative and interactive art. New media objects are (1) 'coded' and (2) 'modular'. They are made up of numerically represented data, consisting of smaller and smaller independent parts, down to the level of digital 'atoms': pixels, points, text, bytes, and bits (Manovich, 2001: 31). Principles one and two allow for: (3) the 'automation' of algorithmic operations – accessing, manipulating, or creating content, for example (Manovich, 2001: 32); (4) 'variability' in the object, with infinite versioning possibilities across customization and scalability, compositing and re-mixing (Manovich, 2001: 36, 124); and, (5) the ability to 'translate' one kind of data – or rather, how that data is decoded / recoded and represented for us – into a different form. All digital files follow these conventions in practice, and so their data can be used and portrayed in various formats. This could mean algorithms that translate sounds into visuals or mouse movements into Morse code.

Manovich goes on to claim that our understandings of media more generally (the 'cultural layer') have shifted along with the 'computer layer' (Manovich, 2001: 46). As a computer savvy culture, we already read the surface of the screen and images differently, and must therefore engage with that difference. At stake, is that computers mediate not only what we see, but also how we see, and where we find meaning. Manovich contends that contemporary media consumers inherently – if also unconsciously – understand his principles of new media, and thus see and think about media materials in relation to them. Our engagement with new media images, I argue by extension, is not only in the suspension of potential that all images offer. We also experience the potency of their code, modularity, automation, variability, and translation – of their production. Here we understand and *feel* the potential for our movement in the image, and the potential past of that image: how it might have been digitally formed and / or transformed.

Pressing a button or a switch, or crossing a threshold, is a different (though not necessarily better) experience from looking, even with all that looking entails. Each is an act you can do, or not do, as a binary input that sets something in motion, for example, a video, a kinetic sculpture, or in Kelli Fuery's example, a toy dog sold as 'interactive!'

that merely barks at you when turned on. The technical strategy of activation provides an easy way to conserve energy in a gallery space for the green-conscious, and in terms of viewer experience it is often deployed as a trigger that gives a minimal sense of authority and authorship – ironic or otherwise. Navigation, then, offers more engagement than activation. While still limited, there are a number of possible inputs and choices that can lead viewers in a multitude of predefined directions. A website, DVD, or 'Choose Your Own Adventure' book of 'interactive fiction' are examples of navigable work. This strategy is generally utilized to again give an impression of command or choice, and sometimes a sense of exploration and possibility, while the artist or designer still maintains control of all possible outcomes. When combined with other artistic strategies, navigation can make for interesting sensory possibilities.

In Janet Cardiff's *To Touch* (1993–4, Figure 7), visitors elicit and construct two lovers' stories through slow, manual, and tactile investigation. Each participant is invited to draw out and feel monologues and aural moments, her main characters speaking and revealing their histories as we glide over the surface of a well-lived carpenter's table. Our hands caress the grain, marks, and dents of the wood, and her multi-channel sound system proffers tidbits of story to contemplate, which are whispered or uttered powerfully from more than half a dozen speakers across the four corners of the room. Cardiff is a master at creating physiological responses to minimal sonic and / or visual information, and this piece builds on her previous work with tactility and sensibility.

What Cook and Graham call reactive or responsive environments, and what I defined as interactive art in the introduction to this book, would be yet one higher level of engagement from navigation. My own *enter* (described briefly there and in detail in the companion chapter of this book) is a case in point. It is a piece that is more than a navigation of a small range of inputs matched to a small number of outputs (a navigable work), in that electronic sensors such as cameras and microphones are complex enough to pick up a range of motion, and could thus encourage styles of movement. While the computer is always limited in its responses, which are programmed, there are limitless possibilities in how we investigate the space of the situation that program creates. The real potential – indeed the real challenge, artist and philosopher Erin Manning points out – is to keep the participant's attention on the quality of their own movements, rather than the response of the machine. Manning implores us to add nuance by making technology's 'failures felt' through techniques such as lagging, system collapses, and a loss of ground (Manning, 2009: 72). Things like feedback loops, layering of time-based forms, or multiple and proportional sensors can create ever-more affective digital spaces that might highlight the body, interaction, performance, and relation, rather than technology and its coded replies. Analogical reactive art – electronic or physical work that does not use computer-based algorithms – is slightly different from its digital counterpart in that it allows for unlimited input and unlimited output possibilities in its variation. I put digital and analogical reactive art in the same category because our experiences of either, at their best, are entirely parallel. As Manning

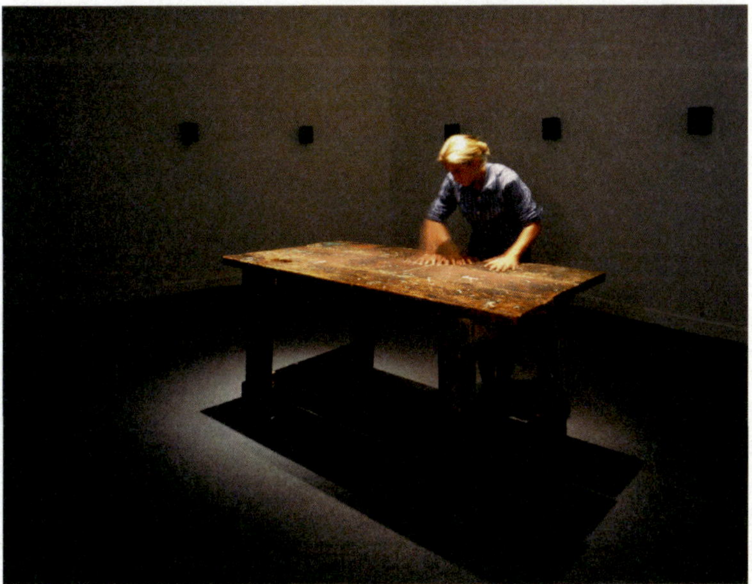

Figure 7. Janet Cardiff | *To Touch*, 1993-1994 | table, photocells, electronic circuits, audio equipment | dimensions variable

eloquently puts it, although in a different context, making 'the digital analog need not be the goal' – media art becomes 'evocative when its techniques make transduction felt, foregrounding the metastability of all moving systems' (Manning, 2009: 72). When successful, we do not just move in relation, we move *the* relation (Manning, 2009: 64).

What Cook and Graham call interaction means 'acting upon each other' – where a computer or another person directly engages us, rather than merely responding to our movements. Participation, then, implies having a say; it requires viewers to contribute at least some of the content, and usually involves human-to-human relationships. Finally, collaboration means working directly with; the production of the piece sees a degree of equality between the participants, rather than small contributions of content. Collaboration is generally between artists, or artists and curators, since it is a reciprocal partnership (Cook and Graham, 2010: 112-14). Interaction, participation and collaboration have, of course, a longer history than electronic art. Although the lines can be blurred between many of the 'levels of engagement' I have listed, as critical tools – digital or otherwise – each creates situations in which our emergent relationships are highlighted. Their definitions, and what each achieves, are useful in thinking the strategies for, and implications of, contemporary interactive art.

The use of technologies and strategies such as these for art need not mimic, and can in fact work against, the same principles employed for capital gain. Massumi reminds us that the 'regulatory principles of the technical process in the narrow sense are utility and salability, profit-generating ability.' Art, on the other hand, 'claims the right to have no manifest utility, no use-value, and in many cases even no exchange-value. At its best, it has event-value' (Massumi, 2011: 53). Game art, as one example, can both use and speak back to the uber-marketable gaming console, linear narrative trajectories, violence, and goal orientation. It provides a very specific context for the interactor, and thus offers distinct possibilities for imaginative intervention into present-day capitalist regimes. Carlo Zanni's avowedly 'boring' (Zanni, 2005) *Average Shoveler* (2004), is an exemplary art-game that challenges our understandings of games, media, news, corporations, and our personal relationships to all three. Where a standard Wii game has us flail to compete, and focus is always on winning (and ending) the game itself, here players endlessly clear New York's streets of snowdrops – each one filled with images from top news stories, falling alongside animated characters that pronounce the headlines, via speech bubbles. These over-the-top stories never cease, the streets are never clean, and, unlike most off-the-shelf video games, no one ever wins. *Average Shoveler* is less a game, and more a critical frame for gaming and media culture.

Jussi Parikka and Milla Tiainen (2012) proffer Tero Saarinen's dance piece, *Hunt* (2002), as a work that appropriates the language and images of digitally-enhanced capitalism and affective bodies precisely to intervene in their reign. The authors argue that as living bodies continuously 'connect, perceive and act with a difference' we must recognize their variability as a 'political existence' with the potential for both exploitation and resistance (Parikka and Tiainen, 2012: 205). Parikka and Tiainen remind us that advertising no longer needs to recognize 'particular target groups' in that they can rather tap into the 'sensation of an excess of possible meanings with respect to a given image /product' (Parikka and Tiainen, 2012: 216). In other words, rather than selling an actual product and what it does, or even branding a product towards a specific gender, age, or race, commercials can simply sell an abstract idea of fulfilled desire through their product.

Provide us a powerfully affective image in an advertisement (an iPod with a blank, human silhouette, an intense face staring into the camera), and we will give the product our own meaning. Couple product power with the supposed infinite choice of interactivity, and credit card details will be very forthcoming.

Media art, Parikka and Tiainen go on to imply, can speak back to such exploitation, and remind us of the body's power and resistance outside the dominant market's regime.

Saarinen's 'jerking body' as he dances, the 'electrified flashes,' and the 'images whirling' do not act as signifiers or metaphors for the power that network capitalism holds over us (Parikka and Tiainen, 2012: 219). What is being danced, write Parikka and Tiainen, 'is the actuality of that encounter of differing scales of bodies': the body of the dancer, the space, the images, the time, and more. While the authors admit that Saarinen's work does not offer a solution to the crucial concerns of creativity and work in relation to media markets, it begins to 'provide a vocabulary relevant for a biopolitical evaluation' of bodies in relation to these concerns, and invites us to experience and launch into 'the eternally recurring chance for relations, creation and a life that might become otherwise' (Parikka and Tiainen, 2012: 219–24). It is, I would argue, an intervention into the dominant discourses of commerce and advertising through opposition, remembrance, and aspiration. Saarinen's body is resistant to exploitation, it re-members itself and its relations outside of capitalism's core structures, and it is hopeful in its potential to materialize differently.

Zanni's work and Parikka and Tiainen's chapter on Saarinen provide a context for how we might think with, against, and around technology, interaction, and processual bodies, beyond how they function and are used to sell us products, culture, and identity. Interactivity and affected bodies are not inherently good. But contemporary artworks such as these, and those by Watson, Kentridge, Davies, Stelarc, and Cardiff, are not goal orientated, are experientially exploratory, and thus have the potential to challenge and intervene in how we position, reposition, and proposition ourselves and our bodies in relation to other formations, both material and conceptual.

Using while forgetting technology to study embodied performance is not an entirely new idea, but rather continues along several extant trajectories of artistic thought. Near the birth-time of video installation (in many ways a precursor to, and now sub-genre of, new media art), film scholar Margaret Morse argued for kinesthetic insights into this kind of work (Morse, 1991: 153). Painter and writer Barbara Bolt asserts that beyond representation, art takes on 'its own momentum, its own rhythm and intensity,' and through its 'radical material performativity' it starts something on its way (Bolt, 2004: 1, 10, 61).

Curator and historian Carolyn A. Jones asks us to think about digital art in a 'broadened sensorial context' (Jones, 2006: 8). Artist and academic Ken Feingold has argued for the importance of touch, vision, and an affective body moving through space as integral to participation in and 'materialisation of the work' (Feingold, 2002: 127).

Digital art scholar and philosopher Erkki Huhtamo asks for a taxonomy of movement, while declaring that an 'interactive work challenges one to undergo a transformation from an onlooker to an "interactor," an active agent' (Huhtamo, 2007: 71). While curator, scholar, and critic Andreas Broeckmann asserts that digital artworks hinge on 'non-visual aspects such as narrativity, processuality, performativity, generativity, interactivity, or machinic qualities.' He does not ask us to talk about the tech, but 'to embrace these practices,' so that we may 'expand the categories of art theoretical reflection' overall (Broeckmann, 2007: 196–7).[9]

Like Broeckmann, I seek an expansion – indeed a rethinking – of art, where the work of the art is embodied experience and practice, is moving–thinking–feeling. New media and mediation supply us spaces for this work – frames for affection and reflection. Anna Munster asserts that 'we require a conception of the digital that neither capitulates to a transcendental idea about "technology" nor disposes so lightly of the human' (Munster, 2006: 13). I follow her in proposing our discourses shift from sign and technology to situation and performance. I argue that art (and philosophy) is an encounter with, and intervention into, the various and ongoing ways we relate and perform.

## Notes

1 The turn from the optic (seeing as a disembodied observer) to the haptic (seeing as touch) is discussed in a number of recent works that address film and video in particular. For example, 'Touching to See,' an analysis of filmmaker Michael Snow's work (Arnaud, 2005), and *Touch: Sensuous Theory and Multisensory Media* (Marks, 2006). Marks explores the affective and embodied experience of new media artworks as well as film and video. She rethinks the perceptual event and extends the haptic-optical synaesthetic strategy to the sense of smell, and to the erotic (in her meditation, on the screen as skin). For Marks too the notion of digital culture as immaterial and transcendent requires critique. She brings her explorations of the haptic and material into the realm of code, arguing that both we and data embody a materiality, on social and global levels.

2 See, for example, *Techniques of the Observer: On Vision and Modernity in the 19th Century* (Crary, 1992) and *Visual Pleasure and Narrative Cinema* (Mulvey, 1989).

3 A similar work worth mentioning in parallel to *audio space* is Carsten Nicolai's *static balance* (2007), which 'works both as a sculpture and as a system to conduct and distribute sound' (Nicolai, 2007).

4 German art historian and media theorist Oliver Grau defines 'virtuality' as, simply, 'an essential relationship of humans to images' (Slayton, 2003: xi). While this may be an oversimplified definition of virtuality, it can be flipped over to interesting effect: our experience of images is always virtual as well as actual. Broadly defined images affect all of sensation and perception. Grau claims that he is solely interested in images: 'no more, but also no less' (Grau, 2003: 308) – naming vision and seeing and looking as more than what appears /is apparent.

5 In 1991, Francisco Varela, Evan Thompson, and Eleanor Rosch first used the term 'enaction' (after Jerome Seymour Bruner) to describe a 'dynamic interplay between self and world ... they envision mindbody and environment coming into existence through a mutual process of "codependent arising"' (Varela et al., 1991: 110).

6 Shannon is most famous for his Masters manuscript, *A Symbolic Analysis of Relay and Switching Circuits,* which used Boolean algebra to first theorize the digital computer and circuit design (Shannon, 1940).

7 In fairness to *WIRED* and its editors, Wheeler did infamously postulate 'It from Bit,' and explains his theory in a free-form essay, as follows: 'every it – every particle, every field of force, even the spacetime continuum itself – derives its function, its meaning, its very existence entirely – even if in some contexts indirectly – from the apparatus-elicited answers to yes-or-no questions, binary choices, _bits_' (Wheeler, 1998). Wheeler and I part ways here. But unlike the *WIRED* article, Wheeler is careful in constructing a system that folds back on itself; here, the questions it generates also birth and perpetuate it – continuously and implicitly, in all its forms. 'Is the universe actually made of information?' is thus misleading; after Wheeler wrote 'All things physical are information-theoretic in origin,' he was quick to add, 'and this is a participatory universe' (Gleick, 2007). The latter half of the statement suggests both a potentially performance-based origin and a more nuanced, collaborative incipience between information and matter (we participate to exist /we must exist to participate).

8 Rosi Braidotti reads Deleuze and Nietzsche from a feminist perspective to similarly explore embodiment as emergent, rhizomatic, interrelated, as an interface of forces. Here affectivity is pre-discursive – not as a 'before,' but as an unthought /non-thought within thought (Braidotti, 1994: 166).

9 This plea for renewed dialogue echoes several other theorists and critics over the last twenty years. One such call was in Simon Penny's 1995 anthology, *Critical Issues in Electronic Media*. This collection was a response to the new conditions surrounding art and technology. In his introduction, Penny asserts, 'The new digital media promise new territories for artistic practice. But they demand a reconsideration of art production and consumption. The new dimensions and capabilities of the new forms (interactivity, instantaneous multiple distribution, ephemerality) demand the generation of new aesthetic models, new ethical models, new institutions… and new conventions of consumptions' (Penny, 1995b: 3).

# Chapter 2

## The Implicit Body as Performance

### Introduction to (a) Movement

In Camille Utterback's art installation, *Untitled 5* (2004, Chapter 4) viewer–participants' sweeping gestures trace painterly marks that cumulatively layer on top of a projected canvas. These splatters, blotches, and scores then interact with each other, as well as new contributions, over time, producing ongoing and animated compositions – both visual and embodied. In Mathieu Briand's artistic 'systems' (1996–2006, Chapter 5), spectator–performers literally share, swap, and interfere in each other's 'viewpoints'. Wearing custom headsets and earpieces, we see and hear what people in other times and spaces are looking at and listening to, while they simultaneously experience and respond to our own eyes and ears. In both cases, not only is vision inextricably linked to bodies – as argued in the last chapter – but the movements, affects, boundaries, and borders of 'body' and 'embodiment' are themselves brought into question.

While a step in the right direction, merely seeing vision as inherently embodied will not necessarily advance understandings of embodiment. Anthropologist Marilyn Strathern argues that reinstating 'the body' as 'the medium' of vision makes it an explicit thing, and 'seems to share with rather than obviate an earlier representationalist obsession with uncovering facts about the world' (Strathern, 1994: 243).[1] Understanding vision, data, and embodiment as always mattering, in other words, is not quite enough towards supporting what is at stake in interactive art. After all, it would be a mistake to think we know what a body *is*. We should not fall back on discourse and structure alone for reading and understanding 'bodies'. An art philosophy for interactive art can help with encountering embodiment, and art, in a broader sense.

Brian Massumi (2002: 4) asks if we can find a way to engage with the body outside of representation without 'contradicting the very real insights of poststructuralist cultural theory'. 'Our entire vocabulary has derived from theories of signification that are still wedded to structure even across irreconcilable differences' (Massumi, 2002: 27). He does not wish to undo the important work of cultural studies' linguistic model for understanding race, gender, class, or other forms of identification, but is looking for 'a semiotics willing to engage with continuity,' a processual and relational approach to embodiment (Massumi, 2002: 27). 'When a body is in motion, it does not coincide with itself. It coincides with its own transition: its own variation ... In motion, a body is in an immediate, unfolding relation to its own ... potential to vary' (Massumi, 2002: 4–5). In contradistinction to pre-existing structures (be they genetic or linguistic), Massumi avers that 'the body is in a state of invention' (Massumi, 2002: 103). It is 'an accumulation of relative perspectives and the passages between them ... retaining and combining past movements,' continuously 'infolded' with 'coding and codification' (Massumi, 2002: 57, 98, 83). Massumi (2002: 4) implores us to put 'movement, sensation, and qualities of experience' back into our understandings of embodiment. The body '*moves*. It *feels*. In fact, it does both at the same time ... Can we think a body without this: an intrinsic connection between movement and sensation, whereby each immediately summons the other?' (Massumi, 2002: 1). Massumi beckons us towards an embodiment that *is* moving–thinking–feeling, a body that is more than its signs and significations, more than what we see or look at, more than skin, flesh, and bone.

N. Katherine Hayles goes so far as to make a distinction between the 'culturally constructed' body that is 'naturalized within culture', and our experiences of embodiment, which are 'contextual, enmeshed within the specifics of place, time, physiology, and culture' (Hayles, 1999: 196, 297).[2] She asserts, 'One contemporary belief likely to stupefy future generations is the postmodern orthodoxy that the body is primarily, if not entirely, a linguistic and discursive construction' (Hayles, 1999: 192). This is somewhat parallel to Mark Hansen's work, following the early phenomenology of Maurice Merleau-Ponty, where he distinguishes between the 'body-image' and the 'body-schema.'[3] The body-image is an understanding of the body and identity. It is a 'predominantly visual representation of the body, a primary resemblance' (Hansen, 2006: 37). The body-schema, on the other hand, is a 'preobjective process of constitution' (Hansen, 2006: 39); it is becoming a body. The body-image describes and is generated by a primarily visual or language-based comprehension of the body as an object – it is *observational*. The body-schema 'lies in the interactional domain specified by embodied enaction' – it is *operational* (Hansen, 2006: 38–9). The cognitive science and philosophy duo, Shaun Gallagher and Jonathan Cole, assert that the body-schema is 'a system of motor and postural functions that operate below the level of self-referential intentionality,' and Hansen builds on this, saying that it is a '*prepersonal* sensory being-with' (Gallagher and Cole, 1995; Hansen, 2006: 21). It includes non-conscious, sensorimotor perceptions and actions, the parts of our bodies that we may or may not be aware of, which are activated when we move and interrelate in and with our surroundings. The body-schema 'forms an infraempirical form: one that is immanent to bodily life without being reducible to its empirical contents.' (Hansen, 2001a). It is an in-process and variable relation to itself and the outside.

Massumi never separates into two 'bodies' in the same way as Gallagher, Cole and Hansen, but rather asks us to re-member the potential that the moving and continuous body *is*. He points to the Zeno paradox as a useful illustration of how contemporary thinking often misreads movement – bodily or otherwise – as serial points of stasis. Zeno's infamous arrow flies through the air, but never gets to its target. For his arrow to reach the bull's eye, it must first get halfway there; it must also get halfway to that halfway mark; and halfway to that, and so on. In fact, the arrow must move through an infinite number of markers – thus making it impossible to reach its goal. Of course movement does not work this way. To map out all the possibilities through which the arrow must travel in order to hit the mark is to see the arrow as only going between many static points, rather than as in motion. If this is the case, it only *is* when it *isn't doing*. Accordingly, now imagine the criss-crossing paths of many arrows across three-dimensional space: post-event, completely mapped-out points of stasis turned into a uniform grid of mediated, understood, unmoving, and ultimately limited possibilities. This is how we have unfortunately come to view the subject, and the body, through contemporary theories of construction. Massumi reminds us that the body is never actually in a position, but always in passing. This approach to the body also includes the folding in of what the body *might become*. Here is an incorporeal dimension to the body – a virtual and not-yet body that embodiment moves towards, in its moving.

I call the body we 'see' as positioned the *static body*, and the body in passing – what Massumi sometimes calls the body without an image – the *continuous body*. This is not parallel to Hayles' or Hansen's dual bodies; my continuous body *includes* the static, the moving, and the incorporeal – all our images, actions, and potentials – *in it*. We of course *relate* to understandings of the body, to its materiality, *and* to incipience, as part of embodiment's continuous becoming. These are, in other words, not really separate bodies. I use the terms static and continuous as heuristic devices that help to conceptually engage with re-thinking bodies and embodiment, as well as different modes of artistic intervention. It is useful to remember and think of them both, so as not to forget how they work together, in continuity.

Bodies are not plottable points (like Zeno's arrow), but, to use a figure from mathematics, topological: an enfolding and unfolding membrane. The one side that is the same side that is the other side of the Möbius strip, for example, could be taken as the continuous body – each of image / language and material / action is open to the other, in fact *is* the other in their corresponding movements. And the strip's continuous folding could be thought of as the virtual body's force: always accelerating towards the bodies that it might become. Möbius strips live in both two- and three-dimensional space, and are greater than the sum of their parts. They have a dynamic form that is 'neither accurate nor fully visualizable. It is operatively vague… a qualitative space of variation referenced only to its own movement' (Massumi, 2002: 183). Like an animated Möbius strip, the body *is*: in and around.[4] This approach to the body as topological, as always and actively relational, opens possibilities in embodiment discourses that go well beyond Strathern's wariness of simply reinstating the body from behind vision. It moves cultural theory out of its 'representationalist obsession' and into a space where we might understand embodiment as 'deliberately incomplete' (Strathern, 1994: 243). Embodiment only *is* through its ongoingness and continuity. 'The body' is not a static 'thing,' but rather an active relation to other forces, matter, and matters-in-process. Both human and non-human continuity, affect, movement, and relationships are precisely what constitute and differentiate both humans and non-human matter.

Cultural studies as a discipline has shown that examining and challenging the body's stop-points can be extremely productive. Judith Butler's early work, for example, questions the essentialized identities (and essentially static attributions) of race and gender with the images and inscriptions constructed through social practices (Butler, 1990). She wonders how we might differently understand, and challenge, such constructions. In thinking through the a priori and Nietzsche in her second book, Butler (1993) asks which bodies come to matter and why. She reminds us of the importance of power (regulatory norms and matrices of intelligibility) and that materialization takes place: it is a series of practices that produces, over time, the effects of insides and outsides (boundaries, surfaces, and depths). In her analyses, she provides a very cogent and provocative critique of constructionism and its instantiation of an a priori body: the tabula rasa body, biological material that is inscribed by the social, cultural, political, etc. Studies like Butler's pave the way for Massumi and others to examine and challenge not only how bodies are formed, but also how we might become otherwise in that formation.

I am arguing that we encounter these philosophies in and with art's practice. I discuss how feminist performance art, for example, intervenes in construction (the static body), and go on to contend that interactive art is ideal for experiencing and practicing the body's movement (as moving) and continuity (as continuous). With interactive art we could rehearse, for instance, varying modes of embodied meaning-making, differentiation, or spatialization, as they – and we – relationally emerge.

My focus is not on new vocabularies (whether Massumi's [2002: 27] semiotics, or Huhtamo's [2007: 87–8] taxonomies), but rather a framework for critical encounters with, and examinations of, contemporary art. While we have production models and visual vocabularies for making and reading art that challenges the static body (the stop-points of the body, the representational), we need to also find ways of introducing, engaging, interrogating, and rehearsing its continuity (the body's incipient and relational emergence). I turn now to the field of performance studies to argue that interactive art can bring a continuous understanding of embodiment to bear, as contemporary art philosophy. Here the implicit body is staged to intensify and interrupt the body's performance, calling attention to the relations it enfolds.

## The Body as Per-formed: Emergence, Potential, and Relation

Performance studies as a discipline uses a combination of anthropology, cultural theory, and postmodern reflection, as well as practices of theatre and dance and more. Performance 'is a very inclusive notion of action,' where 'theatre is only one node on a continuum that reaches from ritualization in animal behavior (including humans) through performances in everyday life – greetings, displays of emotion, family scenes, and so on – to rites, ceremonies and performances' as 'large-scale theatrical events' (Schechner, 1977: 1). Various interdisciplinary scholars have called performance (and this is by no means an exhaustive list) 'processual' (Zarrilli, 1986a: 372), transportative or transformative (Schechner, 1985: 126), or an 'activating force or energy' (Drewal and Drewal, 1983: 102). It is a 'liminal space' (Schechner, 2002: 24), in-'between modalities' (Kirshenblatt-Gimblett, 1999: 1), that is not 'reducible to terms independent of its formation' (Kapferer, 1983: 7). In her chapter 'In Excess of the Already Constituted: Interaction as Performance,' Nicole Ridgway builds on these foundations, and performance becomes a figure of thought that encompasses bodily emergence not *in* the between of pre-existing entities (as Richard Schechner and others suggest), but *of* the relation of them together (Ridgway, forthcoming). For her, the body is relationally performed and always emergent.

Both inside and outside of performance studies, there is currently an interesting convergence around the concept of emergence in contemporary thought. The scientific field of emergence, for instance, is related to theories of complexity, where a great number of agents that follow 'a few simple rules of interaction' will behave collectively, 'self-organizing' into an 'emergent intelligence' (Johnson, 2002: 33, 41).[5] Like the movement of the topological Möbius strip, the relationship between the system's basic components generates a surplus effect: the sum is greater than its parts. Whereas 'distributed cognition replaces autonomous will' in the various scientific disciplines dealing with complexity, 'emergence replaces teleology' in the humanities-based fields of philosophy and cultural studies that Ridgway et al. are speaking to (Hayles, 1999: 288). In both science and the arts – where we now see that much of the work in complex systems happens from the bottom-up, rather than top-down – emergence theory highlights the enormous potential of active (and performed) relationships.

Emergence in the humanities is not 'a shape or structure. It is more a bundle of potential functions localized ... separated from each other by dynamic thresholds rather than by boundaries' (Massumi, 2002: 34). Unlike in the Zeno paradox, where position and stasis come first, 'with movement a problematic second,' here position is secondary to movement; it is 'movement residue' (Massumi, 2002: 7). In this shift the problem for theory is no longer one in which we try to explain how change occurs in relation to an extant position, but 'to explain the wonder that there can be stasis given the primacy of process' (Massumi, 2002: 7). In thinking emergence, movement *is*, and positionality is always an *emergent quality* of that movement. Movement and position are not binary opposites, and emergence is not merely the passage between them. Rather, movement and position pass into one another: they form a dynamic unity. To embody this dynamis, this complex passing into, emergence needs to be conceptualized processually. Process is not ontological, but ontogenetic: it develops. Processes are drawn out, are equal to emergence, and emergence is itself processual. In other words, emergence must be understood as emergent itself, as full of unfolding and enfolded potential. When applied to the body, this means our conception of the static body emerges from an emergent embodiment (its continuity), which itself emerges from the interval (continuous continuity) of its potential. The body is an emerging emergence.

If our approach to bodiliness is to map (only the possible points of stasis, like Zeno's arrow), then we are always looking back, after the event of embodiment (the flight of the arrow), and merely seeing it as a series of positions with a singular end – as one not-really-changing, and immobile, 'thing.' If we, rather, follow the movement / positionality dynamic, then we are in the realm of potential. Possibility, says Massumi (2002: 8) is 'backformed from potential's unfolding. But once it is formed, it also effectively feeds in. Fed back, it pre-scripts'. Possibility allows for variation, but only in what a thing already is, whereas potential 'is un-pre-scripted. It only feeds forward' (Massumi, 2002: 8). Potential is 'the immanence of a thing to its still indeterminate variation, under way' (Massumi, 2002: 8). The body is full of and producing potential: always potentialized and, through movement, potentializing.

Ridgway's aforementioned study of digital art 'inter-actions' draws on Gilles Deleuze to name the figure of performance as a way to think through the movement and potential that is emergence. She juxtaposes the Deleuzean notion of *pre*formism – the already preformed or completely given, rather than produced – with *per*formance, 'a taking place, something in process and, by definition, unfinished' (Ridgway, forthcoming). Performance, she writes, is 'a movement and unfolding of the [relation] that is always supplementary and incomplete' (Ridgway, forthcoming). For Ridgway the topological, emergent, potentialized, relational, and interactive are encapsulated in one word: *per-formed.*

Karen Barad also turns to performance, more specifically a rethinking of performativity, in order to put forward a theory of emergent materialization. She offers 'a materialist, naturalist, and posthumanist elaboration' of performativity, one of 'discursive practices' that gives 'matter its due as an active participant in the world's becoming' (Barad, 2003: 802–3). Here discursive / discourse, Barad says explicitly, is not a 'synonym for language ... signifying systems, grammars, speech acts, or conversations' (Barad, 2003: 819), but rather the constraints that enable what *can* be said, what *counts*. Barad understands that 'performativity has become a ubiquitous term in literary studies, theater studies, and the nascent interdisciplinary area of performance studies,' and wants to push it further to incorporate 'important material and discursive, social and scientific, human and nonhuman, and natural and cultural factors' into the 'production of the matter of bodies' (Barad, 2003: 807–8).

This processual figure of performance is used specifically for understanding interaction in Ridgway's paper, all of matter and ontogenesis in Barad's, and embodiment (as well as materialization) in this book. It incorporates the forces of matter and culture, bodies and art – whether present or nonpresent – as always a part of relational formation. This is not the same figure of performance put forward by cultural theorists (and many performance studies scholars) in the early 1990s. The latter refers to a mostly language-based discourse and performance of identity. It is derived from ideas laid out by Erving Goffman, in his classic *The Presentation of Self in Everyday Life,* as well as J.L. Austin's (1962) understanding of 'performative utterances', spoken words which make an ontological change (easily recognizable examples being weddings or declarations of war). Judith Butler provides an interesting example of this earlier figure of performance in her first book when she asserts that gender is performed. We maintain, she writes, a 'tacit collective agreement to perform, produce, and sustain discrete and polar genders as cultural fictions' (Butler, 1990: 140).

The theories surrounding socially constructed identities, and how they adhere to certain bodies, has been and continues to be very productive for cultural studies. Interrogating the feedback loops between one's own body-image construction and the 'cultural fictions' of identity has lead to many breakthroughs in the liberal arts, as well as fine arts. But there is a more apt approach to interactive art, and what it does. As Barad eloquently puts it, construction is an 'invitation to turn everything (including material bodies) into words; on the contrary, performativity' can be 'precisely a contestation of the excessive power granted to language to determine what is real' (Barad, 2003: 802). Interactive art can continue, and feed back into, the projects that Butler et al. began. The figure of performance this book puts forward does not sit between, for example, me and my desire to be something or someone (per Goffman); it is not a means to an end (even if that end is an unreachable fantasy, as Butler initially avers); and it is not based solely on the inscribing practices we perform in order to construct identity. Here performance is an emergent and relational process. The conception of the performed body acknowledges the constructed body *and* the material body, but understands these – along with the incorporeal dimension of the body, its relational activities – as *potential*. This figure of performance as applied to the body enables a much richer encounter with interactive work, and enables such work to further research in, and practices of, art philosophy.[6]

The body, this book contends, is a performed and emerging emergence. It is a process that is constituted in and through and with its relations. The performance of embodiment *is* our potential; it *is* our relationality. And this understanding of the per-formed (not pre-formed) body foreshadows and stresses what is at stake in interactive artistic encounters: an intervention in movement and continuity – in the emergence, potential, and relationality of the body.

## Interaction is not Relation

In contrast to Ridgway's definition, in the introduction to his 2011 book, *Semblance and Event: Activist Philosophy and the Occurrent Arts*, Massumi (2011: 21) unambiguously excludes what we commonly call interaction from qualifying as relational. Here he is specifically speaking back to the digital revolution's overhyped and ill-defined 'interactivity' at large. A distinction between interaction and relation helps in understanding what digital and interactive artworks *cannot* do, as well as what they have the potential *to* do, outside of purely technical terms. It is important to note that all of matter, not just the body, is active, continuously variable, and relational. Massumi reminds us that matter goes from 'something doing to the bare fact of activity; from there to event and change; then on to potential and the production of the new; coming to process as becoming' (Massumi, 2011: 2). Subjects and objects are inter-given; they only exist as in-process relations to other in-process subjects and objects, relaying nested movements and potentials across themselves and each other, as they continuously form. Like Ridgway's 'excess of the already constituted,' Massumi writes of how 'creation' is *felt*, 'coming-into-its-own out of a prior moreness of the world's general always-going-on' (Massumi, 2011: 3). All is always emergent, and of the relation.

On the other hand, the 'inter*action*' of new media art, is merely a 'going back and forth between actions, largely reduced to instrumental function' (Massumi, 2011: 46). Here technology foregrounds only what is possible in its limited system, not the broad experience of moreness and potential. This is not merely to say that the purported choice and individualism of interactive products (art, design, etc.) are an illusion, as discussed in the last chapter. Worse than that, Massumi is declaring that we, as participants, are instrumentalized interactors, and thus become less dynamic with interactive art, rather than more so. Interaction becomes a game with a goal, and we must behave in a specific way to win it. There can be 'a kind of tyranny to interaction' (Massumi, 2011: 47), that forces particular and thus predictive movements, which then may as well be static because they are conceptually, and perhaps sensibly, pre-formed.

Barad too is critical of interaction when offering her concept of intra-action. She asserts that with intra-action, relation is primary and individuation is secondary. In intra-action (and performativity), component phenomena only become determinate, material, and meaningful through their own relational performance. They do not pre-exist their relation, or differentiation. Interaction, on the other hand, assumes a prior existence of independent entities. It is, she argues, about that which is extant. Ridgway differs semantically: her *inter*action is closer to Barad's *intra*-action and Massumi's relationality. Massumi and Barad's criticisms of interactivity, however, make clear that the frame of interactive and digital art, specifically – its utility – is very limited when compared to a wholly actualized and actualizing performance.

Erin Manning similarly cautions against the alleged virtues of interactive art. Manning puts it in the context of a dancer working with gesture-tracking software, asserting that the coded parameters of the system tend to draw attention away from qualities of movement rather than towards it. Viewers of such performances cannot help but wonder where the sensor is, how the software works, and how the dancer controls it. They have a concern for the technology, rather than for the dancer. 'The question shifts from "what can a body do" to "what can technology do"' (Manning, 2009: 64). Interactivity becomes a limiting factor, not only closing off the body, but focusing on utility rather than relation. Manning (2009: 65) argues that 'This is not a plea to return to a pre-technologized body' but 'to explore the potential of technogenesis in relation to the sensing body in movement', to emphasize qualities of movement and emergence *with* technology, rather than technology itself.

Kelli Fuery too is very critical of the term interactivity – though more so of how it is used in the commercial realm. She attempts to bring together the abstract ideals of interactivity as it is sold and the realities of what it is and can be. She contends that there needs to be a cultural knowledge of how to 'participate interactively'; an understanding of the practices that technology and interaction establish (Fuery, 2009: 28). Fuery poses that interactive works do not merely ask us to interact, but position us *as* interactive more generally. Interaction is not something one stops and starts, and so highlighting our interactions is highlighting how we are '*becoming interactive*' (Fuery, 2009: 44). Interactive art, then, is making literal the kinds of assemblages we are always a part of, and thus accenting how we and culture are changed by, through, and with them.[7] Although these assemblages are technological, again we are asked to concentrate on movement and relation, to forget technology and interaction as thing / utility.

Speaking of the work of artist Fabian Marcaccio, Dag Petersson argues that 'knowledge does not form materiality; knowledge is formed by materiality,' and the body of movement in interactive art 'has a capacity for conceptualization that is not opposed to the materiality of the conceptualized' (Petersson, 2003). Petersson's materiality is a constellation of parts that conditions knowledge. Instead of the traditional hierarchical order of the metaphysical opposition in which reflection trumps action (body and movement), what this knowledge has is a composition in, around, and with forces of and on movement, both real and virtual. We compose component parts through our very moving–thinking–feeling, and interactive art can bring that relational performance to bear.

Massumi illuminates and entwines these points when he asks if we could use interactivity to create a 'semblance' of a 'situation.'

> What interactive art can do, what its strength is in my opinion, is to take the *situation* as its 'object.' Not a function, not a use, not a need, not a behavior, exploratory or otherwise, not an action-reaction. But a situation, with its own little ocean of complexity. It can take a situation and 'open' the interactions it affords. The question for interactive art is, How do you cleave an interaction asunder? Setting up an interaction is easy. We have any number of templates for that. But how do you set it up so you sunder it, dynamically smudge it, so that the relation potential it tends-toward appears? So that the situation's objectivity creatively self-abstracts, making a self-tending life-movement, a life-subject and not just a setup. How, in short, do you make a semblance of a situation? These are technical questions, essentially about framing, about what it means to frame an event situationally or house a dispositional life-subject. You can get there technically – in fact whatever the nature of the object involved, it is always a question

> of technique – but when you do it's not because you've [built] a better functioning machine. It's because you've built into the operation shifts in emphasis from interaction to lived relation. You're creating ways of making the lived relation really appear. You're operating on the qualitative level of thinking-feeling, where you are polling styles of being and becoming, not just eliciting behaviors. (Massumi, 2011: 52)

In other words, where a painting can suspend the potentials of vision to create a semblance that virtually appears, interactive art might suspend the dynamics of a situation, so that relations are *virtually felt*. Here is a 'practice that pries open existing practices, of whatever category, scale, siting, or distribution, in a way that makes their potential reappear in a potentialized semblance of themselves' (Massumi, 2011: 53).

Interactive art, I continue where Massumi left off, can interrupt relationality. It can create a space of intervention that brings a situated moving–thinking–feeling to a higher power. Moving–thinking–feeling, as I describe it in interactive art, must disposition, destabilize, and re-work. Here we encounter moving–and–thinking–and–feeling as they are: at once autonomous *and* with one another, as emergent agencies *and* effects *and* affects. Each of the activities of moving and thinking and feeling is moved and felt and thought, before and after and during the others. Moving–thinking–feeling is both virtual and actual, virtualizing and actualizing. Moving–thinking–feeling is intensity itself, is a lived relation or suspended potential. In moving–thinking–feeling, art is always both a limitation and an amplification. It attunes us to a small number of ideas, relations, bodies, materials, or matters, and simultaneously magnifies how they act, relate, *are*.

This moving–thinking–feeling is how I propose we approach interactive art, and how we look to the future of its production, experience, practice, and analysis. Interactivity's limitations enable a grounded and provocative appreciation of what the most successful interactive art can do. It cannot make relations, or frame all of relation. However, an always relational body can be staged so as to suspend aspects of its own performance. Interactive art can concentrate and ask us to virtually feel our existing practices as they are practiced, and provoke us to engage with what those practices imply. The goal should not be to elicit specific behaviors or gestures, but to inaugurate techniques and approaches for encountering, understanding, and taking greater agency in, our continuous, relational performance.

## The Implicit Body as Performance

Staging an implicit body as performance does two things. First, it situates embodiment as always per-formed: emergent and relational. And second, it implicates (other) conceptual–material formations in that (in)exact ongoing performance. Here we interrupt, and interfere in, the per-formed to make it virtually felt. It is a situation where we might experience and practice embodiment, with a recognition of what Jane Bennett calls the 'agentic capacity' of humans and non-humans, matter and matters (Bennett, 2010: 33). In the foreword to Richard Schechner's book, *Between Theatre and Anthropology*, anthropologist Victor Turner asserts that performance studies practitioners such as Schechner are less 'concerned with *stasis* than with *dynamis*,' and are, as such, 'committed... to interference' (Turner, 1985: xi–xii). I, too, am concerned with practitioners who disrupt and provoke. Like N. Katherine Hayles, I 'view the present moment as a critical juncture when interventions might be made... into prevailing concepts of subjectivity' (Hayles, 1999: 5) and, more importantly for the project of this book, embodiment.

Hayles' use of the word intervention is I believe a purposeful allusion to contemporary art practices. The term 'art intervention' – in use since the late 1960s and popularized more widely by the 2004 exhibition, *The Interventionists* (Thompson and Sholette, 2006) – hints at some sort of subversion from within a dominant paradigm. The works that fit into this field tend to involve references to and engagements with previously existing artworks, audiences, or venues / spaces. The infamous graffiti artist, Banksy, for example, is disruptive and anonymous with his interventions. His art ranges from illicitly hanging his own work alongside 'the greats' in museums, or self-referential and humorously critical documentaries about street art, to printing his own money and putting it into UK circulation, or designing ironic children's story books for religious extremists (Banksy, 2010). Each uses context and media to speak back to power by provoking laughter, discomfort, and / or thoughtfulness around the issues at hand. The accent on and interrogation of cultural norms and accepted hierarchical structures present in such pieces is itself an artful and productive mode of inquiry and practice.

Interventionist art, especially with regards to the body, has seen a great deal of successful work in the performance realm over the last three decades, in particular with explicit body art by female artists in the 1980s and 1990s. The 'explicit body' is a term coined by Rebecca Schneider to describe performances that speak to the body as a 'mass of orifices and appendages, details and tactile surfaces' that 'in representation is foremost a site of social markings, physical parts and gestural signatures of gender, race, class, age, sexuality – all of which bear ghosts of historical meaning, markings delineating social hierarchies of privilege and deprivilege' (Schneider, 1997: 2). The body made explicit in performance 'explicate[s] bodies in social relation' (Schneider, 1997: 2). The explicit body, which is named in reference to the Latin root explicare, to unfold, uses an 'explosive literality' in order to unfold and 'peel back layers of signification' (Schneider, 1997: 2). This explicit unfolding exposes 'not an originary, true, or redemptive body, but the sedimented layers of signification themselves' (Schneider, 1997: 2). The explicit body in performance is a body inscribed by a history larger than the body itself. We are peeling away to reveal which bodies have come to matter, and why. In explicit body art, the cultural inscriptions of race and gender, for example, are interrupted and intervened in as inaccurately mattering more than matter itself. Explicit bodies shock us into remembering that bodies are both more and less than what culture constructs them to be.

Schneider's explicit body in performance 'renders the symbolic [as] literal' in order to 'pose a threat ... [to] implicit structures of comprehensibility' (Schneider, 1997: 1–3). Explicit body performance deploys the material body to collide the literal against the symbolic order of meaning in order to implode the binary logics of capitalism and patriarchy. What follows are brief descriptions of three feminist performance artworks from a very large field, chosen because of how they exemplify Schneider's thesis, as well as stress a common focus on interrupting language and identity.

In the work of Karen Finely, the explicit body intervenes in the spectacle of engenderment. In one scene in *The Constant State of Desire,* she challenges Freud's theory of penis envy (that women have children as a replacement for the phallus) by literally 'strapping on' and wielding an infant across the stage. Finely does not offer herself as an object of desire but rather desecrates herself as an object of male desire, as a commodity to be consumed (Dolan, 1989). Confounding the expectations of conventional theatrical spectatorship, Finley de-idealizes and de-sacralizes the body and draws attention to female bodies as sites of prohibition (Fuchs, 1989). By taking on signifiers that actively identify a body, such performances reveal these markings and draw us to the place where meaning collapses (Diamond, 1989, 1995). Here the explicit body literalizes the legislative frontier, that aspect of power, which both authorizes and invalidates representations, and gestures to that which is un-representable.

The confrontational use of the literal body to draw attention to its representational inscription can also be seen in the work of artist VALIE EXPORT. In her 1968 *Action Pants: Genital Panic,* EXPORT offers the filmmaking / viewing public at an art cinema in Munich an up close view of herself wearing pants with the crotch cut out. Moving from row to row, EXPORT's actual genitals confront the fetishized representational genitals of pornography. She 'repudiate[s] the representational static sign' of the female body in film, and instead stages an 'interventionist act' (Stiles, 1969). This performance amplifies the reduction of women to their sex, and makes explicit the relationships between spectacle, body, visual image, and objectifier / viewer.

A final example, one that Schneider herself often points to, the Guerrilla Girls (GG) began asking questions about women and people of color in the art world – their lack of power and recognition – in the early 1980s. They found their initial protests lacking progress, and so began (and continue) to play out a visual pun on 'guerrilla warfare' in order to get the attention of the media: GG wear ape-like suits, and hang or carry provocative political signs, which might ask questions like, 'Do women have to be naked to get into the Met. Museum?' (Metropolitan Museum of Art), and highlight statistics that show that the vast majority of artists in the Met are white males, while almost all the nudes are female (Figure 8). Calling themselves the 'conscience of the art world,' they remain anonymous to this day, and have gained international recognition as the 'masked avengers,' who fight against discrimination through posters, talks, publications, and films that expose 'sexism, racism and corruption in politics, art, film and pop culture ... with facts, humor and outrageous visuals' (Guerrilla Girls, 2007). According to Schneider, the Guerrilla Girls 'make explicit a social contract which has historically marked women and people of color as less evolved, more "primitive," than the implicitly higher primate,' the white male (Schneider, 1997: 1).

As evidenced here, within the framework of the performance art, body art, and Happenings movements, the notion of the explicit body is extremely productive. It unfolds and reveals to us our stories, preconceptions, and social relations. This kind of art draws attention to the dominant structures of representation and meaning-making, and works to reveal the body as a site of inscription, surveillance, and power. It asks the spectator to grapple with the body's explication in discourse and in art practices (for example, in primitivism), and attempts to make visible the relations of seeing – who sees and who is seen – embedded in these discourses and practices.

Ursula Frohne and Christian Katti assert that body and language, as concepts and materials, gained new significance in the art realm with the introductions of performance and conceptual art, and their importance continues to grow as artists engage with and use new media. But, they continue, we need 'to develop a critical concept of media that neither presupposes nor excludes the categories of body and language ... to address the political implications for changing notions of the body and language under the impact of electronic space and communication' (Frohne and Katti, 2000: 9). This book takes up Frohne and Katti's challenge to develop an approach to new media art that neither excludes nor presupposes the body (or language). It aims to develop a critical approach to digital artworks that disrupt not

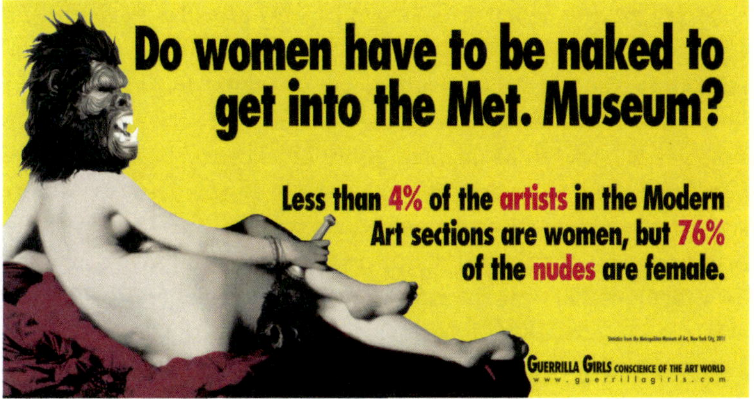


Figure 8. GUERRILLA GIRLS poster I Copyright © Guerrilla Girls I Courtesy www.guerrillagirls.com

only inherited structures of representation, but also the embodied relations inherent to that which is (materially) per-formed.

Following performance art and under the conditions of digitality, there's potential for an/other shift in subject /object and performer / audience hierarchies, and thus a shift in how we might read explicit inscriptions and/or come to sense, perceive, and perform our embodiment. To pick up on Schneider's pun, the flesh is not only a site *for* inscription and thus unfolding, but also an activity *of* writing and mattering and enfolding, a continuous topology that does not uncover or discover bodies, but emerges *as* bodies (both legible and illegible), as not-yet-bodies, as bodies in process; these are implied and implicated bodies, in relation and drawn out. Where the root of explicit is *to unfold*, to imply is *to enfold*, and the relationship between the two is neither dichotomous nor dialectical. Inside becomes outside becomes inside; implication feeds into explication and vice-versa, in a continuous and transformational performance akin to the Möbius strip. This continuum is not a binary between emergence and positioning, between regulatory operations and becomings, or even between implicit and explicit. It is a both /and, a processual formation that is of the relation of both body and bodies, both virtual and actual, both material and conceptual.

South African digital artist Tegan Bristow provides an elegant example of such work. Her *Chalk Vision* (2007–8, Figure 9) uses a camera to track participants' movements in real-time, drawing chalk-like lines over a black background in the wake of every action, which then slowly fade back to nothingness. Move quickly, and large swathes of powdered sketches appear and slowly dull; slower gestures conjure smaller patches of white pigment, which seem to vanish more rapidly. Stand completely still, and disappear entirely. The piece began as an investigation of movement with dancer / choreographer Athena Mazarakis in a full-length performance piece entitled *Coming To*, and was later turned into various interactive installations, videos, and prints. The key to the installation version is that it does not represent or intervene in 'the body' as construction or even as a material thing, but rather presents movement, itself, as productive. It shows and *makes felt* 'the energy' we put into 'performing, in a different way' (Bristow, 2012). With *Chalk Vision*, vision is in tune with all of sensation – our virtual and actual movement and potential are emphasized, over time.

The drawn lines that are both anticipated and left behind in our ongoing performance with Bristow's installation make *difference* appear. We see not only our movement *as* movement, but also that motion in relation to the environment around us. If we run past a chair, sketched outlines of that chair become visible and then wash away. If we sit in the chair and remain static, both chair and body wither. And here, we move–think–feel without moving. We sit still, and that stillness is *still moving* – an activity that is affective in its stillness. In this way, *Chalk*

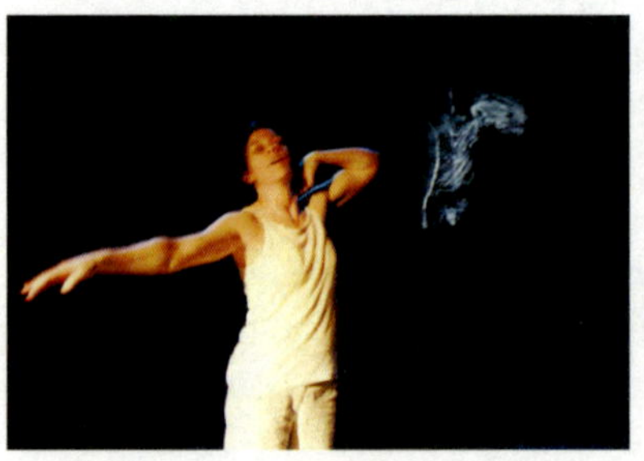

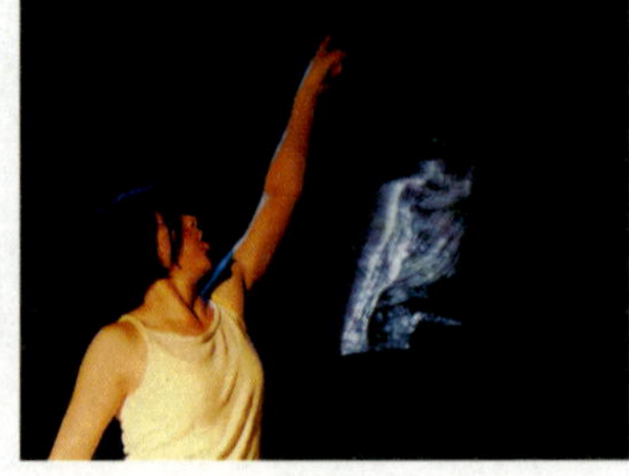

Figure 9. Athena Mazarakis with Tegan Bristow's *Chalk Vision* | part of *Coming To* | photo copyright Christo Doherty

*Vision* invites us to focus not on a drawing or text or image or body, but on embodied and continuous creation and relation. It is a framing of intensive experience, of moving–thinking–feeling, both as they happen, and about to happen.

Interactive artworks such as *Chalk Vision* and its various iterations *introduce* us to embodiment's performance, as it is felt. They foreground incipient formation. Nicole Ridgway asserts that interaction is often thought of as 'doing something.' But, she continues, 'as a combination of attention and distraction, intention and passivity' it is also a receiving and enduring, 'woven through with the reciprocities of sensation, affectivity and conscious reflection.' 'It speaks to not only the ability to effect, but the ability to be affected' (Ridgway, forthcoming). Art like Bristow's has the potential to highlight active composition and not merely reflection. It may 'unfold the space between subjects and objects such that subjects and objects are implicated in the space of unfolding. Here interaction encompasses a taking place that inaugurates rather than enacts an *a priori* script' (Ridgway, forthcoming). Interactive art can be a site that frames emergence. It stages neither just a doing or making, nor all of relation; it is an *inauguration* of their processes.

Moreover, interactive installations have the power to provoke a *rehearsal* of the possibilities and potentials in embodied transformation. Hansen beautifully captures the power of corporeal interventions when translating and paraphrasing French philosopher Alain Milon's *La Realité Virtuelle: Avec ou sans le Corps?* The body in interactive art, he argues, 'furnishes the opportunity to pose the question of the person and its status' (Hansen, 2006: 14). Here the body 'forms an "obstacle and a resistance to all forms of transparence" and is living only "when it is opaque, complex, confused, flexible and in perpetual mutation"' in relation to the outside (Hansen, 2006: 14). Implicit body art – interactive art – I argue, intensifies features of this ongoing mutation, the ongoing transformation of the 'living' body. Like a directional microphone, *Chalk Vision* picks up and amplifies specific facets of our continuous relations over time, and gifts us with a stage to *practice* being and becoming.

All the world's goings-on, according to Massumi, are not made of *objects*, but *events*. An event is a 'substanceless and durationless moment ... whose reality is that of potential – pure relationality, the interval of change, the in-itself of transformation' (Massumi, 2002: 58). Nothing pre-exists the event of occurrence. *Things*, and I use this word as purposefully ambiguous, are *per-formed*. Art, its perception and materialization, has the power to frame and highlight events as they occur – to make them perceptible and felt. With *interactive* art, I am arguing, aspects of action, affect, and occurrence are framed, in *practice*. Bristow's technological rig has us take account of, and purposefully shift and change, how we might per-form otherwise.

Such event-spaces, I contend, are what Massumi calls situations.[8] In his study of a Hollywood film set, he asserts that the 'good graces of a rig' can make 'a technology of the event' through 'strategies of performance' (Massumi, 2002: 55, 63, 277).[9] In other words, the 'rig' of a set, stage, or art installation may produce a space that invites a performance, which is ripe with potential and transformation. A *situation* refers to the 'potentialization of a context' (Massumi, 2002: 265), circumstances that frame and amplify an event. The 'technological rig' of interactive art, I argue, does precisely this. It stages an implicit body as performance, creating a unique situation that might intervene in the eventful emergence of embodiment. The proscenium that stages an explicit body can be thought of as a rig, a situation for intervening in the body's cultural construction – the static body. Interactive art, then, situates and intervenes in the body's ongoing constitution – the continuous body. Explicit body art unfolds and explicates inscriptions, while implicit body art enfolds and implicates incorporations.

An inscription is a sign. It is normalized and abstract, a system that can operate 'independently of any particular manifestation' (Hayles, 1999: 196). Incorporation, on the other hand, cannot be separated from its context – it is embodied. Hayles writes that an incorporating practice like a wave cannot be separated from the body: 'it exists as such only when it is instantiated in a particular hand' making a particular movement (Hayles, 1999: 197). We could, she continues, abstract that sign from an embodied or material gesture by 'representing it in a different medium, for example by drawing on a page the outline of a stylized hand with wavy lines indicating motion' (Hayles, 1999: 201). But then it is no longer incorporated; it is inscribed outside its particular instantiation. Incorporating practices are part of a performing body, which is modulated by inscribing practices, which then feed back in between sign and potential, construction and constitution, static and continuous: in and out and in again. This can be applied to an understanding of what interactive art *does*.

Where static and continuous bodies together make our experience of embodiment, and inscribing and incorporating practices make clear the signs and performances that feed into them, explicit and implicit body artworks disrupt and intervene into these practices, respectively. Explicit body art, to use the language of performance and dance, *unpatterns* habitual understandings, calling attention to the contradictions in commonly accepted power structures; implicit body art does the same to habitual actions, accenting movement and transformation through relational mobility. Both suspend potential.

Hansen asserts almost this much when he claims that *Bodies in Code* are 'the technical mediation of the body schema' (Hansen, 2006: 19). Interactive art is a 'technically triggered experience' that can 'stage ... the excess of the body schema over the body image to increase [the participant's] agency as an embodied being' (Hansen, 2006: 19–20). He looks at the mixed reality movement within interactive art to argue that inviting action and acceleration, rather than producing illusion and simulacrum, creates more immersive spaces. Interactive artists, he asserts, are 'exploiting the margin of indetermination' (Hansen, 2006: 30) in the process of body-making. Interactive art intensifies the experience of bodiliness through its engagement with embodiment as inherently relational and emergent. I take Hansen one step further in contending that here we might practice *modes* of embodiment, philosophies for how we *could be*.

Referring back to Zeno's arrows, and the post-event, 3D, mapped-out structures that make up the contemporary subject, I like to say that artists like Finley use the explicit body to not only frame the body's constructions, but to put a given and signified 'possibility' for the body – the arrow's stop-points – in quotes. Explicit body art can performatively literalize, ironize, and call into question the sacred classifications of 'race,' 'gender,' 'woman,' 'child,' or 'phallus,' depending on the *explication*. Actually, to borrow a phrase from Walter Benjamin, they are 'quoting without quotation marks' (Benjamin, 1997: 48).[10] To quote is not only to restate, but also to re-site (with an 's'), and to re-*situate*. This 're-giving is neither a simple iteration nor a repetition,' but rather a 'process of reworking' where possibilities – inscribed, incorporated, or otherwise – are 'able to be revealed' (Benjamin, 1997: 50–3). Quotation marks, asserts Benjamin, are used to indicate 'the presence of different moments of historical time – chronological time,' to give or remove the temporal conditions for that which is quoted. To quote without quotation marks, then, 'signals the disruption of context' (Benjamin, 1997: 53). In other words, the context becomes *potentialized*. A quotation without quotation marks re-cites and re-situates, suspends, amplifies, challenges, and intervenes in, that which is (not) in quotes.

Staging explicit bodies in performance puts Zeno's stop-points in crisis through the tactic of quoting without quotation marks. Here artists re-cite and re-situate our structured inscriptions and supposedly static identities, asking us to look at what is both inside and outside of the quote, its history, presence, and disruption, all the while bringing 'ontological and temporal considerations to bear' (Benjamin, 1997: 53). Finley, EXPORT, and the Guerrilla Girls interrogate their respective subject matters with the spectacle of missing quotation marks around aspects of their supposedly static bodies, how we read their explicit inscriptions. And where explicit body quotes surround Zeno's positions and put them in crisis, *implicit* body quotes do the same to movement, to the body's continuity. Interactive art such as Bristow's *Chalk Vision* suspends and intervenes in the *potential* that is the body before it is reduced to what is *possible*. It interrogates ontogenesis, the body's passage and emergence, and challenges that which occurs, and plays a role, in its per-formance.[11]

In interactive art, in addition to challenging 'gender' or 'child,' we can poll styles of 'individuation' and 'temporality' – as embodied and processual conceptual–material formations. The process of embodiment, like passage, precedes construction – and every relation is implicated. Interactive body art is a situation, a potentialized context that invites us to engage with the experiences and practices from which an implicit embodiment emerges. The work that this book addresses does not focus only on our social inscriptions, but also attempts to create uncertainty in our contextual (or decontextualized) incorporations, dispersing, interfering with, and intervening in, our continuous materialization. Such art re-cites the potential of emergent bodies at large, and can more fundamentally incorporate and / or re-situate its ongoing relations to that with which we interact, and their *implications.*[12] By staging an implicit body as performance, interactive art can magnify our bodies' *emergent relations with* the forces, concepts, and materials that make up and embody, for example, language, society, or space. These 'sensible concepts' get to be *conceptually sensed* and virtually felt. They are situated and intensified as always a part of how we move and create (with) them, just as they move and create (with) us. To imply in Latin is not only to enfold, but also to involve and entwine, and in the best cases of art, to inter-act, re-work, and per-form.

Interactive art not only engages a performed embodiment, but intervenes in its implicit and indeterminate processes. The implicit body in interactive art situations, staged via technologized rig-events, is complexified, confused, and suspended. In fact, interactive art stages a body whose inter-actions are once removed from a situation, and brought to a higher power: it creates a semblance of a situation. According to Char Davies, such works 'temporarily deautomate habitual perception and facilitate a "seeing freshly"' (Hansen, 2006: 111). Interactive artist Rafael Lozano-Hemmer claims that the motivation is a 'modification of existing behavior,' to 'create a situation where... the participants relate in new, "alien" ways' (Lozano-Hemmer, 2001b). By setting the stage, interactive artists create productive tensions between the per-formed and the pre-formed, shifting our experiences of 'body,' and having us practice how bodies might become otherwise.

## A Relational Approach

Curator and art theorist Nicolas Bourriaud has also called for a 'thematic framework' that understands participatory, relational, and interventionist art and installation (Bourriaud, 2005: 7). In his *Relational Aesthetics,* however, socioeconomic status and identity are engaged through face-to-face dialogue between peers, rather than embodiment and materialization being practiced through interaction. Bourriaud asserts that the 'aura of art no longer lies in the hinterworld represented by the work, nor in form itself, but in front of it, within the temporary collective form that it produces by being put on show' (Bourriaud, 1998: 61). For him the power of art lies in the 'momentary social groupings' of the exhibition (Bourriaud, 1998: 17). Bourriaud writes that many artists from the 1990s had begun to engage such groupings as a dominant force in the *work* of their art, and contends that we need 'aesthetic criteria' to analyze and judge the coherence of this art's form, and 'the image of human relations reflected by it' (Bourriaud, 1998: 18). Here art is 'an activity consisting in producing relationships with the world with the help of signs, forms, actions and objects,' and it is critiqued by asking questions pertaining to what Bourriaud calls the co-existence criterion: 'Does this work permit me to enter into dialogue? Could I exist, and how, in the space it defines?' (Bourriaud, 1998: 107, 109).

What Bourriaud defines as relational artworks take the forms of 'invitations, casting sessions, meetings, convivial and user-friendly areas, appointments, etc. ... vehicles through which particular lines of thought and personal relationships with the world are developed' (Bourriaud, 1998: 46). They are public encounters, events, and collaborations that go beyond aesthetic consumption. These works deal with relationships between people, whether individuals, groups, networks, or some combination thereof. Thai-born and New York-based Rirkrit Tiravanija, for instance, is probably best known for his performance-based events, where he provides free meals for his participants, with the hope of collaboratively exploring dialogue, sharing, and gifting between them. The artist would set up a dining table and working kitchen, and cook lunches and dinners for both invited and walk-in guests. He would carry on conversations, ask and encourage participants to interact socially with one another, thus provoking and creating the relationships that shape the work itself, over time. Tiravanija's other work includes setting up reconstructions of his own apartment in the gallery space, organizing reading libraries in museums, and setting up communal artist residencies, towards the same end of social interaction – among other sociopolitical goals. His work, argues Bourriaud, breaks 'with the manipulation of references and citation' most common in 1960s performance art, Fluxus, happenings, etc, and instead works to 'deeply reexamine notions of creation, authorship, and originality through a problematics of the use of cultural artifacts' (Bourriaud, 2005: 8–9).

Tiravanija's work places people in relation to one another. Rather than attempt to move the world towards a pre-determined ideal (as in the aforementioned art movements) he and his contemporaries ask us '*to inhabit the world in a better way*' (Bourriaud, 1998: 18). Bourriaud writes that artists such as Tiravanija use interpersonal relationships as a starting point in their work, and are making temporary 'micro-utopias, the interstices opened up in the social corpus' (Bourriaud, 1998: 70). A relational aesthetic framework thus seeks to explore 'the invention of relations between consciousness' and 'the social setting for the reception of art' (Bourriaud, 1998: 22). Relational artists set up human to human relationships in order to invite investigations, along with better understandings and perhaps practices, of society, and how we operate with/in it.

As art critic and theorist Claire Bishop notes in the introduction to *Participation* – her edited collection that aims to show the trajectory leading up to and beyond relational aesthetics – the 'point of departure' for relational aesthetics and its historical antecedents 'is the *social* dimension of participation' (Bishop, 2006: 10). This is opposed to the participatory activities found in what Bishop disdainfully refers to as 'so-called "interactive" art' (Bishop, 2006: 10) in which a *continuously embodied* participant is activated. Bishop quickly dismisses the kind of work discussed in this book, arguing against 'the opposition of "active" and "passive"' viewers – and thus nullifying the potential difference in understanding bodily activity in the gallery space – as well as stating that the 'trajectory' of interactive art has been 'rehearsed elsewhere' (Bishop, 2006: 16, 10). Unfortunately, Bishop's stance only serves to solidify the opposition she argues against – active and passive viewers, social and corporeal interaction – and the examples she gives for the 'rehearsal' of interactivity discourses fall very short of comprehensive study.[13]

In her September 2012 piece for *Artforum,* Bishop perpetuates what she calls the Digital Divide in her separation of the sphere of 'new media' art from the mainstream art world. She sings praises of the few relational artists that cross over from their world to the digital, all only occasionally working in video, and entirely ignores those digital artists who practice intensive situations in and with new media's forms. She directly asks, 'While many artists use digital technology, how many really confront the question of what it means to think, see, and filter affect through the digital? How many thematize this, or reflect deeply on how we experience, and are altered by, the digitization of our existence?' (Bishop, 2012). Bishop's polemical stance is in the interest of debate, but with it she shows a willful ignorance of the very large number of artists who do precisely what she is asking for. Perhaps the question is not in what digital artists have mostly failed to produce, but in what mainstream theorists and critics have mostly failed to engage with/in their work. New media art, I argue, can and does directly stage themes of affect. Its work continuously addresses 'digital' existence (and performance), and so much more in our being and becoming.

Bourriaud, many of the artists he writes about, and most of the theorists that follow his lead (Bishop included) largely ignore the following: the body as more than a vessel for consciousness and identity; recent technological innovations in art;[14] and embodied interactions in the gallery space. These three areas of investigation admittedly have little to do with his thesis or the work that Bourriaud and his peers discuss; but their lack nonetheless reveals a large gap in relational art dialogues. I take inspiration from Bourriaud's and Bishop's texts, but proffer an approach and framework for embodied experiences and practices in addition to social participation. Here yet other criteria can be productively applied when approaching artworks that engage with relationality as their point of departure. Like Bourriaud, I too want to move beyond the utopian promises of my art form's progenitors. But while relational aesthetics is 'devoted ... to the world of exchange and communication, the world of "commerce,"' (Bourriaud, 1998: 42), the implicit body approach concentrates on emergence and corporeality, matter and matters, as framed through affect, movement, and sensation. Instead of critically asking about dialogue and existence, it interrogates continuity, being, and becoming. Both modes of interactive art place forms in relation to one another and make temporary and exploratory corpuses within the gallery space. They both explore relationality, the goings-on at an exhibition, interactivity and participation. In the case of the works discussed in this book, however, these formations are both material and virtual, in addition to social, and the corpus is embodied as well as in discourse. The interactivity interrogated with the implicit body approach asks us to relate in a different way: through – and as – flesh, in addition to our socioeconomic standings in the world.

One example of a work that might be productively approached in this way is Brian Knep's *Healing Pool* (2008, Figure 10). Knep explores biologically-inspired generative algorithms in interactive installations for galleries, museums, and public spaces. *Healing Pool* is a room-sized Petri dish featuring a floor that is covered with projected 'cells,' which participants walk through / over, leaving tears and empty space in their wake. The installation then 'heals' itself by growing new cells

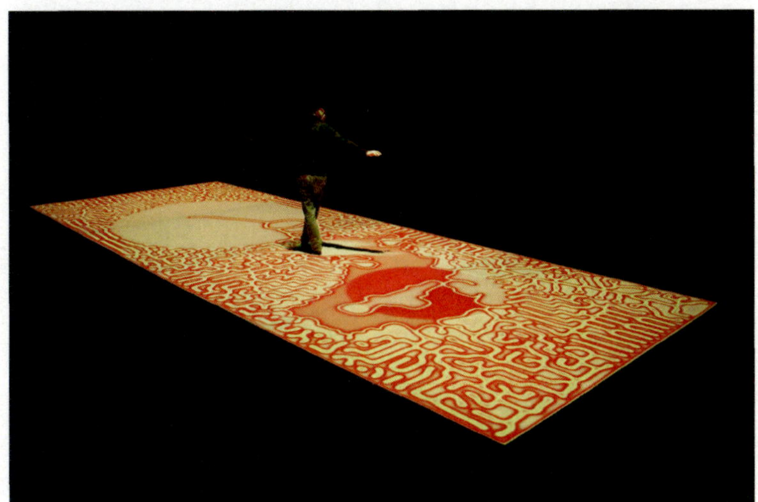

Figure 10. Brian Knep I *Healing Pool* (Mois Multi), 2010

as seams and scars, never again to repeat any of its previous patterns. Knep's work pushes at the boundaries of how we move–think–feel and practice growth, healing, organic structures, and temporal relations. It is a work that is mostly playful on its surface, and extremely subtle in its visual difference over time. So subtle, in fact, that it is very easy to miss the artist's doubled gesture towards emergence theory: both how simple systems can create complexity, and how our collaborative embodied interactions, which seemingly change little, have lasting and forever-changing effects.

Knep shows both the similarities and differences between the works presented in the rest of this book and those Bourriaud writes about. Like Bourriaud's relational artworks, a piece such as this goes 'beyond its traditional role as a receptacle of the artist's vision, it now functions as an active agent, a musical score, an unfolding scenario, a framework that possesses autonomy and materiality to varying degrees' (Bourriaud, 2005: 20). As this chapter has argued, here is a situation, a potentialized context ready for transformation among agents – the *work* is in the event that continues to occur in and with its space. We must focus, as with all relational art, on the styles of engagement this piece generates, the relationships that create and transform the art and the viewer, experience and practice, over time. But in Knep's case, with the implicit body approach, we concentrate on material as well as social relations. We engage with pre-conscious movement and affect, while Bourriaud's relational art is reflective only on our identities – social, economic, political, etc. – in the world. In other words, while the works that Bishop, Bourriaud, and others write about encourage relationships, participation, and interactivity, they are similar to explicit body performance art in their engagement with how we *understand* our selves in the world – challenging the *static* (socioeconomic) body. Artworks that stage an implicit body have us encounter how we move, transform, and *are* (continuous). The difference is key.

Bourriaud proclaims that relational art is a 'set of artistic practices which take as their theoretical and practical point of departure the whole of human relations and their social context, rather than an independent and private space' (Bourriaud, 1998: 113). By comparison, implicit body art takes as its point of departure the whole of *embodied* relations, and their material and conceptual, encountered situations, rather than an individual and extant body (or 'consciousness') that passively consumes an a priori world. Neither work asks us to move towards utopia, and the latter provides circumstances where we might investigate and rehearse the constitution of body, matter, *and* meaning. Interactive art asks us to explore performance and corporeal relationships as powerful means of being and becoming, thinking, feeling, and beginning to know.

Bishop (2004) follows Bourriaud by asking what criteria and critique befit relational art. I ask the same for interactive installation. How can we best encounter art situations that push us to chase or stutter or build or write with our bodies? What modes of analysis should be practiced for rigged-up installations that intervene in our incorporating practices, events that beg questions of how we relate corporeally? What do such artworks imply and enfold? We need a framework that enables a moving–thinking–feeling through of interventions in movement and continuity, which is sensitive to cross-modal perception and intensive experience, counter to the disembodiment discourses often found in digital domains, beyond technical utopias, and open to the productive paradox(es) that being bodily *is*. I do not turn to art in order to explain philosophical theories, but rather, understand art as the practice of contemporary philosophies, where we investigate, and further research on, embodiment and relationality, together. I do not concentrate only on the social aspects of participation, but also on the material activities that constitute per-formed bodies and that with which they relate. At stake are the agencies at play in a continuous embodiment that is interactive, relational, and implicated, deeper insights into, and potential strategies for, interventions in our ongoing enfleshment.

## Notes

1 Strathern's is a critique of specific 'feminist quests' that try (and fail) to escape dominant Western understandings of embodiment (Strathern, 1994: 243).

2 This should not be confused with the Cartesian split of mind and body. In Hayles' thesis, our physical consciousness is *part* of embodiment (the

flesh), and 'the body' is how we understand it. In a later paper, Hayles critiques her own 'dualistic thinking', and says both the body and embodiment emerge from a 'relational flux' (Hayles, 2002: 298).

3 Many embodiment theorists have criticized phenomenologists like Hansen because, with their philosophy, every experience centers on a human perception. Erin Manning asserts that we must recognize the potential of virtual effects and bare activities – where being and becoming exceed the human, in what she calls the more-than-human (Manning, 2010a). Object-oriented philosophers who embrace phenomenology – like Graham Harman or Ian Bogost – claim a move to 'non-human' perception, a 'deep commitment to objects' in themselves (Grusin, 2012b). But as media theorists Richard Grusin and Jussi Parikka point out, they offer a distinctly '*human-centered* discourse about objects' (Grusin, 2012b, my emphasis). 'Objects' are implicitly things to be perceived (by humans), and explicitly more singular and static than matter (Parikka, 2011a, 2011b).

4 The Möbius strip was chosen for this analogy because it is the simplest and most well-known topological figure. Elizabeth Grosz (1994) and José Gil (2006) similarly think the body in this way. Grosz's use of the Möbius strip is actually critiqued by Hayles, who says that a topological figure makes it 'difficult to chart gradations within the continuum,' and she instead suggests an 'interplay between two intersecting axes... the field itself is generated by the interplay between these end points.' She makes the case that the 'polarities defining the end points of the axes acknowledge the historical importance of dichotomies' (Hayles, 1999: 195–6). I would rebut her in saying that our understandings of history and future (the supposed end points of her axes) also feed back into, and are affected by, the entire formation. Further, in the specific case of a relational embodiment, it is precisely because we want to look at continuity (the Möbius 'continuum') and *not* 'gradations' (Zeno's stop-points, which might lie between, or at, the axes end points), that a topological figure is a far better analogy.

5 Emergent complexity explains how ant colonies (long mistakenly thought to have central decision-makers, or pacemakers) can perform mathematical formulas to figure out precisely where are the most efficient places for garbage dumps, their dead, or the queen in relation to the colony (tested in nature as well as captivity), and reveals how and why cityscapes form, merge, and change due to human behavior and external forces. Emergence theory has been used to develop genetic algorithms

that adapt software to new operating systems, create intelligent voice and character recognition programs using a large number of small, parallel programs instead of one massive decision tree, and recommend music and books to Amazon shoppers worldwide. For a popular science explanation of the field of emergence, see *Emergence: The Connected Lives of Ants, Brains, Cities and Software* (Johnson, 2002).

6 A study of gender, race, or other identity-based classifications through the lens of the per-formed is beyond the scope of this text. Such a study is taken on in part, however, in Lanei Rodemeyer's forthcoming book on Lou Sullivan and transexuality, *Diaries of a Transsexual: Lou Sullivan and the Body's Voice*. Its premise was outlined in Rodemeyer's paper, 'From the Diaries of Lou Sullivan: Intersubjective Discourse and the Intersection of Embodiment' at the Intercorporeality and Intersubjectivity conference at University College Dublin, June 6–7, 2008 in Dublin, Ireland (Rodemeyer, 2008).

7 Worthy of mention here is Fuery's reference to the oft-forgotten differently-abled, who are rarely considered in new media theory and production. How can we better engage those with physical or mental differences that might not interact with new media in the same way, and how can 'typical' bodies experience and practice with them (Fuery, 2009: 43)? This is very fertile ground for research both in and beyond the arts, humanities, and sciences. Some of my own art investigates stuttering through interactivity, and a number of artists, including David Rokeby, Erin Manning, and Patrick Lichty, have written about their or others' work in relation to the differently-abled and / or neurodiversity with digital technologies.

8 Massumi's concept of 'situation' first appears in a footnote in *Parables For the Virtual* (Massumi, 2002), and later in his hopes for interactive art in *Semblance and Event* (Massumi, 2011).

9 In Massumi's original example, it is a 'technology of the event that is also a technology of the self and a technologizing of the self' (Massumi, 2002: 63). This sequence of critical proclamations comes out in an ironic but thoughtful study of one of Ronald's Reagan's early performances.

10 This phrase comes from Walter Benjamin's unpublished notes, some of which are translated and cited by Andrew Benjamin in *Present Hope: Philosophy, Architecture, Judaism* (Benjamin, 1997).

11 Quoting without quotation marks as a frame for interactive art is put forward with an understanding that quotation marks are themselves signs, and thus inscriptions. This is a gesture towards reconciling the feedback

loop between the incorporations we perform in and with our relational activities, and the critical distance we must apply in order to utilize an implicit body approach.

12 This is not the first time the word 'implication' has been used to refer to enfolding potential. Philosopher Gilbert Simondon's work on emergence briefly labels 'implicit form' to be 'a bundling of potential functions, an infolding or contraction of potential interactions' (cited in Massumi, 2002: 34–5). Nigel Thrift discusses implication in his *Non-representational Theory* (Thrift, 2008). And quantum physicist David Bohm also puts forward an 'implicate order,' which assures us that 'objective indeterminacy' happens on all levels (Bohm, 1980; Massumi, 2002: 37).

13 Bishop names *Ambiente / Arte: dal Futurismo alla Body Art, Installation Art in the New Millennium,* and *Installation Art: A Critical History* (Celant, 1977; Oliviera, 2003; Bishop, 2005). The first is an outdated exhibition catalogue from 1976 with no interactive works that resemble those being produced today and studied in this book; the other two are surveys of installation art more generally (the latter of which is by Bishop herself) that include very few (in Bishop's case, no) digitally interactive pieces, and are a far cry from the careful and insightful critiques that both Bourriaud and Bishop aim for with their own proposed aesthetic frameworks.

In *Installation Art,* Bishop is more careful around issues of embodiment and interactivity than she is in *Participation,* but it pertains to cross-modal perception rather than action, such as with Minimalist art, or to the *potential* for interactivity, for example in relational art. In the latter case, her portrayal of the 'embodied viewer… insists' *only* on the 'presence of the viewer [as] the key characteristic of installation'; these bodies, she says, need their 'senses of touch, smell… sound [and] vision,' but are not active beyond perception (Bishop, 2005: 6). I do not wish to devalue affect and perception, or such work and our experience of it, but to convey that it is only *suggestive* of embodied *practice.* When Bishop writes about works that 'discourage you from contemplation and insist that you *act,*' the 'acting' she writes about is interpersonal and propositional. In her words, these artworks ask viewers to 'write something down, have a drink, or talk to other people' within a given space (Bishop, 2005: 10). The pieces are exclusively sociocultural in their emphasis; while they can provide interesting outcomes through the collaboration of participants, they do not highlight material investigation or call for a rehearsal of physical techniques.

14 The influence of global technologies, most specifically the Internet, makes an occasional appearance in *Relational Aesthetics*, and more so in Bourriaud's follow-up book, *Postproduction*. Bourriaud does not write about digital interactive art directly in either of these books, however, and in fact reveals disdain for new media when he says that the 'traps' of 'calculated' and 'so called computer graphics… synthetic fractals… images' and 'gadgets,' explore 'arcane mysteries' and merely act as 'illustration' (Bourriaud, 1998: 68–70).

# Chapter 3

## A Critical Framework for Interactive Art

### Relational Specificity

An implicit body approach for understanding interactive art (and embodiment) must move beyond concentrating solely on the apprehension of art (and the body) through signification (or technology). It must focus on the amplification of bodiliness – of affect, proprioception, and sensibility – that takes place in the potentialized context interactive art creates. A framework such as this needs to be sensitive to the historical languages used for understanding art, materiality, and visuality, while taking account of embodiment and matter's emergence from and with their relations; it must directly address our interactions, and the relational per-formance of body, matter, and matters.

This is not to say that a separation of body and matter (or their matters) ever finally occurs. In this emergence, all of matter, sensible concepts, and their bodies, flesh or otherwise, have relational agency in their coming-into-their-own 'out of a prior moreness of the world's general always-going-on' (Massumi, 2011: 3). Like Whitehead's 'mutual immanence,' here is a 'fundamental ... togetherness of things'

(Whitehead, 1970: 164). The body / world and body / concept couplings in the artworks I describe should be understood as an implicit body, staged: as the suspension of specific and limited conceptual–material relations, and our experience and practice within the space of the installation. Here some of the intensities of relational performance are virtually felt by an individual participant or participants as part of the interactive situation.

As we have come to expect from most well-written criticism in the contemporary art domain, the implicit body approach begins by recounting a given artist's individual inquiry and process, and a description of the artwork itself. This is not to privilege intent over experience, but to understand the stage that is set in the gallery, and get a *feel* for the work, as best as we can, in writing. The framework also attempts to re-member *how we inter-act* – our literal, physical actions over time and in space, our affect, movement, and sensation, breathing, running, and grasping, for example, described in detail as the *work* – the work of art, and the work of embodiment. In implicit body case studies, actual (and actualizing) activity and its qualities are genuinely given priority over the projections we might look at or the sounds we might hear within the gallery space. Interactivity is engaged as affection and reflection, as (the) work.

The framework also, and more importantly, endeavors to analyze *how and what we relate with,* in and of these interactions. Interaction (however limited) and performance are, of course, inseparable from emergence and relationality, but they are given individual due so as to ensure a concentration on both our literal movements, and what and how they per-form. The implicit body framework attempts to name and unpack the (unnamable) 'sensible concepts' of a work, the physical experience of ideas, the being and becoming that is virtually felt as we interact. I call these *implicit body thematics.* I have chosen to use the adjective (or adverb), 'thematic,' rather than the noun, 'theme,' because this is more reflective of a sensible concept: adjectives must always be in relation to something else. Implicit body thematics differ from traditional conceptually based themes in that they aim to investigate the materiality and form of our conceptually sensed relations. Thematics require relational activity: incipient, actualized, and reflected upon. Any number of implicit body thematics can be applied to a given piece in order to bring more insight into its study, through describing the limitation and amplification of potential and relation. While we must be careful not to pre-scribe meaning, to better understand interactive art and embodiment – what is at stake in staging an implicit body as performance – we must approach the multiplicity of ways that we relate, as they are inaugurated and introduced to us, with as much specificity as possible.

## The Implicit Body Framework

Most succinctly, the four areas of examination in the implicit body framework are: artistic inquiry and process; artwork description; inter-activity; and, relationality. Respectively, they will show what kinds of questions the artists were exploring in production – taken from interviews with, and texts by, the artists themselves; how each installation works both technically and in a sensorial context; what viewers see, do, and experience through their inter-active engagement with the piece; and, some of the complex relationships that are suspended and intervened in through this embodied dialogue. The latter two areas of examination are the most crucial to the implicit body approach and, I am arguing, those which are most often left out in critical readings of interactive installation. This is not meant to be prescriptive, but rather to insure the most descriptive and critical examination of what individual works stage, situate, and inaugurate, and the conceptual–material formations we experience and practice in that encounter. There will, of course, be a blurring between each of the implicit body framework's four areas. But the strength of my approach is in naming, framing, and attempting to think them all. It includes the intent of the artist, the content and materiality of the installation, the inter-activities of the participant and software, and the relational feedback loops that affect and are affected by their interactions. I turn to Golan Levin and Zachary Lieberman's collaborative project *Messa di Voce* (2003, Figure 11) to model the implicit body framework.

The first area of analysis simply gives us an initial context for experience and practice. It covers the artist's approach to their own work: how they critique what it is doing, reapply that in production, and speak about it thereafter. This obviously affects our readings of, and encounters with, the rig or stage of the art. The conceptual frame for the *work*, the gallery, title, and text descriptions in situ, online, and in print, all feed back in to how we understand, interact, and engage. The Levin and Lieberman team (sometimes referred to as Tmema) is known for its interactive installations, performances, Internet art, technical contributions, teaching, and research in the fields surrounding digital art. Both members have highly influential instructional and exhibition practices, and both have contributed greatly to open source and educational developments for new media creatives more broadly. Their shows are highly charged with anticipation, and a desire to act. *Messa di Voce* lives as both an interactive installation and feature-length operatic performance – the latter with experimental singer–performers Jaap Blonk and Joan La Barbara. It grew out of several Tmema collaborative projects where the artists were exploring 'the aesthetic implications of making the human voice visible'; they wanted to use interactivity to invite a practice of the relationships between emergent images, sounds, and bodies (Levin and Lieberman, 2004: 1).

Since we are not experiencing the moving–thinking–feeling *work* of the art 'in the flesh,' the implicit body framework's second area of examination calls for a detailed description of the piece – what it looks and sounds and feels like, how it responds to us in the gallery or performance space. Tmema's *Messa di Voce* software, for example, 'augments the speech, shouts and songs produced by a pair of vocalists with real-time interactive visualizations' (Levin and Lieberman, 2003a). Multiple computer vision techniques are employed to track both the locations of the performers' heads, and the orientation of their bodies. The artists' computer system additionally evaluates the audio signals from the performers' microphones, extracting features such as pitch, spectral content, and autocorrelation data. In response to real-time position, movement, and sound, a creative array of visualizations is projected onto screens immediately behind the performers, appearing to emerge directly from the their mouths.

In *Messa di Voce*'s 30–40 minute, semi-improvisational theatrical event, Tmema and their collaborating performers serialize 12 audio-visual and performative vignettes – solos and duets, which each use drastically different particle system / generative algorithms (what Lieberman calls implicit, rather than explicit, animation) – in relation and response to Blonk and La Barbara's embodied song and dance. As demonstrated in Figure 11, and in online videos, these complex interactive animations, individually, turn emphatic breathing into throbbing geometric shapes; transform man-made and storm-like sound effects into generatively forming clouds; convert vibrato sounds into rippling waves of water; map song and movement to the body in space; rework face distorting, raspberry-blowing, and baby-esque sounds as animated and circular music boxes (which can be re-triggered by the performers' movements in order to play back the audio that created them in the first place); and, stage operatic and duel-like battles between the singers, where their weapons / charges include smoky fluids, porcupine suits, and painterly forms.

Each new scene in *Messa di Voce* builds on the last, asking for more or less activity from the performers both in their bodies and with their embodied music-making. The show begins with one of its singers standing completely still and simply breathing geometric shapes into existence on the screen behind them. This scene slowly transforms itself, performatively, visually, and sonically, as the singer and scenery erupt into a flurry of storm clouds. This in turn sets the stage for an operatic duet that ripples out into the projected motion of water, which in turn morphs into an intense 'battle' between two competing and embodied noise machines / performers, each emitting and directing enveloping billows of smoke from their mouths and bodies. According to the artists, '[u]tterly wordless, yet profoundly verbal' (Levin and Lieberman, 2003a), *Messa di Voce* is designed to accomplish the 'fiction that the voice can be seen' (Levin and Lieberman, 2003b: 4) and thereby provokes 'questions about the meaning and effects of speech sounds, speech acts, and the immersive environment of language' (Levin and Lieberman, 2003a).

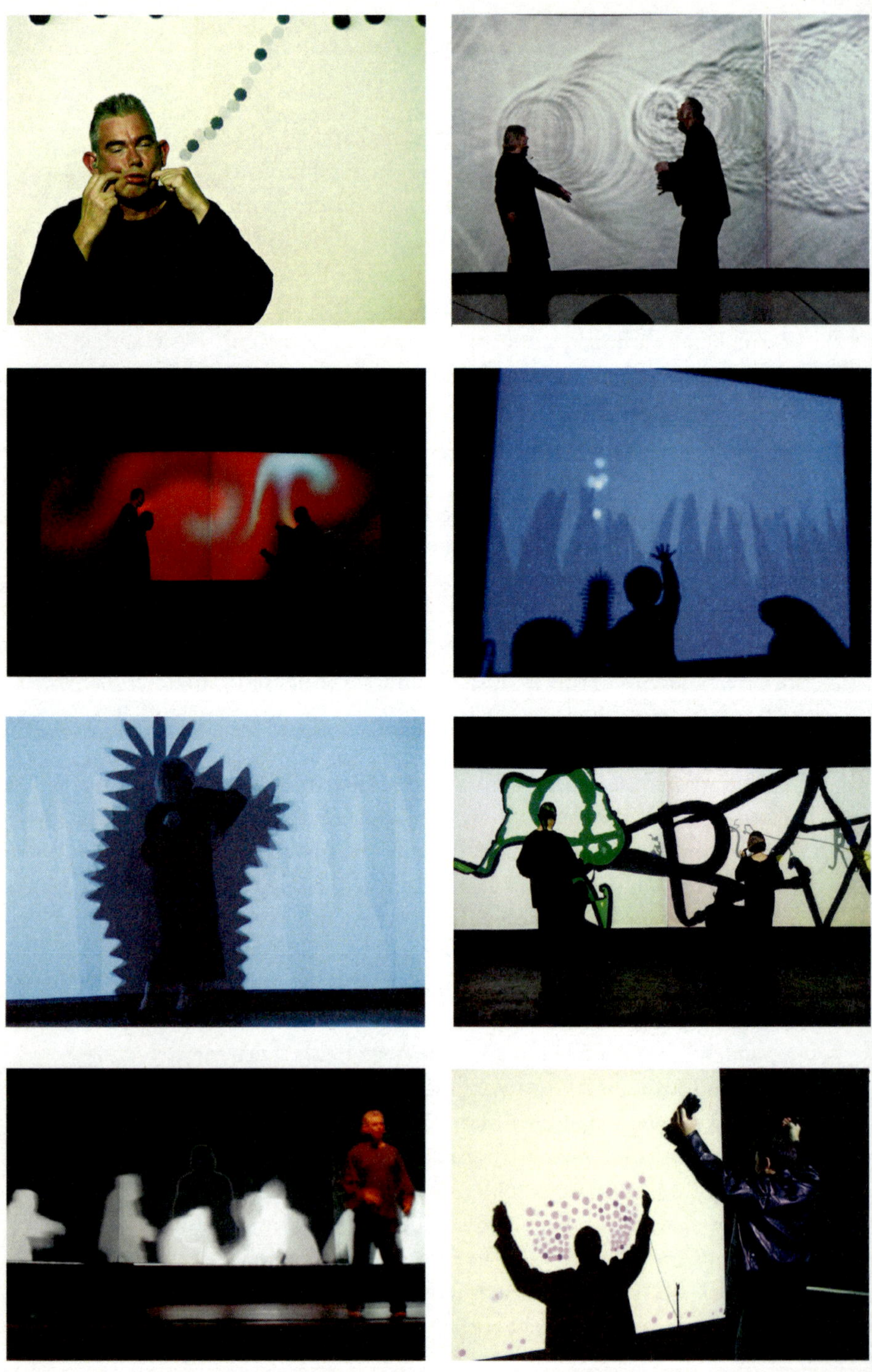

Figure 11. Tmema (Golan Levin and Zachary Lieberman) with Joan La Barbara and Jaap Blonk | *Messa di Voce*, 2003 | Courtesy of the artists

The performance version of this piece is meant for audience members to watch, while the installation uses the same software in an interactive and participatory mode, granting gallery-goers encounters with each of the aforementioned scenes so they might spawn geometric shapes or storm clouds, perform sonic battles as tidal waves or smoky fluid, and so on. Both versions present the possibility for playing out, intervening in, and amplifying an embodied interactivity, and relational embodiment, through the situations they create. But how do we practice and read that play / intervention / amplification?

Traditional readings of interactive art and new media tend to stop here: after the first two areas of examination in the implicit body framework (inquiry and description). I maintain that it is the latter two areas – inter-activity and relationality – that enhance understandings of interactive art and embodiment because of their engagement with the per-formed elements of body, matter, and matters. In other words, most visually-, technically- and linguistically-based writing on interactive art explains that a given piece *is interactive,* and *how it is interactive,* but not *how we inter-act.* This, the third area of examination in the framework, is vital towards understanding what is put in (absent) quotes and thus at stake. The viewers' and artwork's inter-activities must be discussed intensively.

The third part of my framework is similar to Susan Kozel's description of her dance works in *Closer* (Kozel, 2008) 'without recourse to explanation or analysis' (Craig, 2010) before she unpacks what is practiced in those movements. This exercise, I contend, holds three aspirations. First, to avoid further descriptions of technology and the interface; second, to move away from reading semiotic gestures or the elicitation of specific behaviors (rather than rehearsing specific conceptual–material relations); and third, to introduce the potential for polling *styles* of being and becoming as we move, affect, and feel affection. Here the art's context becomes potentialized.

It must be noted that since its focus is on the primacy of action and experience, page-bound but demonstrative studies of interactivity are no small task. Although the large number of images presented attempt to show bodies moving–thinking–feeling, they are quite literally a series of snapshots (sequentialized images, Zeno stop-points);

and the process of writing out how participants are interacting in these photos simultaneously renders incorporation as inscription. I highly recommend readers visit the artists' online video documentation (provided via the bibliography), but even then, the artworks will not be experienced as interactive, in space, and in relation.

In other words, I can describe in text and images what an artist intends and how he or she tries to realize it; and, I can point to videos that show what a piece looks like and does with the participants who engage with it, but the *interaction itself* will always be absent. How we move, sense, and think-feel, and even more importantly, what this highlights in *doing* and *making*, how we *relate* and perform, the *work* of the work of art, the inter-activities that are integral to it, and how they attune us to our embodiment, can never be sufficiently captured and presented. I am asserting that although such an endeavor cannot completely succeed, it is precisely interactive art's resistance to representation that the implicit body framework demands we address as staged.

In the case of *Messa di Voce* one of the more fascinating aspects of the work is how its performer-participants – whether Tmema's operatic collaborators or interacting 'viewers' in the gallery space – almost automatically exhibit grand physical gestures along with their enunciated sounds. Circular arm sweeps are instinctually deployed along with songs of 'Ooooh.' Repetitive, seemingly angry hand-waves from under the chin / neck and outward across the stage or room are spontaneously executed in tandem with tongue-rolling cries of 'PHBTTTTTTs' that are worthy of a two-year-old's appraisal. Each scene beckons atypical techniques that should be studied – not merely mentioned as possible – precisely because of how atypical they are. These awkward interactions are a re-situation and intensification of the body's relational activity. They are no more or less relational than our ongoing and processual embodiment in the everyday, but they are exactly *not* everyday, in that they are both out of the ordinary and put in quotes. The 'Ooohs' and 'PHBTTTTTTs' and their accompanying gesticulations are, this book has effectively argued, interventions in movement and continuity – in the emergence, potential, and relationality of the body – and can thus offer insight into embodiment and materialization at large.

The affective dancing of the interactor in interactive art must be described in detail in order to ask, as the fourth area of examination in the implicit body framework does, 'What materials and bodies and sensible concepts emerge from this moving–thinking–feeling, in and of the relation? How might this work deepen our understandings and experiences of embodiment, materialization, and articulation? What techniques can be learned and practiced in the situation it creates?' *Messa di Voce*'s activities, expounded in the last paragraph, for example, might be said to bring to light the 'shape' of our sounds and signs. Soothing arm sweeps usher in sorrowful 'Oh' songs while angry spittles, hand-waves, and chin-juts are accompanied by rolling tongues. And although these two gestures are on opposite sides of the emotional and emotive spectrum, each shows how both movement and language emerge and define one another in their mutual immanence. Our interactions in *Messa di Voce* highlight how material bodies know, perform, and relate to their visual, linguistic, and sonic communications. They reveal the performative, real-world implications of how what we say affects, is in fact a parallel to, what we do. Body and sign , and the forces that create and change them, are staged and implicated as continuously emergent from their relation, as made concrete – conceptually and corporeally – through a concurrently physical and symbolic enactment.

The fourth area of examination in the implicit body framework asks us how and what we move–think–feel in our inter-actions, how our conceptual–material relationships intervene in our transformation with the world around us. It invites us into our own potential to vary by means of how we interrelate, and then rehearse in the interval. In other words, where the explicit body *in* performance uses the stage to put aspects of the static body in quotes (Chapter 2), the implicit body *as* performance *rigs* quotation marks around a continuous body *and* its contrapuntal relation to something *else*. The implicit body framework attempts to analyze and examine interactive art as a materially performative proscenium for, and artistic framer of, 'embodiment and X' – X being a sensible concept (language, society, architecture, other matter, forces, and matters) feeding back between the artwork and its participant. This formula is not meant to say that embodiment and X are ever separate and explicit 'things,' or that they are 'added together' per se; like static and continuous bodies, it is another heuristic device to show the implicit body framework as able to de-contextualize and re-contextualize potential, and highlight our interactive and amplified bodily performances of / with meaning or community or space.

Interactive artworks like *Messa di Voce* attune participants to an exploration and practice of their embodied relationships and processual categories – implicit body thematics – such as meaning-making, temporality, spatiality, visuality, and bodiliness itself, among other matters. Each of these categories can and should be paid attention to individually in new readings, and each additional reading with any one of them would be a slightly different utilization of the implicit body framework – all of them implementing the concepts and approach laid out in the preceding chapters. Here we deepen understandings of the work itself, as well as those of embodiment, relationality, and potential, through and with the interactive installation. Where sensible concepts are the physical experience of ideas, what I call implicit body thematics are an approach to experiencing, inter-acting with, and rehearsing, how we per-form that which is conceptually sensed. They are used to explore, practice, and analyze interventions into the performance of what *is* and *can be,* as they emerge.

## The 'with' of Implicit Body Thematics

The practical and critical application of the implicit body approach must be attended with the same nuance of the concepts and materials it engages. The framework needs to show deference to the complexities of emergence, while still enabling a critical and thorough investigation of the body's suspended relations in interactive art. One major difficulty in unpacking emergent relationships between 'embodiment and X' is that to set up and discuss the relation of two things (which are precisely *not* things), we must first name them; and by naming them individually, we run the risk of treating them as explicit and separate (and as things). If we are to engage with them together and as continuous, with how they are always already implicated in one another through and with and as a reciprocal immanence, it is necessary to start with the 'with' of their relation. Here I think alongside Jean-Luc Nancy's conception of 'being-with,' which for him is the precondition for emergence.

Following Heidegger, while also critiquing him, Nancy (2000) breaks with the concept of single and undivided entities, and instead asserts the primacy of relation. He puts this understanding of being in relation to others (matter, people, ideas), into the broader conceptual frame of a community. In his thinking, according to Nancy scholar Ignaas Devisch (2000: 244), the 'primal ontological conditions of our community,' and of our being, are not found in the subjective I, the Other or the We, but in the '"with", "relationality", and the "between"'. Being is *always* being-with because one cannot be without being in relation to other beings (who are beings in relation as well). Community and being make one another, emerge from their relations – material, conceptual, and always plural. While interactive artworks cannot possibly encapsulate all that this notion of a community *is*, they can accent both being-with more generally, and highlight some of the sensible concepts we might emerge-with *as* a being(-with).

One of Nancy's most lucid explanations of the relationality of being can be found in his discussion of the word and concept, people. The term 'people' articulates that we are all of a similar category: human beings with common characteristics. Still, there is not one person who can represent all of people, and not one individual who can be said to make up the whole of what it means to be a person. People, in turn, can exist only as they are 'numerous, dispersed, and indeterminate' in their generality (Perpich, 2005: 80). Feminist philosopher Diane Perpich explains that for Nancy, the existence of people can 'only be grasped in the paradoxical simultaneity of togetherness (anonymous, confused, and indeed massive) and disseminated singularity (these or those "people(s)", or "a guy", "a girl", "a kid")' (Perpich, 2005: 80).[1] And the term 'people' does not have any meaning or origin outside of this 'coexisting collection, this being-with, of plural singularities' (Perpich, 2005: 80).[2] Nancy's plural singularities are all individuals, but each singularity can only exist through being part of the plurality, the people. This plurality exists 'with,' and is formed by, those self-same singularities. The word 'with,' as Nancy uses it, is not descriptive, but the 'prerequisite for, and makeup of, every action, material and meaning' (Devisch, 2000: 250, 245). It is the continuous relation from which everything emerges, and that interactive art, I contend, has the power to intervene in.

'We' (the people, the community, the world), like being, are constituted as a shared becoming that Nancy calls 'partagé': that which is divided or shared out. The world and its spaces and people are inextricably linked, constituted and maintained as individuals, only through their ongoing and shared divisions, together. Bodies, meaning, and how they relate are 'never monolithic or totalizing but always shared out or divided between different subjects, between subjects and things, and between one thing and another' (Perpich, 2005: 77). With his concept of partagé Nancy complicates the relational 'logic' of being-with: 'we' emerge as and through our relation to 'we,' and our mutual emergence arises as something in common *and* shared out across our difference. Communities and subjects (both plural singularities), meanings and concepts and materials, all appear together. None is the cause of the other, nor are any the same. We 'constitutes an inchoate performative: in the process of being formed' (Nancy, 2007: 106). 'We' (like 'I') is, in other words, a per-formance: relational, emergent, in process. We begin, are always already beginning, with 'with.'

This understanding of collective per-formance includes the emergence of being from, and in, 'all directions at once' (Perpich, 2005: 78). In other words, people and communities and bodies and language and space and meaning and world appear *with* each other. I contend that interactive art can focus us on partagé: that which is divided and shared, that which relationally emerges. Implicit body thematics point to the specific sensible concepts that are *always* performed with us, but highlighted by the best interactive art situations. Applying such an approach to *Messa di Voce* facilitates an examination of how the performers' real-time bodies, the live sounds and animations, are all involved and entwined with one another. By turning the spoken, sung, and sometimes awkwardly playful voice-sounds of performers into graphic and interactive elements, the artists create dynamic instantiations of the continuous relationships between body and sign (both visual and sonic). Levin and Lieberman have utilized our embodied en- and unfoldings to play out the processual and reciprocal performance of language with flesh. Over the course of this performance, they give voice to how bodies and signs move, feel, deteriorate, and interact 'with' each other, and their own potential to vary.[3]

And this is just one possible relational analysis of *Messa di Voce* and the interactivities in its space. The implicit body framework – and its fourth area of thematic examination – is used to accent how body and language emerge together, and might be rehearsed differently. *Messa di Voce* could also be beneficially read as a 'with' in the between, and of, time. The performers encounter and practice with the animated echoes of their past bodies and sounds, bringing a vitality to the potent present and its virtual future. Their temporally juxtaposed matter and matters inter-act as an emergent, static *and* continuous body; they exist only as relational, across time, always already implicated with/in one another. Or one could add to this engagement by looking at the shared potential of body and space – whether the latter refers to the stage, or the building, or the dynamically spatialized flux between bodies / performers. And so on. Each relation is a sensible concept that is always 'with,' and approached as actively per-formed *and* a prerequisite for performance.

Every thematic is both a theme and an action, a careful reading of the 'with' of the incorporating practices we always perform and embody. They are intensified and virtually felt – put in absent quotes – with interactive art. When I write about relational couplings such as body-language, social-anatomies, or flesh-space in interactive art, there is an implicit 'with' both in and between my terms. Neither body nor language, for instance, can become without the other; this thematic approach is intended to explore artistic interventions in the shared emergence of embodiment *with* meaning-making. And since bodies emerge not only with language, but with society (social-anatomies), with space (flesh-space), and with a plurality of other sensible concepts, the thematic approach offers the possibility for multiple kinds of encounters with, and analyses of, any given interactive artwork. Thematics advocate a specific exploration within a mass of reciprocally emergent categories. In other words, implicit body thematics provide a platform for moving–thinking–feeling with and through body-(with)-language and / or social-(with)-anatomies, and / or flesh-(with)-space (the list is ongoing), individually and with a difference, while still attendant on the continuity and relation of the others. Within any given thematic, the body is always understood as potential and in relation 'with' both the conceptual category of that thematic, and all others, and all matter and matters, all at once. Implicit body thematics are, put differently, themselves emerging and in relation. But as tools and as guides, they point to discrete possibilities for enhanced experiences and practices with, and understandings of, interactive art and embodiment.

The implicit body framework is a practical approach to interactive art, a mode of inquiry for interventions into incorporating practices, a method of digital arts criticism that acknowledges the complexities of our embodied interrelations and aims to deepen the modes of rehearsing with, reflecting on, and questioning of, all of the above. If interactive art offers a situation where we might practice philosophy, then the implicit body framework offers a philosophy for the practice of interactive art. Each is a moving–thinking–feeling where affection and reflection are in tune.

## Moving–Thinking–Feeling Forward

The implicit body framework examines interactive art as a potentialized context, a semblance of a situation, where bodies can conceptually sense a suspended and intensified relation. Here discrete aspects of the unlimited possibilities in the body's relation can be virtually felt, and practiced. This approach calls attention to performance and relation in order to better understand interactive art and embodiment, together. While it explicitly reads the relational 'with' of 'embodiment and X,' it is also careful to interpret these as always already in relation to a multitude of other sensible concepts, forces, matter, and matters. The framework facilitates a concentration on inter-activity and a precise relation, while still recognizing the greater openness and distributed agencies across not only embodiment and materialization, but the ocean of complexity and more-ness of the world with which, and from, they emerge. The remaining chapters of this book put the implicit body approach to work within intensive case studies of interactive installations (Chapters 4, 5, and 6) and brief explorations of what I call potentialized artworks (Chapter 7). Through various thematics, I introduce a depth to the field, and model the potentials of moving-thinking-feeling and rehearsing 'with,' while examining the import of, works of digital art.

## Notes

1 This is an unreferenced Nancy quote / translation taken from 'Corpus Meum: Disintegrating Bodies and the Ideal of Integrity' (Perpich, 2005).

2 When I presented this concept in the Center for 21st Century Studies, at the University of Wisconsin–Milwaukee, Professor Maria del Pilar Melgarejo pointed out that *Being Singular Plural* might be better said as *Being Multiply Plural.* Here we are 'with' through our plural multiplicities, since even as individuals, we are never only 'one,' and never wholly singular. Nancy addresses the body as always multiple and plural in his writing on exscription and limits, discussed in the following chapter.

3 Contemporary dancers William Forsythe and Norah Zuniga Shaw (Chapter 6), Troika Ranch, Jeannette Ginslov, Merce Cunningham, and Philippe Decouflé use interactive technologies to similar effect.

# Chapter 4

## 'Body-Language'

### Embodiment as Meaning-Making

This chapter discusses – as process, sensible concept, and critical approach – the implicit body thematic of body-language, and applies it to the work of Simon Penny and Camille Utterback. These artists were chosen because of their conceptual and practical interests in the emergence of language, meaning, and discourse as they relate to our continuous embodiment. The internationally acclaimed Utterback, first of all, avowedly attempts to 'bridge the conceptual and the corporeal' with her work (Utterback, 2006). Her main interest lies in how 'we use our bodies to create abstract symbolic systems, and how these systems (language for example) have reverberations on our physical self' (Utterback, 2006).

Cutting-edge technology plays a central role in how Utterback understands her practice. She explains that interactive media provide exploratory possibilities of the connections between physical bodies and representational systems. Like Tmema, her interfaces often utilize 'computer vision' technologies, more commonly known as interactive video. Here the combined use of digital video cameras and custom computer software allows each artwork to 'see,' and respond to, bodies, colors, and /or motion in the space of the museum or gallery. Utterback believes it is important to get beyond the mouse, keyboard and screen. She hopes to 'refocus attention on the embodied self in an increasingly mediated culture' by creating a 'visceral connection between the real and the virtual' (Utterback, 2006). At their core, her artworks ask participants to encounter a performance of bodies and meaning.

*Text Rain* (1999, Figure 12), Utterback's well-known and award-winning collaboration with Romy Achituv, is an interactive installation that invites viewers in front of a large screen to catch individually falling characters of text with their bodies (and by extension, anything they are attached to or holding). Participants between a plain white wall and video screen use their arms, legs, heads, and chests in a mirrored black and white video projection overlaid with colored and animated letters. Each character 'lands' on the edges of bodies or objects darker than the white background, and 'falls' when they are removed. 'Like rain or snow, the text appears to land on participants' heads and arms.' It can be 'caught, lifted, and then let fall again' (Utterback, 2000).

As the letters accumulate along a ridge of collaborating bodies, or on an up-close, outstretched, and immobile arm, viewers may occasionally 'catch' a recognizable word or even an entire phrase. Evan Zimroth's 1993 poem *Talk, You* was selected for *Text Rain* because it resonates with artists' intention. Like the artwork it inhabits, it creates 'metaphorical bridges between the physical and the linguistic'; it is an investigation of 'how "meanings" come together and fall apart through transient "syntactical" spatial relationships' (Blake, 2006). When *Text Rain* is installed in international cities, the artists most often translate the poem into the language and alphabet of its host country, so as to insure the possibility of word recognition. But reading the poem, 'if participants can do so at all, becomes a physical as well as a cerebral endeavor' (Utterback, 2000), in how we must literally catch a phrase.

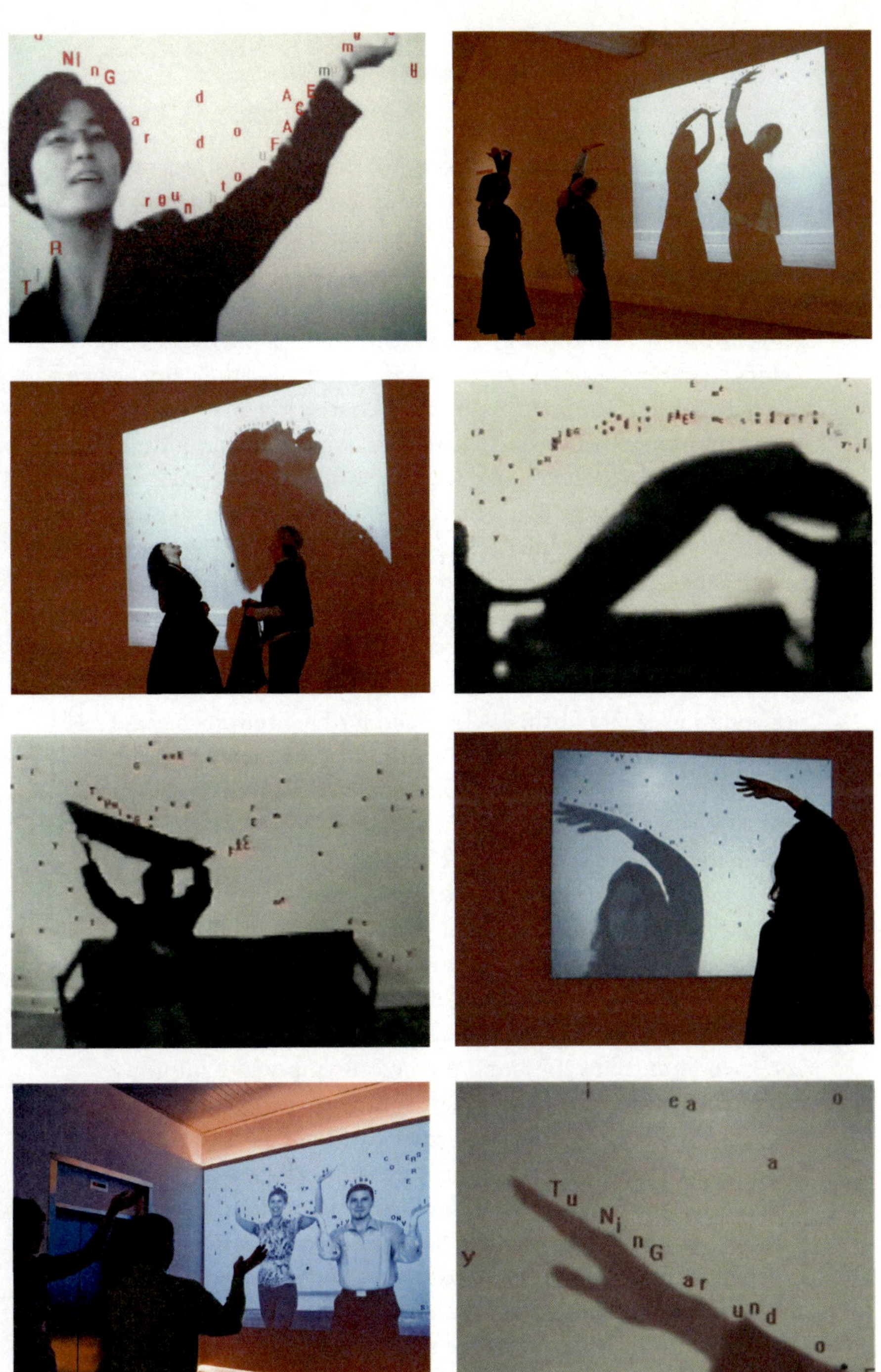

Figure 12. Camille Utterback and Romy Achituv | *Text Rain*, 1999 | photos by Kenneth Hayden and / or courtesy of the artists

Utterback writes that the tension between the 'abstract realm of ideas and the corporeality in which we live and interact with these ideas' (Utterback, 2006) is central to all of her work. It is not interactivity as a concept that garners her interest, but how embodiment and concepts relate and manifest. *Text Rain* is not about the body or language. Reading it in this way would (mis)understand these as static 'things.' It rather stages an experience and practice of their emergence together. An implicit body approach encourages a closer look at our and their inter-activities, and the relational performance Utterback's work intervenes in. I undertake an analysis of *Text Rain* as a situation, and the body-language thematic couples the shared arrival of, as Utterback says, 'the conceptual and the corporeal'.

As seen in the images provided (or in online videos), viewer–participants that encounter *Text Rain* most often attempt to gently catch words with their hands and arms, treating the language-drops as fragile treasures to be handled (and read) with care. They sway their upper bodies back and forth, catching and pushing the alpha-numerals with their heads and shoulders. Sometimes performers work together creatively, using, stretching, and waving picnic blankets to collect and read poetic phrases, or play out the metaphor further, with upturned umbrellas that both shield them from the onslaught of the Symbolic, and simultaneously elicit and make legible that which was initially unreadable. At a New York exhibition in 1999, I witnessed a crew of five participants wandering – apparently aimlessly, at first – and laughing, mouths open, in and around the interaction area, trying to catch the falling letters with their mouths, in their jaws, on and around their upturned faces. I like to think they were attempting to introduce an expression that was on the tips of their tongues.

While the interactive experience of *Text Rain* 'seems magical – to lift and play with falling letters that do not really exist' (Utterback, 2000) – so, one might argue, does the indoctrination into language itself. Whether a child is learning to communicate for the first time, a traveler is slowly beginning to understand a new, foreign language, or a graduate student finally manages to internalize a complex text – for the sake of this particular argument, let us say Lacan's 'Mirror Stage' (1949/2006) – each situation revolves around a self-referential, undeniably fragile, perpetually challenging, and extremely gratifying – and corporeal – relationship to abstraction. We test and play with words and meaning, see how they *form* in our mouths, *roll* off our tongues, *flow* on the page, in our ears, and in space, in order to find the right ones, and ourselves, within them. In *Text Rain*, 'it is our intuitive mental manipulation of language that is frustrated ... We manipulate the abstract symbolic space of language both physically – with our mouths and hands, and mentally – with our thoughts' (Utterback and Achituv, 2000). Body and language are mutually immanent.

Utterback and Achituv ask us to sensually and conceptually weave in and around our simultaneously incorporating and inscribing relations to language and text. We catch and toss continuously moving meanings that may contrapuntally be read as actually trying to capture us. Whether standing still, dodging the droplets, or actively collaborating with other reader–participants, *Text Rain* puts our incipient feedback loops between the conceptual and material in (absent) quotes: 'body-language.' It re-cites and re-situates how bodies and language/ meaning emerge together, from and as their ongoing relations.

Utterback's work is exemplary in its amplification of the relational 'being-with' of flesh and discourse. It invites us to experience and practice language as a sensible concept. I parallel the body-language thematic to Jean-Luc Nancy's idea of exscription: the relation between the performance of embodiment and the process of meaning-making. Body-language was chosen as a key implicit body thematic for this book exactly because of how it might at first seem to resemble explicit body art, given that both kinds of work address bodies and signs. While explicit body art interrogates inscription and its signifiers, however, implicit body art intervenes in an embodied exscription, the enfolding, unfolding, and with-matter processes of signification and constitution. Simon Penny and Utterback have been selected for study in this chapter both because of their stated interests in corporeality and semiotics, and because of their recognized status in the field of digital art. With Penny's work, I reference other published readings in order to show where the implicit body framework can provide different and deeper insight. And Utterback's installations will be examined further, as setting stages for rehearsing our ongoing and embodied relationships to art and art history more generally.

## Exscription

Like Jean-Luc Nancy's philosophical approach to being, exscription is a nuanced approach to understanding reciprocal emergence: this time of bodies and / with meaning. It is a purposefully tautological appreciation of how bodies and meaning make one another, through their making of one another. Like a topological figure, exscription is relational and self-referential, and can thus be best understood through the lens of exscription itself. I use exscription to ask for an engagement with how bodies and meaning are constituted through their continuous relations, in our experience and practice with interactive art. For Nancy, 'bodies make the world go round' (Perpich, 2005: 78–9), but like Marilyn Strathern, he does not presuppose *what* a body is, only *that* it is – and it *is,* only when it is in, and of, and making the world.

Nancy's body is 'not of essence or substance' (Ridgway, 2008: 335). It is

> neither fullness nor void, neither outside nor inside, neither part nor whole, neither function nor finality. It is… 'folded, refolded, unfolded, multiplied… evading, invading, stretched, relaxed, excited, shattered, linked, unlinked.'… it is 'a whole corpus of images stretched from body to body: colors, local shadows, fragments, grains, areolas, half-moons, fingernails, body hair, tendons, skulls, ribs, pelvis, stomachs, meatuses, froths, tears, teeth, foams, clefts, blocks, tongues, sweats, liquids, veins, pains, and joys, and me, and you'. (Nancy, 1992: 16, 104–5; Perpich, 2005: 85)

In other words, Nancy's understanding of body (le corps) is not in fact a body but bodies (corpus): folded, enfolded, and unfolded with other bodies, matter, images, and discourses.

As with the complex being-with of community and people, Nancy sets out to write an embodied discourse that is also *not* a discourse, in that it explores the interrelationship of body and discourse, body with discourse, discourse with body. Nancy's 'corpus' is a constant reworking of the conditions of embodied thinking. It is, according to Jacques Derrida, an 'implacable deconstruction of modern philosophies of the body proper and the "flesh"' (Derrida, 2005: 63). Here, bodies emerge with matter and meaning, *as* matter and meaning. Key to Nancy's approach is an effort to 'eschew both the tendency to arrest the affect, plurality and difference of the body, as well as the tendency to reinstate the body as something un-representable' (Ridgway, 2008: 334–5). On the one hand, Nancy argues that 'discourse can represent or signify the body, that is, write *of* or *about* the body,' but it cannot '*write the body*' (Perpich, 2005: 84). On the other, he reminds us that one cannot write *without* a body, that the body *haunts* all writing, language, and signification, and must therefore be present in, and a condition for, every inscription. In other words, while we may not be able to produce any successful language or discourse that is 'embodied' as bodies are, we also fail to produce any discourse without the body already in it.[1] After all, we need bodies to write. Both language and bodies are implicit in every-thing, every constitution, every action, every communication, every meaning, and every text: corpus.

In her paper on Nancy and 'dis-integrating bodies,' Diane Perpich argues that in 'the Western philosophical tradition, the body has been construed in opposition to speech and language: it is ineffable, passive, impenetrable, unintelligent, and as such opposed to the intelligible articulations of discourse' (Perpich, 2005: 84). So, according to this tradition (or at least to a dominant movement within it) bodies and discourse are mutually exclusive.[2] How then, can we access the body through and with language? How can the putatively incorporeal (language, meaning, text) 'touch' the corporeal (bodies, matter, things)?

Nancy suggests that how bodies are accessed by language (and writing), that this touching of corporeal and incorporeal, is not *inscribed* in language (and writing), but rather *exscribed* outside of it. Bodies and meanings mutually emerge outside of, and with, each other; they touch implicitly, en- and unfolding as relational. Nancy asserts that the act of writing, for example, 'exscribes meaning every bit as much as it inscribes significations. It exscribes meaning or, in other words, it shows that what matters ... is outside the text, takes place outside writing' (Nancy, 1994: 338). And here both matter and its matters matter.

In this thinking, outside and inside are not to be understood as oppositional. Rather, in the bodily and relational thinking that Nancy proffers, inscription and exscription, outside and inside, bodies and discourse / writing, happen together; they are not opposed, they *are-with*. This 'with' that is the pre-condition for all things (and non-things) is 'neither substance, nor phenomenon, nor flesh, nor signification. But *being-exscribed* [l'e tre-excrit]' (Perpich, 2005: 84). Signification is 'located meaning,' but exscription 'resides only in the coming of a possible signification' (Ridgway, 2008: 331). In being exscribed, the body both *makes* sense, and *comes* to sense, along *with* signification. When Nancy writes that bodies and meanings take place outside, he means that they take place neither in discourse nor matter alone. 'They take place at the limit, *as the limit*' (Nancy, 1992: 18, 20, emphasis added). Here, 'bodies *are* meaning ... they are the limit and expression of meaning' (Ridgway, 2008: 335). Every-thing is defined by being outside another outside another outside.[3]

Nancy thinks corpus and bodies (and discourse) as continuously incipient thresholds that allow us to appear as distinct from one another, but that also serve as points of connection, and contiguous existence. Bodies, and meanings, emerge through their relational margins of contact, the various borders and limits they engage with. Interactive art asks us to play at these limits, amplifies and intervenes in a processual embodiment *as* and *at* these limits. The implicit body thematic of body-language more specifically puts the relational activities of 'enfleshment with signification' in quotes, inviting us to experience and practice at their mutually emergent borders.

Bodies and language and meaning and signification and discourse – which I purposefully slip between throughout this chapter – and what comes to matter in and with them, work together reciprocally. The body-language thematic, then, is an approach to analyzing how bodies (and meaning) are continuously reconfigured, re-cited, and re-situated; they are per-formed, they are touched. 'Bodies are first masses, masses offered without anything to articulate, without anything to discourse about ... discharges of writing rather than surfaces to be covered in writings' (Nancy, 1992: 197). These are neither written bodies, nor bodies on which writing takes place, nor bodies that are signs of themselves. For as Nancy himself asserts, 'the body is not a locus of writing ... it is always what writing exscribes. In all writing a body is traced, is the tracing and the trace – is the letter, yet never the letter ... a body is what cannot be read in writing' (Nancy, 1992: 197). It is a body only in the touching of, in being touched by, the Other (whether Other refers to body, signification, world, matter, meaning, or writing). And this touching is always already interrupted, syncopated, exscribed.

In touching and being touched (in our active and incipient relations) we encounter the limit, we encounter bodies and meaning. If the claims made by Jacques Derrida and Zsuzsa Baross that the self 'comes into being only in and through the sensuous relation with the other, in and through exposure to the limit, to that which is not self (but is nevertheless internal to it)' (Sullivan, 2004: 7) are accepted we can see how touch, and by extension the body, is not simply an object of the self's perceiving consciousness (or an expression of its affective interiority), but is also a body in and through exscription. The body-language thematic invites examination of how interactive artworks magnify touch, that encounter with contact and limits, and, as such, are interventions in the movements between meaning and body as 'with.'

Bodies and language are staged and highlighted as *together*. We encounter their limits, play with them *as* limits, and rehearse how they *might be* in amplified limitation. Here meaning and bodies are of the relation. They are shared, conceptual-material formations, that come to be-with. With interactive art, we remember: being *is* being-with, it is partagé or shared, and here that being is shared with meaning; it is exscribed.

And therein also lies the fundamental difference between staging an explicit body *in* performance, and staging an implicit body *as* performance. The explicit body challenges the stasis of bodies and signs: the latter inscribes the former – with race or gender or class, for example – and an explicit artwork intervenes in these 'things' that are presupposed. An implicit body approach – and, by extension, the body-language thematic – takes no-*thing* as its subject. Here we encounter processual matter and continuous bodies, relata and incipient actions and meanings. This work is part of a self-critical corpus, highlighting and exploring relations between the processes of materialization and signification.

The body-language thematic focuses on interventions in the continuous relationships between embodiment and meaning-making – the activities of *writing-with-the-body*. The artworks discussed in this chapter solicit such embodied writing as 'traced,' as 'the tracing and the trace,' inviting us to per-form and interrogate 'bodies with discourse.' Such work remembers that meaning is exscribed; it sets a stage for the practice and examination of 'embodiment and signification' as incipient, active, and mutually appearing.

## Symbolic Traces: Simon Penny

Artist, technologist, and academic Simon Penny has conducted research since the mid-1980s, which takes the form of arts production, writing, teaching, and engineering projects, that in early incarnations centered on the premise that technology has been the major force for change over the last century. In his edited collection of texts by artists and academics circa 1995, Penny argues that 'as we move out of the first technological era, that of industrial production, into the era of the digital, a profound warping and rifting occurs across the cultural surface' (Penny, 1995b: 1). He unequivocally asserts that computers mediate our relation to the world. Simon Penny's oeuvre invites us to explore relationality and meaning-making through technological mediation.

Penny's work in the 1980s consisted of anthropomorphized kinetic sculptures (*Stupid Robot* [1987]), robotic projection machines (*Great Arcs* [1987]), and other artworks that integrated gadgets such as radio receivers (*Lo Yo Yo* [1988]) and / or infrared sensors (*Pride of Our Young Nation* [1990–1]). He often invested his energies in creating illusions of sentience (*Petit Mal* [1989–95]), *Sympathetic*

*Sentience* [1995 and ongoing]) or in sociopolitical simulations of our 'organic' communication systems (such as the Internet, in *Big Father* [1990–1]), in order to intervene in our experience and understanding of each. Many of these pieces use the history and currency of media to ask us to engage with how we behave as human beings.

Penny's somewhat more recent work sees a range of projects that 'focus their attention on the experience of the user as an act of communication, on the social space of the interface, and on the dynamics of interaction' (Penny, 1995a: 58).[4] He explicitly calls for an enhanced critical inquiry into our embodied cultural practices in the new technological age. Like Jean-Luc Nancy, Penny couples body and language, embodiment and sign, inside and outside, and attests 'to the unacknowledged but pervasive power of physical behaviors in social and cultural formation' (Penny, 2005). For Penny, as for me, embodiment and interactivity play essential roles in the act of producing meaning, and thus need to be studied, challenged, and critiqued, together. He asserts that his art acts as 'an intervention into certain prevailing attitudes regarding embodiment and interaction' (Penny, 2004). To that end, as a label for what he does, Penny prefers the 'rather clunky "digital cultural practices" to either new media or media art, partly because' he now thinks 'the notion of "media" is an irrelevant focus' for investigation and interrogation (Scholz and Penny, 2006). This hints at how 'media' or a 'medium'-based work is thought of as a thing, an object to be seen or perceived rather than a stage for encountering performance. Penny is speaking back to the same discourses critiqued earlier in the book, and instead allying himself with the processual, potentialized 'practices' of meaning-making within a larger culture. His artworks, I argue, use digital technologies to intervene in the relational emergence of bodies and discourse.

Much that drives Penny's production comes out of his critical assessment of VR (Virtual Reality). It would be, he argues, 'an oversimplification to claim that the body is not present in VR,' but it would be a similar 'oversimplification to claim that the body is *in* VR. The body, we might say, is partially present. It functions as an "effector," but the sensorial feedback is almost exclusively visual (with the occasional addition of sound)' (Penny, 1995a: 61–2). Penny attempts to reclaim the body in Virtual Reality from the hegemony of vision. Not that vision is ever only vision alone, but that intensive experience requires vision to be folded *in*. Penny says that the material body – and all that bodiliness *is* – is neither fully present in, nor fully absent from, VR and its immersive image. In the 1990s and early 2000s, he worked with collaborators to create a much more interactive rig for VR, one which distills, and intervenes in, the body as always and never both inside and outside of the image, discourse, signs, writing.[5] Penny et al., in other words, wanted to create a situation that would engage both the static and continuous body, both inscription and exscription, in Virtual Reality.

Penny first created a machine vision system that is an even more advanced and complicated version of the kind that Utterback utilizes in *Text Rain*. It similarly uses analysis and interpretation of live video images from the interaction area (in this case, infrared images) to 'see' and respond to the viewer–participant. But Penny's set-up employs the use of four cameras, along with customized hardware and software, in order to calculate every embodied movement in three-dimensional space, over time. In other words, this system, which later became known as the Penny / Bernhardt TVS or Traces Vision System, combines its multiple video inputs mathematically to create a semblance of the body's full, voluminous form in real time. This interface, which has been used in much of Penny's work,[6] invites a complete, moving, affective, and sensual sensorimotor body into the interactive and three-dimensional experience of Virtual Reality. Rather than only seeing the moving body through a singular camera eye, flat like a video screen, it recognizes the body as a moving and three-dimensional sculpture. I examine Penny's most well-known TVS piece, *Traces* (1999, Figure 13), with the body-language thematic.

Unlike the customary Head Mounted Display goggles commonly used for Virtual Reality explorations (such as with Char Davies' work), *Traces* is placed within a stereo-immersive CAVE (Cave Automatic Virtual Environment). Here participant–viewers wear specialized glasses that act like the stereopticon in William Kentridge's work to turn eight 2D / flat images into four 3D and sculptural forms.[7]

These 3D videos, which are rendered in real-time, are projected on the three walls, the ceiling, and floor of the CAVE, to create a virtual space that surrounds the entire body. It is important to note just how enveloping a CAVE, and the interaction in *Traces,* really is. While the still images presented in this book can only show the 2D projections on the flat surfaces surrounding the active performers, any given participant in *Traces* sees these floating 'images' as three-dimensional moving sculptures in the immediate space around them.

*Traces* takes the TVS's real-time model of the whole moving body and places it within the stereo-immersive CAVE. The software 'sees' the moving body as a collection of 'volumetric pixels' or 'voxels.' Each viewer is thus more than a disembodied eye looking at a screen; he or she is an actively embodied participant in a responsive 3D space. *Traces* aims to privilege bodily intervention and investigation over high-resolution visual elements. The artist did not endeavor to produce a '"world" which is "navigated"' – its 'graphical representations are minimal, texture mapping and other gratuitous eye-candy' are avoided – but rather a responsive and interactive environment that encourages physical exploration (Penny et al., 2001: 47–9). Penny did not want 'to present a panoptic spectacle for the user, but to turn the attention of the user back onto their own sense of embodiment' (Penny et al., 2001: 47–9). He asserts that all 'attention is focused on the ongoing bodily behavior of the user' (Penny, 1999), where participants' interactivities are integral to, indeed *are,* the work.

There are three modes of interaction in *Traces,* where each builds into the next. Dubbed an 'autopedagogic interface,' *Traces* introduces the 'complexities of the environment' and how it responds to movement 'gradually and transparently' (Penny et al., 2001: 49), so that participants can learn how to engage their encounters on the fly. This is not to say that *Traces* only responds to specific gestures or behaviors, but rather that styles of movement and stasis, acceleration and stimulation, can be experienced and practiced. It is not a language per se, but a kinesthetic mode of meaning-making that emerges, and is virtually felt, through the participant's interactions in space.

In the first, 'passive,' trace, every movement, small or sweeping, draws real-time lilac-colored voxels that slowly fade to nothingness, like trails of ephemeral bricks behind each flickering action. These traces of our bodies look and feel like 'volumetric and spatial-acoustic residues of user movement that slowly decay' (Penny et al., 2001: 47–9). Penny describes this interaction as dancing a sculpture. When the software crosses into its 'active' trace mode, the small cubic voxels no longer fade at a standard rate. Instead, participants' movements seed 3D cellular automata characteristics: elements of relationality and randomization mean that each voxel may shift to any number of varying colors, for any amount of time, before disappearing. In the final, 'behaving' trace, performances in the CAVE initiate animal-like, flying statuettes that move in Reynolds flocking patterns in and around the viewer. These user-spawned 3D animations – playfully called Chinese dragons by the artists because of their segmented spherical appearance – follow complex, interactive and generative behaviors that make them swoop and flock and tease. These interactions, the mutually constitutive relationships between / of body and image, inside and outside, embodiment and signification, are intervened in, and their per-formance is productively interrupted. They are staged as in relation: separate but together, different but in common, inscribed and exscribed.

With the passive trace, the shape of a participant's volumetric avatar (the common noun for human representations in cyberspace and virtual worlds) is entirely dictated by their movements in the CAVE. Their activities leave trails of slowly fading blocks in their wake, and so audience members tend to spend time exploring their own motion and its fantasy-like remnants around them. They may drag their arms and legs in exaggerated gestures akin to Tai Chi, or swish their limbs through the air in order to try and tease more interesting patterns into existence. As *Traces* slowly progresses into its active trace mode, the movement of its interactor still generates voxels in real time, but rather than simply disappearing, these begin to follow a cellular automata algorithm, where a 'discrete dynamical [system] is completely specified in terms of a local relation' (Perron, 2004). Such equations are simplified mathematical models of spatial interaction, where the 'state' – in this case, color and fade – of each voxel is co-determined both by its own activities / data, and its neighbors'.[8] Here 'the number of neighbors a voxel possesses determines whether it will persist into the next time-step' in the fade, 'and also determines its colour and level of transparency' (Penny et al., 2001: 60). The generative programming in the active trace mode gives the person / avatar's embodied voxels their own life-like quality, compiling 'structures of varying stability in places where the user has been. It changes shape, sparkles and percolates in unexpected ways' (Penny et al., 2001: 60). Whereas the passive trace leads to an investigative and fantastical exploration of the body in relation, the more randomized elements of the active trace avatar forces compromise, negotiation, and suspension on the part of the participant–performer. They must watch and listen to and play with the expressions of the outside, with more care, in a way much more integral to the compilation and completion of their-and-its 3D forms.

With the active trace, performers relate their movements to a greater discussion. They engage more cautiously, with slow mime-like stutters or sometimes frustrated swipes, as they birth and transform the surrounding environment and its three-dimensional responses; and this environment, in turn, influences their own movements, again. Body and discourse *appear* and are *felt,* virtual and together, as a corpus that occupies the inherent coupling of an active embodiment with the outside, even in its use of representative forms. A performer's awkward inter-actions with *Traces* during the active trace magnify bodiliness itself as relational meaning and vice versa. Here we are a being-with the (virtual) world, and said world and meaning mutually emerge; they are inaugurated, rather than enacted as an a priori script. *Traces* offers direct but unpredictable contact and syncopation between embodiment and signification. The 'work' is an introduction to, and intervention into, bodies-with-images; it challenges their movements and readings and relations, amplifying how both are per-formed, together.

In the final stage of *Traces,* aptly called the behaving trace, the viewer–participant's motions spawn 'semi-autonomous agents' that fly around the space and interact with them and each other. As seen in the provided images, these are snake-like animals, 'thrown off' by interactor's movements 'as though the user is shaking off water droplets' (Penny et al., 2001: 60). After they fly from the performer into the 3D environment in front of them, these self-governing creatures follow a relatively simple set of rules to create a complex 3D animation. The software might tell several dragons to flock and swoop together, while others meander at the edges or fly directly to the center of the action. Thus, the animations in the behaving trace may follow an interactor's movements, or 'break away as a flock following its own artificial life dynamics' (Hayles, 2002: 307). The dragons exhibit their own organic behaviors, together and apart from each other and the participant. Our experience with them is virtual and actual, virtualizing and actualizing, static and continuous. As a kind of reciprocal play, people lie on the floor, jump, dance, kick, and dance again. They 'emerge from the CAVE sweating, panting and red faced' (Penny et al., 2001: 48–9).

Performers build up their own active participation along with the increasing behavioral patterns of the semi-autonomous agents in *Traces'* space. What begins as embodied exploration becomes a physical investment in interactive and generative creation, through flicks and jabs, running and jumping, swiping and diving. *Traces* responds to our bodies, but over time, we must also be more responsive to it, attempt new styles of movement and perception, looking and doing. A body-language thematic reading suggests that there is a dialogue, a corpus, between these two things (which are not things), as they find embodiment and the per-formed and performative (body-) language that gives them meaning, together.

Mark Hansen and N. Katherine Hayles have also both written about *Traces*.[9] They in fact often turn to art in order to grow their technology-inflected philosophies of embodiment. In counterpoint, I am vying for an experience and practice of art *as* philosophy. The difference is in the articulation. My approach is to encounter *Traces* as a situation where we move–think–feel and rehearse how language and meaning and concepts and philosophies manifest *with* embodiment. The sensible concept / thematic of body-language was chosen for *Traces* in order to focus precisely on meaning-making (philosophy, language, discourse) and its emergent relation to 'body.' Here the framework, which is informed and supported by Hansen's and Hayles' theories, offers insight into how *Traces* suspends and potentializes – and helps us better understand, among other embodied performances – the relation of flesh and discourse.

One of Hansen's key arguments in his *Bodies in Code* is that humanity and technology evolve together. He says that human embodiment and experience – which are always technologically mediated – are the primary factors in our evolution, and goes on to argue that contemporary artists' 'varied use of digital media has pointed the way toward an introjection of technics into embodiment' (Hansen, 2006: x). In other words, digital art enables us to bring the surrounding world, the technologically-mediated world, into our body-schema.

Hansen asserts that *Traces* 'demonstrates that the disclosive power of the body schema is an essentially technical power' and that, 'in the end, it emerges only through the technology that makes it possible in the first place' (Hansen, 2006: 48). Our experience of our 'body proper' does not take the form of a representational image, but rather 'emerges through the *representative* function of the data of body movement' (Hansen, 2006: 49). Rather than seeing ourselves as the 'body' the cameras capture, we see traces of our *movements* in space. *Traces* allows us to encounter a 'body-in-code,' in that our body-image ('self-representation') is 'indiscernible from a technically generated body schema' ('enactive spatialization') (Hansen, 2006: 48–9). Hansen argues that the difference between the two '*has been entirely effaced*' (Hansen, 2006: 49). Hansen in fact goes as far as to say that in *Traces,* as in the world at large, 'the entire body schema – the coupling of body proper and environment – is generated by the technical system' (Hansen, 2006: 47). Despite his careful reasoning around the co-evolution of body and technology/ code, however, Hansen winds up privileging the latter. To him, the technical system, and our perception of it, are more essential than qualities of movement, and what they make.

In Hayles' treatise on relationality and the emergence of technology/signification with the body, she argues that interactive artworks are spaces that 'make vividly real the emergence of ideas of the body and experiences of embodiment' (Hayles, 2002: 304). Hayles puts forward three 'modes of relation' for interrogating such work: 'relation of mindbody to the immediate surroundings,' what she calls enactment; 'relation between mindbody and world,' perception; and 'relationality as cultural construction,' enculturation (Hayles, 2002: 304). Hayles parallels these to Don Ihde's work, where Human–Technology–World relations can also be broken into three categories: Human+Technology in relation to the World, or 'embodiment relations'; Human in relation to Technology+World, 'hermeneutic relations'; or Human in relation to a Technological World (such as Second Life or the Internet), 'alterity relations' (Ihde, 1990). Hayles states that these 'by no means exhaust the ways in which relationality brings the mindbody and the world into the realm of human experience,' but are 'capacious enough in their differences to convey a sense of what is at stake in shifting the focus from entity to relation' (Hayles, 2002: 304–5).

Hayles places *Traces* within her mode of enactment: the relation of mindbody to its immediate surroundings. She states that *Traces* 'occupies a middle ground between avatars that mirror the user's motions and autonomous agents that behave independently of their human interlocutors' (Hayles, 2002: 308). This 'performance,' she goes on, is 'registered by the user visually and also kinesthetically as she moves energetically within the space to generate the entities of the Active and Behaving Traces' (Hayles, 2002: 308). It 'makes vividly clear that the simulated entities she calls "her body" and the "trace" are emergent phenomena arising from their dynamic and creative interactions' (Hayles, 2002: 308). Hayles contends that *Traces* 'enacts a borderland where the boundaries of the self diffuse into the immediate environment and then differentiate into independent agents' (Hayles, 2002: 308).

To quote her summation in context:

> Far from the fantasy of disembodied information and transcendent immortality, *Traces* bespeaks the playful and creative possibilities of a body with fuzzy boundaries, experiences of embodiment that transform and evolve through time, connections to intelligent machines that enact the human-machine boundary as mutual emergence, and the joy that comes when we realize we are not isolated from the flux

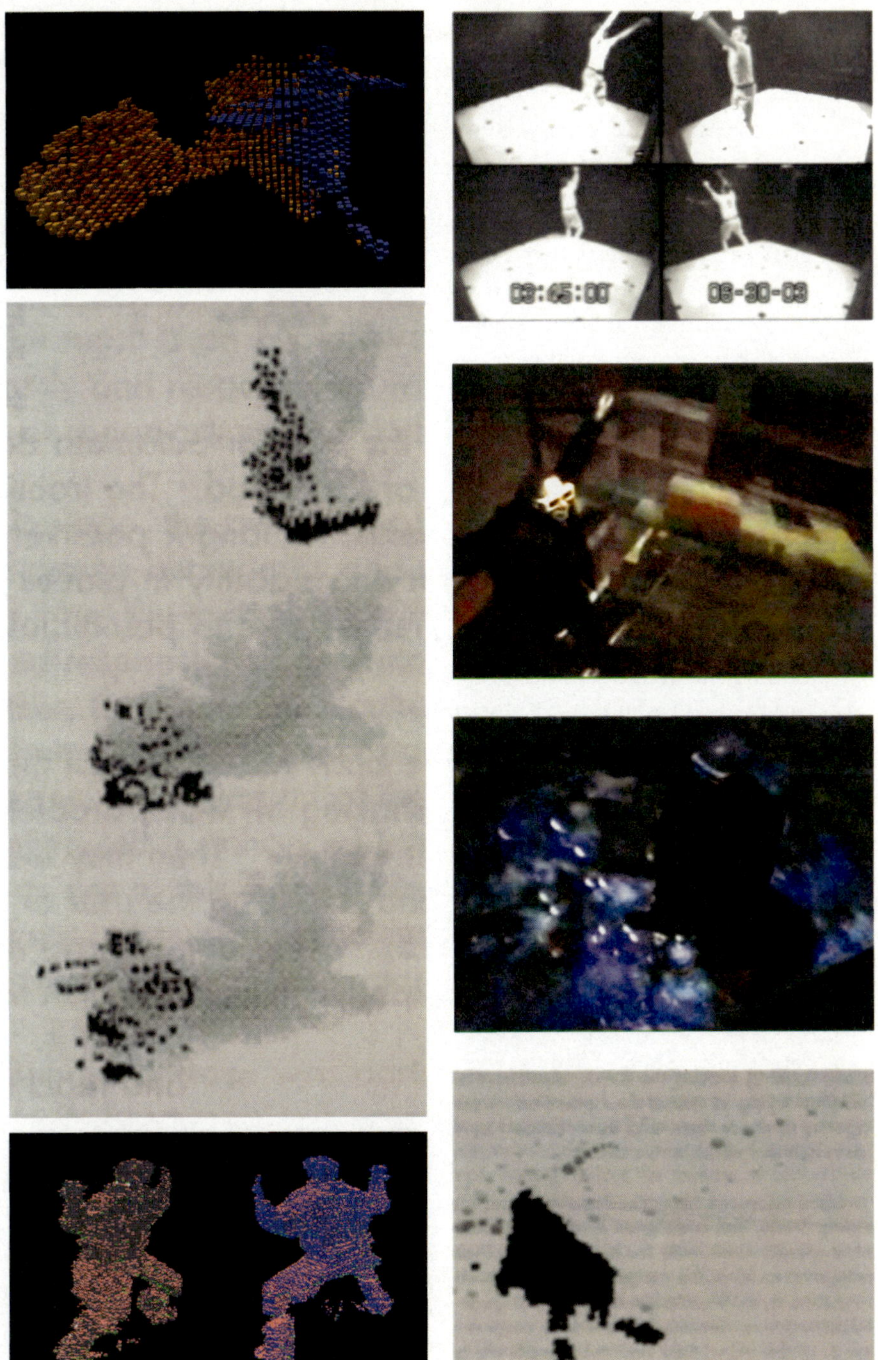

Figure 13. Simon Penny | *Traces*, 1999

> but rather enact our mind-bodies through our deep and continuous communion with it. (Hayles, 2002: 309)

Hayles' body, world, and technology co-emerge, and like in Hansen's text, she asserts that *Traces* supports an understanding of embodiment as relational and emergent.

My approach to embodiment and interactivity is itself not dissimilar to the one proposed in Hayles' paper, and implicit body thematics are not completely unlike her 'modes of relation.' Her reading of *Traces* indeed adds insight and understanding, as is the goal of the implicit body framework, to both embodiment and interactive art. But like Nancy's critique of Heidegger – that the latter set up 'being' before refiguring 'being-with' – I maintain that Hayles (and Hansen) set up a separated artwork / technology and participant before refiguring their dynamics. I am not arguing for an extant body which can 'diffuse' with its environment and then 'differentiate' again, an embodied and artful 'communion' or 'connection' with, for example, the pre-formed (even if fuzzy) 'boundary' of technology – words which unfortunately suggest the two as a priori, despite Hayles' argument for 'mutual emergence.'

We must take the per-formance of body and meaning (or world or technology), together, as (inter-)given. Technology and the artwork are not acting as catalysts or glue that combine two things (which are not things); they act as a rig, a quotation, a suspension and intervention into, matter and matters that are always already in relation and in excess of their always-in-process individuation. These relations are necessary – are in fact the very pre-condition – for being(-with). Interactive art such as *Traces* creates potentialized contexts that underscore the fundamentally relational processes of embodiment, materialization, meaning-making, and so on. And implicit body thematics are in fact more than 'modes of relation'; they are sensible concepts which are *themselves* emergent and in relation; they are used to examine an embodied investigation of a continuous embodiment and x (and x, and x, and x, ad infinitum).

I also add to Hansen's and Hayles' readings a focus on the emergence of embodied reading (and writing). In *Traces*, we *virtually feel* the body contributing to and distorting, while simultaneously being guided by, reciprocally immanent 3D images. We *practice* the formation of embodiment and meaning-making. Bodies move and are thus affected by the image-signs they concurrently create. Here is a semblance of a situation, where (a) body and (a) language are intensively felt as per-formed in relation.

In the passive trace, performers tend towards slow investigative gestures: swooping arms, a dip, or a wave-making slip of the leg, explorations of the magical fades of the voxels in their avatars. In the active trace, when images begin taking on characteristics of their own, viewers' styles become more erratic; they try to control the images around them by ineffectually waving them away, slowing their movements then unexpectedly lashing out, flailing and failing at their attempts to have exacting control over the environment/ embodiment /three-dimensional image (and its meaning). In the behaving trace, they tend to stop trying to control everything in the space, but instead flick and kick their arms and legs in short motions, generating Chinese dragons, and engaging in an ongoing play.

In this final trace, 'movements spawn' inter-active animations that have a kind of relational agency; they are 'cultural artifacts that exhibit' their own 'behavior' (Penny, 2004).[10] The behaviors feed off participants' position and movements in the space, as well as those of other agents, and in turn, their movements respond to these images: shorter and harsher, static then erratic, karate chops and kickball. Here the work is not simply, as Penny and others say, a 'point at which [a] computational system and the user make contact' (Penny et al., 2000: 5). The 'work' *is* the relationship that emerges, and the amplification of what such relationships produce.

Anna Munster recognizes two vectors in information aesthetics. One sees 'abstraction as a means for engaging intensive corporeal experience,' and the other looks 'toward an investigation of biology as a materialization of information' (Munster, 2006: 185). *Traces* highlights both. In body and in language, we are always guiding and making, tracing and transforming, feeding back between what we do, what we see, and what each means in and through and to and with the other.

We look at and read what we perform and produce, together. Bodies interacting in trace-space contribute to the construction and constitution of the image-world in the VR environment that they are interacting with. Since *Traces* does not re-present the body, but rather the body's movements, the images that participants make, read, and respond to are precisely processual and per-formed. These images, like the body, emerge from the (outside / inside) space of relationality, and together they produce meaning. The relationship that the work of *Traces* frames is thus between / with explicit and implicit, construction and constitution, inscription and exscription, body and sign. Its significations and symbols are inscribed, in real time, through our incorporating practices, and simultaneously take on a symbolic life of their own, informing how we perform before, during, and thereafter. Acting together, body and language emerge together. We come to sense, to mean, to be-with. A body-language reading of *Traces* does not support a philosophy of embodiment, but rather shows how the work exscribes both embodiment and (its / our) philosophy. At stake is how we rehearse their performance, and continue to perform them thereafter. Here art is the practice of philosophy. It brings the stakes of philosophy into the room, into our space, into our actions, into how we affect and are affected in our moving–thinking–feeling.

Interestingly, Penny and his collaborators have also proposed an as-yet-unimplemented version of *Traces,* one that is 'networked, so that users can interact with each other's mediated trace-avatars' and the semi-autonomous agents that are spawned off of their volumetric re-presentations across several CAVEs (Penny et al., 2000: 2). In this version of *Traces,* there are many performers, which do not see one another, but only the resulting images from their inter-actions. If there are three CAVES, each performer interacts with the traces and autonomous agents of the other interactors as well as their own.

This unrealized networked version of the piece ties the contact between several audience members to a collaboratively constructed VR image, a shared backdrop that then feeds back into how we inter-act. It maintains an unambiguous kinship to the body-language sensible concept: we relate with and through the movements of our bodies, creating and incorporating a language that lives through those very same movements. But, through its multi-user efforts, it also opens up the possibility of an/other reading, one that engages with the collaboratively constituted social order, and looks towards reciprocity and exchange between several bodies (languages, and meanings). It leads the way toward the next thematic discussed in this book: social-anatomies. After a more in-depth discussion of Utterback's body of work between 1999 and 2010, the following chapter will introduce and describe social-anatomies as a sensible concept and thematic approach to understanding interactive art, and use it in two more intensive case studies.

## External Measures: Camille Utterback

Utterback writes that her work across traditional and digital media attempts to 'draw attention' to 'human bodies and the symbolic systems our bodies engage with' (Utterback, 2004d). She claims an interest in the digital medium as a site for exploring the relation between bodies and representational systems, whether the latter be language, painting, sculpture, or computer code. Utterback avers, 'Interfaces, by providing the connective tissue between our bodies and the codes represented in our machines, necessarily engage them both. How and to what extent new interfaces may engage the body, however, is up for grabs' (Utterback, 2004d). This is where the implicit body framework can be deployed to shed some light.

Utterback allies herself with an interventionist approach to movement and continuity by describing her goals of engaging and challenging the lived relations between flesh and sign. As opposed to interfaces for exclusively utilitarian software, she believes artists can explore more poetic practices for text or spoken language. Here images and texts are readable as marks and signs, but also move with their own behaviors or even misbehaviors. What she calls her 'unusual interfaces' stage our conceptual–material relations to symbolic meaning as always moving. Utterback asserts that our interactions with machines are never neutral. What is at stake is everything from the format of the 'new media through which we will read and imagine, to how we will explore the limits and reaches of our physical bodies, to how our information about our bodies will be captured and represented given new technologies' (Utterback, 2004a). While the artist admits that these stakes are not new, they do need to be understood in the uniqueness of this technological moment. Utterback's artistic practice seeks to focus 'attention on the embodied self in an increasingly mediated culture' and to 'create social spaces focusing on human interactions' in which 'unusual' performances (arising from unusual movement and affect in the interactive arena) (Utterback, 2006) draw us *to* the limit of body and language, and *as* the limit of body and language. Here signification and embodiment are framed as exscribed, body and / with language are staged as per-formed, in relation.

Following *Text Rain,* Utterback embarked on several series that intervene in not only the relational emergence of embodiment and meaning-making, but also in those of body and time, body and vision, body and history, and many other sensible concept couplings. I use the body-language thematic alone to analyze her interactive environments as rigs which suspend and magnify the per-formance of embodiment with the process of signification. I discuss her *Liquid Time Series* (2001 and ongoing), which engages viewer interaction to reveal pre-recorded segments of video images (re-presenting time), and pieces from her *External Measures* series (2001 and ongoing), which create generative and painterly impressions along with participants' movements in a gallery or public space.

Utterback writes that the *Liquid Time Series* (Figure 14) asks us to explore 'how the concept of "point of view" is predicated' on an embodied experience and existence (Utterback, 2004c). Here the 'imagery of time, as well as space, is disrupted by users' motions' (Utterback, 2004c). Participant action temporally and spatially fragments a pre-recorded video clip. Utilizing a coded technique visually similar to slit scan,[11] the video is broken into very thin slices, and each video strip is on its own timeline. In other words, if the video for her first *Liquid Time* piece is in standard NTSC format (the actual format is unpublished), then rather than playing a large singular video clip of 720 x 480 resolution, she has broken her moving image down into as many as 720 individual videos that are each as thin as 1 pixel wide and 480 pixels high; and rather than playing these forward at the rate of 29.97 frames per second, each 'clip' is controlled individually, by the interactions in her situation. An overhead camera and computer vision software track participants' real-time movements in the interactive area of Utterback's projection screen. The slices that are directly in front of them – the 1 pixel wide video strips they face and which take up the same width of their bodies at any given moment – will move forward and backward in time as they move towards or away from the screen. States the artist, 'Beautiful and startling disruptions are created as people move through the installation space. As viewers move away, the fragmented image heals in their wake – like a pond returning to stillness' (Utterback, 2004c). Utterback literally unfurls and enfolds time and space through our embodied relationship to the signs and media she presents – to the language of video and the screen.

The sequenced images shown in my book admittedly do not do justice to what we see, experience, and practice with *Liquid Time*; the fluid unraveling and reconstitution, the viscous un- and enfolding of time in-and-around-and-as space rippling through the installation area, must be performed in person and in body. Since every video slice explores its own space and time as the viewer–participant crosses through its thresholded section and moves or leans forward or back, the projection itself shimmers and flows from his or her interactivities. It then freezes its space-time slices with rough edges and jagged pixilation as one falls static or backs away from a given section of the screen. It is stunning. For those readers with Internet access, I highly encourage viewing Utterback's video documentation on her website, to at least get a sense of the visual aesthetic the three *Liquid Time* pieces accomplish.

In all three pieces in the series – *Liquid Time Series-Tokyo* (2001), *Liquid Time Series-New York* (2002) and *Liquid Time Tenderloin* (2009) – participants interact with images 'from sites in these cities where humans, data, or other physical matter are transferred or in transit' (Utterback, 2004c). In other words, the original 'source' videos that Utterback has cut up contain scenes that might be of a busy street in Tokyo, full of foot traffic under umbrellas trying to escape the rain; it may show crowds waiting for a slowly stopping subway train, underground in New York City; or it could reveal cars driving past a BART station in downtown San Francisco. Our movements back and forth with the installation remember, re-act, and activate the movements of the people and matter on screen. The images of pedestrians walk with the viewers in the gallery space or on the street (her 2009 installation is in a storefront window), umbrellas twirl, trains and cars come to life – but each only in fragmented slices, one sliver at a time. The chaos and fragmentation in each section is anchored by 'static elements' such as 'street signs, trash cans, a person standing oddly still' in the original video (Utterback, 2004c). Her 2010 piece, *Shifting Time – San Jose,* continues this research as a panoramic installation in an airport. Here Utterback additionally folds archival footage into the mix – enabling an encounter with decades, rather than minutes, and with film as well as video media (Utterback, 2012). Each is a play between passage and position, motion and stasis, suspension and acceleration.

As the included images suggest, viewer–performers encounter an actively embodied exploration of *Liquid Time,* but one that is tentative and anticipatory. Participants first '"test" the correspondence by moving parts of their body – tilting their head, waving their arms, etc,' and once they understand how the given interaction works, they '"play" with manipulating their transformed symbolic "self" using their physical body' (Utterback, 2004d). *Liquid Time* audience members often mimic the screen's water-like spurts of sliced and rippling movement, pushing and pulling the moments and slits of time, leaning their heads and torsos and bodies toward the screen or camera to slow an instant, or using fluid but frenetically reaching arms to grow an uncannily familiar street scene. Our moving bodies in front of Utterback's responsive screens perform what might look like novice moon-walking or break-dancing techniques, stringing together a series of ludic gestures that feel, literally and virtually *feel,* like trying to find and make sense in the relations between sign (albeit signifying representations of time, through video media) and flesh.

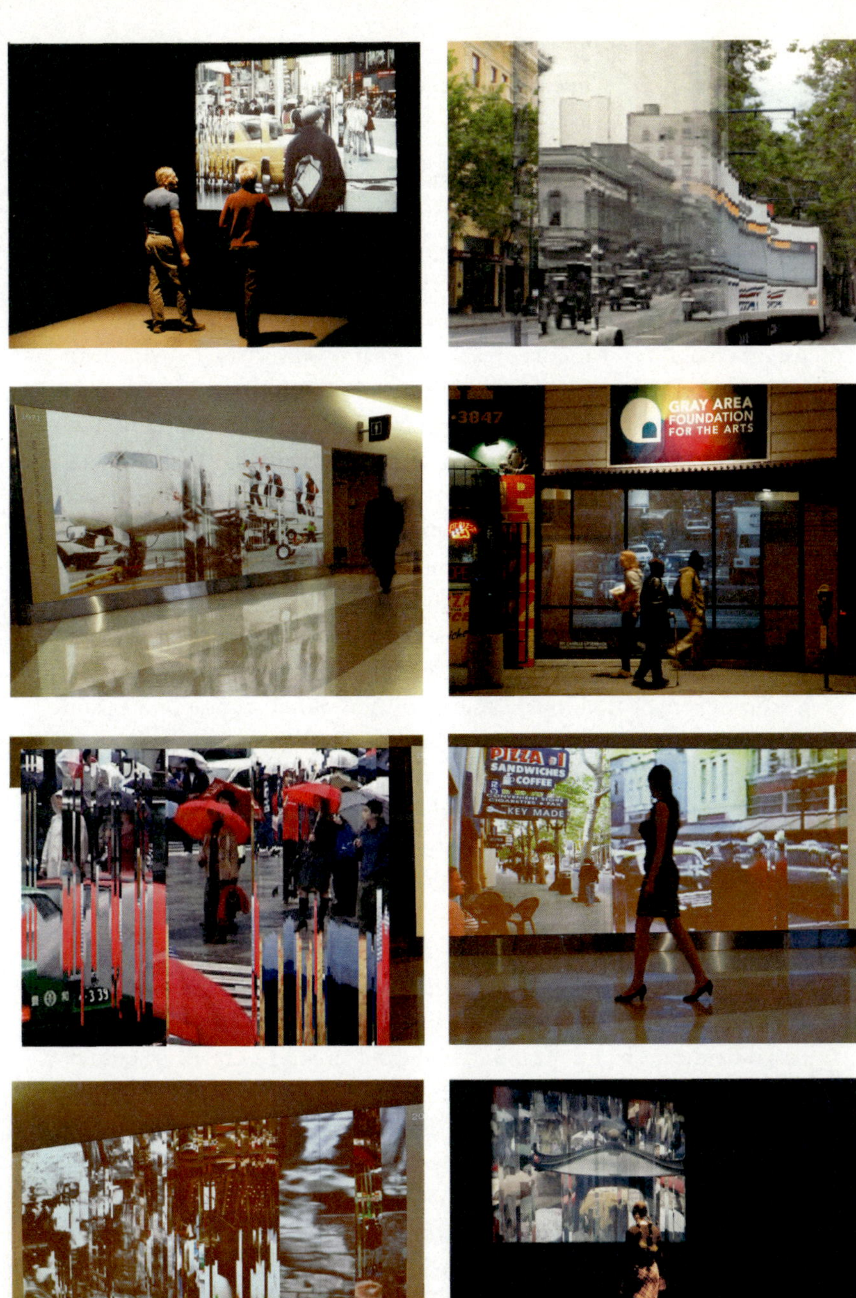


Figure 14. Camille Utterback | *Liquid Time Series – Tokyo, Liquid Time Series – New York,* | *Liquid Time Series – Tenderloin, and Shifting Time – San Jose,* 2001 – 2010 I Screen details and installations views I photos by Thomas Eugene Green and / or courtesy of the artist

While many emergent relations are framed, and could be examined, with Utterback's work, the thematic of body-language invites a focus on the symbol(s) of / in / with embodiment which we attune to in their space. This thematic fits well with the artist's performative intrigue – legible in her stated interests, as well as in her consistent use of recognizable media on screen (text or otherwise) – which sits squarely between human interaction and real-time significations. In *Liquid Time* we scrub back and forth in a symbolic, three-dimensional space-timeline that is immersed in, and physically representative of, the language of video and digital images. Utterback makes use of computer abstraction and human relations to invite 'boundary negotiations' at the 'limits' of body and meaning.

*Liquid Time*'s interactive instantiation puts in quotes how body and discourse, materiality and abstraction, emerge together through their performance and relation. Utterback's interactive experience is a kind of syncopated touch: the rhythm of our emerging bodies and the performing video slices play at one another, interact and relate through an at-once touching and emerging of the conceptual and corporeal. The piece invites us to feel bodies and meaning, together, as always already implicated and enfolded with one another. In *Liquid Time*, we explore and operate a video image, find meaning through the touching of an (inside) embodied exploration with/in a fragmented (and outside) semiotics. Utterback's participants 'come to sense,' feel the mattering of meaning and image and language, through a performative and interactive exploration of what is on screen. Inside and outside, flesh and meaning, body and language, are all exscribed.

The emergent relation of embodiment and meaning-making as exscribed is also worthy of analysis in Utterback's ongoing *External Measures Series*. In these interactive installations, she uses body-tracking software to trigger painterly and animated marks on screen that collectively create 'kinetic sculptures' or 'living paintings' (Utterback, 2002b). The marks look and move like actively reconfiguring geometric patterns, smudging pencil sketches, dripping paint, or seeping molding clay depending on the piece in the series. Their position and velocity within the projected image are initiated and continuously performed by both the location and movements of the participants in space, as well as the marks' own internal logic. Although the overhead computer vision system that Utterback employs in this series is similar to that of *Liquid Time*, her 'dynamic drawings' (Utterback, 2002b) have a completely different aesthetic feel; her canvases are generated as they move, affect, and are affected by participants' gestures and stasis, or presence and absence, in barely predictable and organic ways. And each installation invites a very different style of inter-action.

Utterback's marks immediately appear in response to participants' attendance and movement, and they are animated – leaving trails of what looks like graphite or acrylic or earth – based on the flow, stillness, and number or lack of people in the installation area. An overall composition emerges and continues to transform over time as layers of persistent marks and bodies feed back between interaction, performance, and image. Each piece 'measures' how we move or stand still, and creates an 'external' visualization of that movement and stasis. Participants in turn 'monitor this external data and measure out their actions in response,' creating an 'intricate dance between computer algorithm' and affective involvement (Utterback, 2002b). 'Measure' in Utterback's sense of the word does not refer to measurement, but rather to an active 'measuring up,' a diagram of body-language. It is a play on the moving–thinking–feeling and making of the screen-image – and its ongoing signification – with our inter-active bodies. Her use of the word 'external' is also an ironic pun on interior/exterior between each and the other. Neither body nor matter nor sign are a declared subject (or object). She rather highlights bodies and images as a mapping across each other, an experienced and practiced topological formation.

The first piece in Utterback's series, *External Measures (Rectangle)* (2001, Figure 15), follows our movements, and our relation to each other, to create a collection of angular shapes that fold in on themselves. It was produced, released, and exhibited along with her second work, *External Measures (Round)* (2001, Figure 15), a circular projection where 'lines curve and snap between people like crazy elastic bands, creating a dynamic tension' in the image and space (Utterback, 2002b). Utterback's third *External Measures, 2003* (Figure 15), saw a slightly more organic relationship, where constant procedural

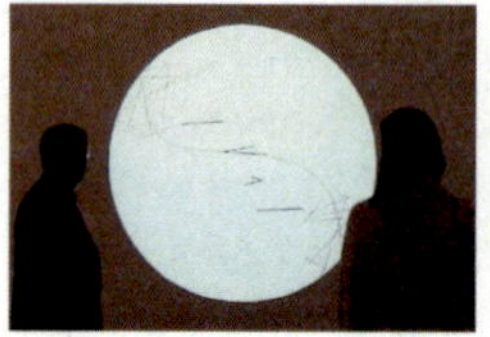 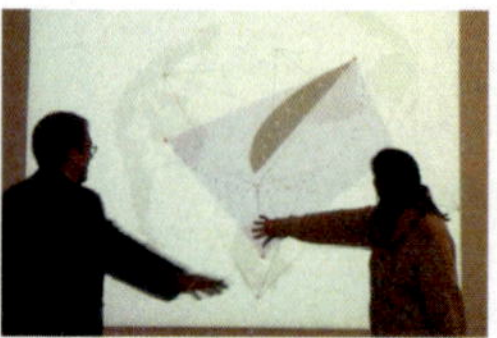 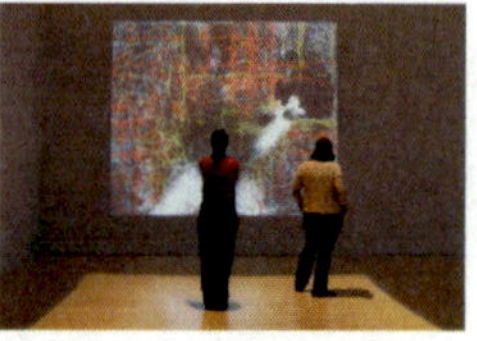

Figure 15. Camille Utterback | *External Measures: Round, Rectangle* and *2003*, 2001–3 | photos by Tom Bamberger and / or courtesy of the artist

animations of slowly moving gray lines are pushed aside by viewers' movements, making way for more sparse but saturated color-lines left in their wake. 'Subtle brown and black swaths are etched between any people in the space' and 'scratchy white lines connect' each of us to our point of entry into the interactive area (Utterback, 2004b). A given participant's appearance alters the traces on the screen by erasing marks in the projection – ones automatically drawn, as well as those left behind by others – and as time goes on and the software continues to draw over the composition, eventually overwrites all traces left behind. *External Measures, 2003* thus creates a 'hypnotic tension between presence and absence, mark-making and erasing, human gesture and algorithmic drawing' (Utterback, 2004b). Here, we literally write with our bodies, are implicitly the 'tracing and the trace' in a staged drawing and meaning-making, inscription and exscription.

In Utterback's *Untitled 5* (2004, Figure 16), visual feedback between multiple bodies and the projection influence one another immediately and over long stretches of time. The artist's goal was to 'create an aesthetic system which responds fluidly and intriguingly to physical movement in the exhibit space' (Utterback, 2005). Utterback uses the same overhead body-tracking system from her previous works, but introduces more generative complexities in her pixel painting that are not only affected by moving bodies, but still bodies, multiple bodies, and absent bodies, and these cumulatively collected marks interact with each other as well. The result is a continuous, hauntingly, and haltingly poetic moving image, which invites participants to make and find meaning in, with, and as an embodied and relational corpus.

Upon entering the space, the real-time shape of our bodies from the bird's eye view of the camera produces beautifully sketched renderings on screen, like body-shaped, black and white pencil-sketched, criss-crossing, mountain ranges on an egg shell background. As we move across the interaction area, the sketched patterns move along with us, while a colored line maps our trajectory as a red-lined path drawn out from our center. When we leave the installation, our trajectory line is overlaid with tiny organic marks. The longer we are still and in the space, the larger these marks are. These tiny spots, which act like splotches of ink or paint, can be pushed from their location by other people's movement in the space. As they are pushed, streaks and smears of color are left behind in their wake, like sponges full of wet pigment and dragged across the surface of a canvas. 'Displaced trajectory marks' also 'attempt to return to their original location,' making yet more 'swaths of color occur.' The 'intersections between current and previous motion' and stillness (Utterback, 2005), between movement paths and who does or does not follow them, connect different moments of time, different bodies in space, the continuous compositions and how we might read them, and the relation of all three.

The behaviors behind *Untitled 5* are never explicitly revealed to its participants; it instead invites us to practice styles of 'kinesthetic exploration' (Utterback, 2005). The embodied sense of 'more,' of a relation to the world's larger goings-on, is always prevalent. For Utterback, a 'visceral sense of unfolding or revelation,' of both 'immediacy and loss' is integral to the work itself. Like the 'experience of embodied existence itself – a continual flow of unique and fleeting moments', *Untitled 5* is both sensual and contemplative in its interactivity (Utterback, 2005). The tensions she discusses result from the suspension and thus intensity of our relations, a kind of attunement to how we inter-act, sense, and make sense.

With *Untitled 6* (2005, Figure 16), a work very similar to its predecessor, Utterback carries on with this interactive methodology, but aesthetically shifts to bold graphics that are less like abstract painting and much closer to Minimalist, sculptural forms – like clay mush dropped from above. And with *Abundance* (2007, Figure 17), she highlights public space and social relationships – topics often explored in installation art of the 1960s through today – by moving her visuals onto the facade of a three-story building in San Jose, and viewer interactions onto the adjacent public square.

Each *External Measures* work – indeed, every time any individual interacts with the variable traces of other / past participants on screen, in any given piece in the series – creates slightly different conceptual–material encounters. They accent multiple relationships with her artwork, and with art- and mark-making more generally. Where one *Untitled 5* viewer, for example, may utilize stillness in order to leave large splotches that later agents may or may not erode over time, another can run and drag illustrative trajectories across an empty field or slowly concentrate their gestures, treading lightly across the stage, so as to smudge a crowded canvas. The interactive experience can be care-ful or care-free, and any performance might produce subjectively stunning images or visual garbage – similar to a professional artist's practice in the studio.

The live relationships and generative algorithms in Utterback's *External Measures Series* become more and more complex as she works with her media over time. They also begin to collectively en- and unfold our relationships to art history and practice more generally. She began with simple shapes and immediate on-screen responses that might allude to early cave paintings or mathematical drawings (*Rectangle* and *Round*); she then moved on to the use of negative space and real-time animated images, reminiscent of both landscape painting and early motion graphics (*2003*); in *Untitled 5* she again pushes forward on this historical arts trajectory, referencing the affective and performative – and in this case, collaborative – possibilities of Abstract Expressionism a la Jackson Pollock; *Untitled 6* turns to the embodied encounters of Minimalism, and *Abundance* remembers happenings, the Situationists, and Fluxus games. Viewers' operational movements in the *External Measures Series* are a playful reminder of, allusion to, and interaction with, the literal, historical 'art movements' of the past; the 'language' of this work could be said to be art itself. Participants are invited to physically relate to the images and trajectories of preceding artists / interactors, creating a lived and enfleshed collage of intertextual and intersubjective expressions and ex-

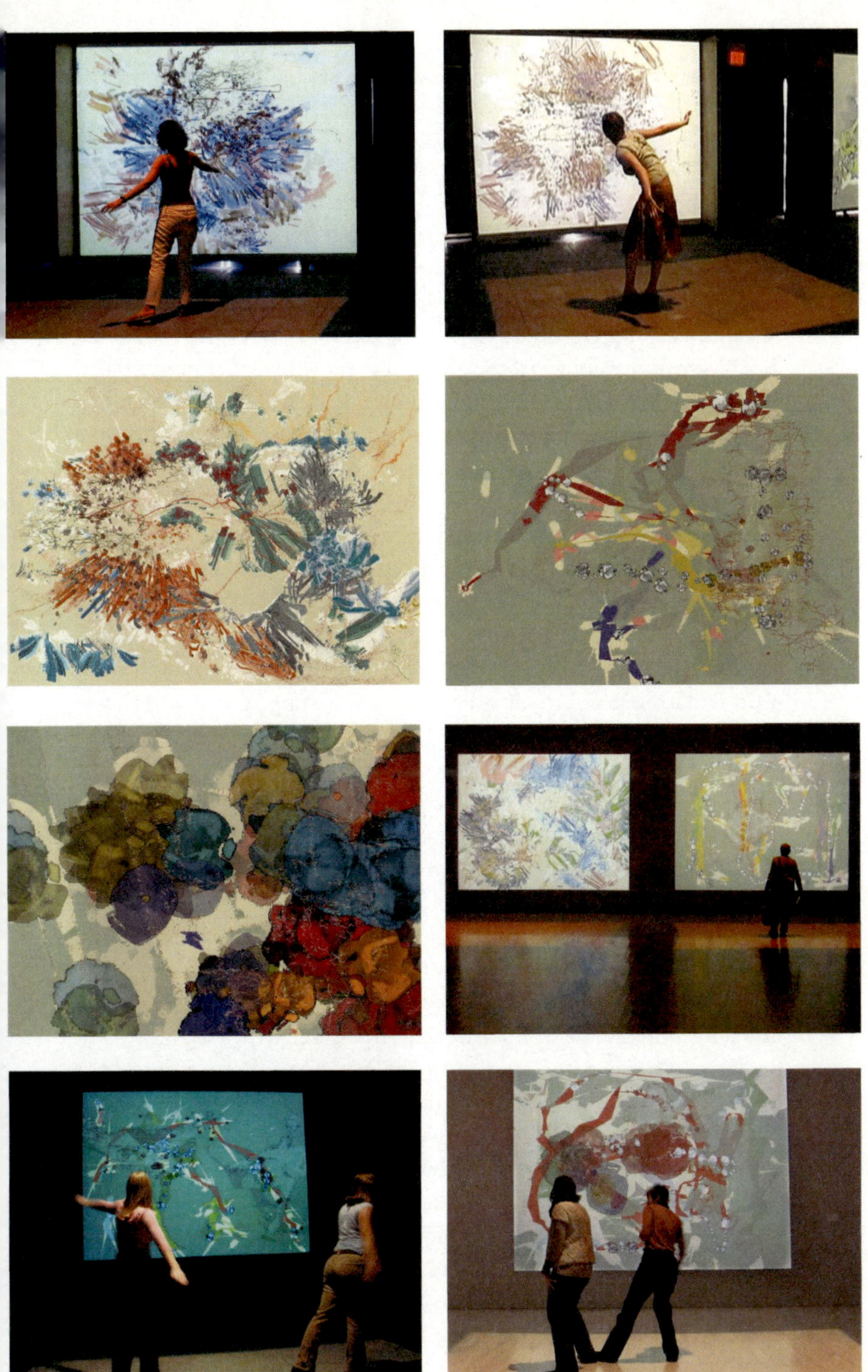

Figure 16. Camille Utterback | *Untitled 5* and *Untitled 6*, 2004–5 | Screen details and installations views | photos by Tom Bamberger and / or courtesy of the artist

plorations. They construct and assemble four-dimensional re-presentations of 'embodiment and art' on a potentialized, two-dimensional plane, and continuously feed back into that image and process. The variable aesthetics and interactions that emerge conjure up memories and re-member-ings of not just Abstract Expressionism's embodied splashes of paint or, in *Untitled 6*, Minimalism's solid forms, but Art Nouveau's graphic arts, Collage and Assemblage's found objects and pasted fragments in formalist composition, the technologically-inspired Constructivists and Futurists, Cubism's goals of incorporating several perspectives and / or times, the absurdity of Dada, or the unconscious revealings of Surrealism, to name just a few. These situational semblances suspend and intervene in the movement styles of creation, the non-representational representations they create, and the relation between the two.

In *The Ground of the Image*, Nancy suggests that the 're- of the word representation is not repetitive but intensive ... mental or intellectual representation is not foremost a copy of the thing,' but an intensified presentation. It is 'a presence that is presented' (Nancy, 2007: 36). Nancy's 'presentation' with its 're-,' Nicole Ridgway explains, is 'the coming into presence of a presence – a presence which is neither representable nor un-representable, but presentation / sense before signification' (Ridgway, 2008). To re-present, in other words, is to present emergent sensation.

Sensation was defined earlier in this book as affect and proprioception. It is before meaning, but that which makes meaning possible. We must *make sense* of, and with, senses, and this can happen nowhere other than in its articulation. Sense, writes Ridgway, 'articulates difference, the fracturing and fraying of the relation of the present to its presence, of the immediate to the mediate' (Ridgway, 2008). By interacting with Utterback's *External Measures*, I am arguing, we make sense in our embodied and intensified re-presentations of her immediately mediated, on-screen imagery. By extension, we are asked to relate to the history of signification and meaning-making in the work of art more generally. In this relationship, in the sensation of making sense of, and mediating, the language of art and / with the

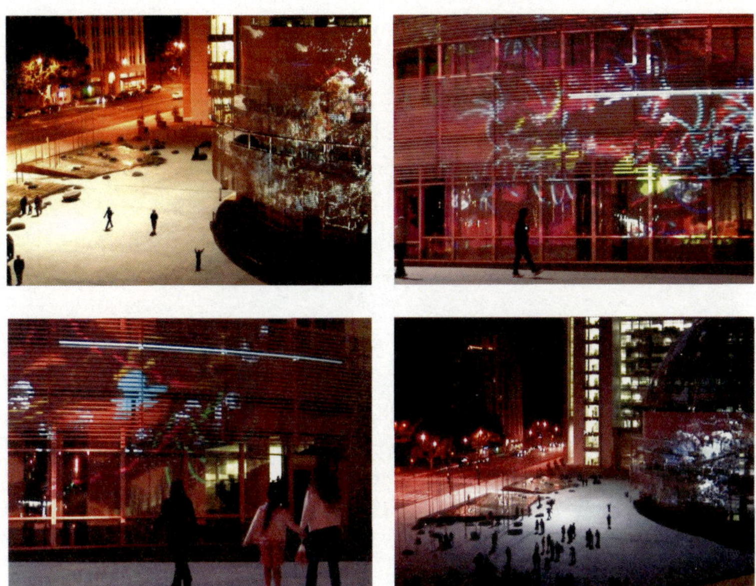

Figure 17. Camille Utterback | *Abundance*, 2007 | images courtesy of the artist

embodiment of images, we virtually feel ourselves, and the work of art, becoming present.

In *External Measures*, staging an implicit body as performance amplifies the inscribing practices of writing, drawing, painting, and making art as simultaneously exscribing, per-formed, and embodied practices. We are invited to re-member, experience, and practice how signs, images, and the discourses that surround them are not mere representations, but re-presentations in the Nancyean sense. The body-language thematic, and Utterback's work, highlight that making meaning always requires bodies, and embodiment always requires meaning be made. This is art about art and artists, images and image production, signs and bodies; it invites us to feel and rehearse how we express and re-present, and how we relate to each of these embodied processes, both historically, and in the moment. We perform new-but-not-new images into existence, and these (now preformed) images feed back in to how we perform, again. Utterback invokes our relationship to her individual artworks in order to evoke our affective encounters with the work that is art more generally. In question are how expressions of meaning and bodies and matter are articulated and presented through inter- and intra-acting agencies: conscious and unconscious, human and nonhuman, present and nonpresent, living and otherwise. Here we encounter the sensible concept, the emergent language, the preformed and performed continuity, of art.

## Notes

1 This is paraphrased from Nancy's reminder that we are always faced with a double failure: 'a failure to produce a discourse on the body, also the failure not to produce discourse on it' (Nancy, 1993: 180).

2 Perpich refers to specific Western philosophical traditions going back to Descartes. Other strains might include Merleau-Ponty's phenomenology in *The Phenomenology of Perception* (Merleau-Ponty, 1962), Tom Cohen's 'non-representational' materiality in *Ideology and Inscription: Cultural Studies after Benjamin, de Man and Bakhtin* (Cohen, 1998: 8, 41), Nigel Thrift's *Non-representational Theory* (Thrift, 2008), or Judith Butler's *Bodies that Matter* (Butler, 1993).

3 This sentence is paraphrased from an uncredited Nancy citation in Derrida's book on Nancy. He elaborates: 'the being outside another outside forms the fold of the becoming-inside of the first outside, and so forth.... Hence, by reason of this folding, here are the interiority-effects of a structure made up of nothing but surfaces and outsides without insides' (Derrida, 2005: 14).

4 Adopted from the fields of computer science and design, 'user' was a common term digital artists such as Penny employed up until very recently. Viewer, performer, or participant, are now more popular terms, in that they differentiate art-based digital experiences from commercial ones. Sometimes practitioners apply all three (and others), with slashes between them, to further problematize what media art situations can do.

5 Penny's collaborators include Andre Bernhardt, Jamieson Schulte, Phoebe Sengers, and Jeffrey Smith.

6 TVS has been used in *Fugitive* (1997), *Body Electric* (2003), *Fugitive 2* (2004), and *Spectre* (2006).

7 In a CAVE, the two images are either polarized at opposite angles and overlaid, so each only appears in one eye through polarized lenses, or else

the images flash quickly between one and the other, while glasses simultaneously and rapidly 'wink' from eye to eye.

8 Such algorithms are sometimes used to show or portray emergent and organic behaviors, most famously in Conway's Life and Wolfram's 1D CA set.

9 Oliver Grau writes about *Traces*, too, but the text contains many factual errors about the piece – how its interaction works and what the artists' intentions were.

10 *Fugitive 2* video available for purchase at http://ace.uci.edu/penny/stuff/index.html

11 Says Golan Levin, 'Slit-Scan imaging techniques are used to create static images of time-based phenomena. In traditional film photography, slit scan images are created by exposing film as it slides past a slit-shaped aperture. In the digital realm, thin slices are extracted from a sequence of video frames, and concatenated into a new image' (Levin, 2008).

12 See also *Metaphors We Live By* (Lakoff and Johnson, 2003).

# Chapter 5

## 'Social-Anatomies'

### Touch with Tact

In the year 2000, then ITP students and now international artist-designers, Ralph Borland (South Africa), Jessica Findley, and Margot Jacobs (both USA), collectively known as The Millefiore Effect, produced the first version of *Front* (2000, Figure 18), a wearable and interactive sculpture. This being the only concrete collaboration between all three, it is hard to construct a narrative around their general approach, but each has gone on to use art, design, and technology as a means for provocation, investigation, and / or innovation.

Borland writes about the politics of technology, and develops creative projects that address social issues. Taking cues from activist groups and under the blanket term 'provocative technology,' Borland investigates 'tools and technologies that combine the attributes of art and design to make objects' that 'may have an immediate function to perform, but that also serve as pointers' to specific 'social conditions' (Borland, 2007). Jessica Findley's other work ranges from collective, interactive experiences that transform how we produce and perceive the landscape at large, to odd engagements with plant life. She is most well known for her ongoing *Aeolian Rides*, where participants in wind-inflated suits ride bicycles through cities around the world (Findley, 2011). Margot Jacobs' subsequent work is focused on design methodologies, and experimental prototypes that change how we engage with technology in the everyday. The team as a whole worked to create a wearable piece that was seemingly integrated with its participants' bodies; these viewers were encouraged to perform publicly, and the dynamics of their interaction were meant to provoke styles of 'behavior we see in few other contexts' (The Millefiore Effect, 2002).

*Front* consists of a pair of plastic suits, which inflate when activated by the sounds around them. It is 'an endless game of vocal battle between two people who wear' custom-designed, inflating and deflating plastic ensembles (Debatty and Findley, 2007). Basically, as participants yell at one another, hacked blow-dryers are triggered to distort their moving forms. Gallery-goers take turns, two at a time, adorning *Front*'s suits then facing each other in a small, marked-off ring. The volume of each wearer's screams inflates their own suit's 'aggressive' parts – pointy horns, boxing gloves, or wings – while their 'opponent' sprouts protective, but ultimately constrictive, forms around their more vulnerable flesh.

In the accompanying, and mostly humorous, video documentation, the team explains that they began with the question, 'How would it feel to express your emotional state through large changes in the shape of your body?' (The Millefiore Effect, 2002). They 'looked for inspiration from animals which could transform their own bodies,' and 'used the volume of their voices' as a 'crude metaphor for emotional state' (The Millefiore Effect, 2002). Once suited up and told to begin, the power of each participant's yells or cries in their face-off (or perhaps body-off) has a physical effect on both them and the other. Aside from the verbal and visceral taunting, pointing, and physical jabs that may come from any given screaming and growling person towards his or her subjected listener, this interaction quite literally amplifies and inflates the potential power hierarchies that emerge from any given relationship. As is demonstrated in the included imagery, we see not only aggressive and defensive positions coming out of any

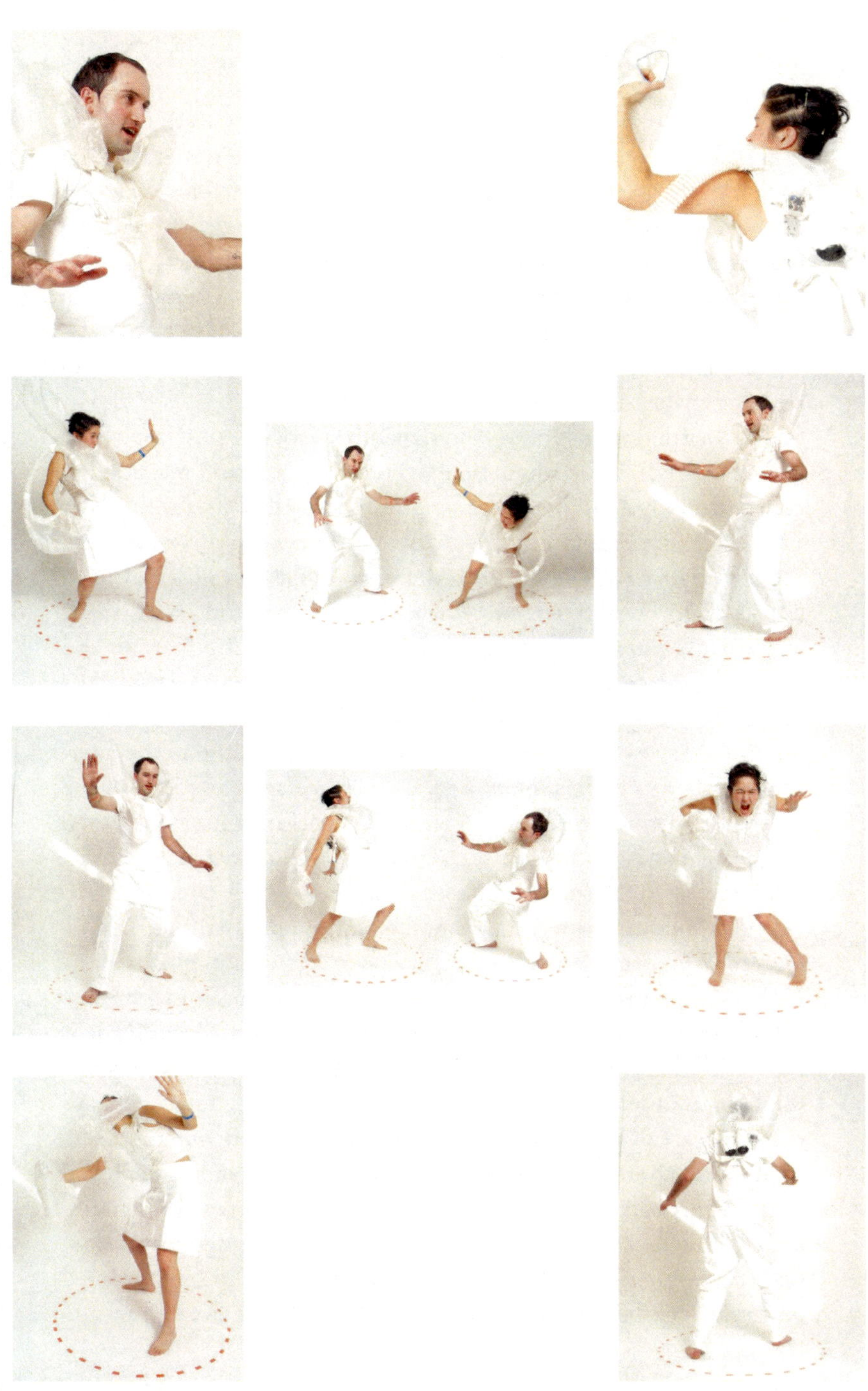

Figure 18. The Millefiore Effect: Ralph Borland, Jessica Findley, and Margot Jacobs | *Front*, 2000

given duel, but also shock in the eyes of the duelers, as they recognize that their own bodies and voices and feelings continuously feed back into their own, as well as their opponent's, tangible forms and emotional states. Although mostly playful howling matches – you can hear laughter in every gallery setting – this is also a serious investigation of how action, perception, and the body itself all materialize from a network of interrelating agents, rather than one affective source.

The tensions between how each participant affects the other, in sign and material, stasis and continuity, accent the body as both virtual and virtualizing. Unforeseen dynamics between suit, opponent, audience, voice, body language, perception, action, and reaction become precisely that 'reality-generating potential' (Massumi, 2002: 123) which emerges from the virtual cusp between possibility and actuality. *Front* remembers both the operational and observational; it asks us to engage our immediate environment and other acting participants and resonating matters within its space. Both armor and disarming, protection and provocation (Borland, 2002), these suits and their integral performances, concretize, intervene in, and make physical our emotions, both visible and invisible, as and in the interaction between bodies. *Front* asks us to rehearse formations of the emergent relationships between embodied performance as governed by our societal rules, and the social role that embodiment has to play.[1] It intervenes in the sensible concept that this chapter refers to as social-anatomies, and the thematic of the same name is a mode of moving–thinking–feeling such work.

The social-anatomies thematic follows on the 'logic' of Jean-Luc Nancy's principles of plurality, builds on the mutually immanent categories that we *are-with* – as a people and corpus. It extends this thinking in order to examine artworks that intervene in how bodies perform – are dispersed, enacted, entwined, interfered, differentiated, shared, and continuously embodied – with each other. It is deployed to think through how interactive artworks stage the un- and enfolding of 'bodies,' all engaged across a sea of flesh, matter, forces, and matters. Elements from the social and the affective body are accented precisely 'together,' to make explicit the implicit, and vice versa.

Touching between bodies is, for Nancy, always a sharing and a separation; like his partagé, it is an instance of both contact and difference. It is touch with tact. Touch is multivalent, incorporating both of the senses of the 'sense of touch' and the sense of 'to touch someone' – to come into contact with, to move or affect. We touch the limit of the other but the other is not immediately given to our touch. Our touching does not fix and confer a singular meaning, where the other is revealed or brought to presence as something completely known, or as an extension or mirror of ourselves. It is touching 'in both a tangible and intangible sense, to gain access to her specificity, to be exposed to it, to be affected by it and to respond to it, not to subsume or annihilate it' (Sorial, 2004: 78). Here neither individual is inscribed within or via the other – they are not touched / moved in the sense that they have accessed the heart of the other, or felt them in all their fullness / presence. Rather, they continuously and collaboratively emerge in and from their reciprocal touching.

In this sense, by engaging with 'bodies,' with 'embodiment and embodiment,' we are also engaging with the process of differentiation, with the contact and difference that produces bodies from within bodies. Each body in this body of bodies (a corpus of / as social anatomy) is 'affected in and through the other, responds to the call of the other, is exposed to the other, as something (no-thing) unfinished and unaccomplished' (Lyotard, 1988: 112).[2] Body and corpus emerge not *of* essence or substance but *as* series: as a series or multiplicity of contiguous states that are neither fullness nor nothingness, neither outside nor inside, neither part nor whole, neither function nor totality. Coming into touch with bodies – coming into contact with the limits that enable something to take place – *produces* a body (and bodies). This is a body that is *multiple* in its circulation of touches and separations as it divides and relates to itself and others (Ridgway, 2008).[3]

The name 'social-anatomies' was chosen for this sensible concept and thematic not only as a gesture towards bodies, but also the organic and elaborate nature of parts and wholes that only *are* in relation to other parts and wholes: anatomical. It is worth mentioning that transgenic and bio art could be developed within and alongside the social-anatomies frame, provoking a discursively practiced question of ethics across various domains – but such a study is beyond the scope of this book. The thematic as it is applied here is intended to add insight into interactive artworks that intervene in the complex system of embodiment by engaging with bodies as (always) *plural.* Through it, embodiment is understood as interrupted by other interacting and relational bodies, and this interruption is highlighted as the process of embodiment-*with*-the making of society. Participants suspend their always-entwined selves with the entire implied network of living, physical bodies. They explore bodiliness as more than the experience of *one's* body, and rather practice techniques of emergence from the relation between *all bodies.* Here one's bodily position is only derived from its relational movement with others' bodies. Social-anatomies are artworks that work to invite bodies to move, and to touch. They interrogate the relational performance of embodiment and bodies as emergent, singular (and multiple) pluralities.

## Body and Society

Nick Crossley asserts that the 'active body and the social world as a stage of action are completely interdependent' (Crossley, 1995: 147). He proposes that embodied action 'is oriented to and articulated with an embodied world, such that it cannot be understood independently of that world: that is, of the dangers, exigencies, rules and requirements of that world understood as a moral-practical (and perhaps political) world' (Crossley, 1995: 147). In other words, performing bodies make and rely on the social world and order, and vice versa. Crossley is not only concerned with what is done to the body in society (and how it is represented), but also with what the body does in and to the social world: how they actively construct and produce one another.[4] He maintains that the world in which we act is made up of situations that require specific, social accommodation from us. And we are, reciprocally, a relational part of, active in, and instantiating, a collaboratively embodied culture. Here we, as continuously embodied and individualized agents, emerge along with the social world around us. We collaboratively *make* the societies we interact in, *as* we are acting *in* them.

The crux of Crossley's argument underscores Nancy's bodies that touch, along with what the implicit body thematic of social-anatomies aims to call attention to, and have us practice. Others are available to us, and we are available to them, in our actions. And in focusing on shared activity and experience, 'in focusing upon behaviour, we arrive at an understanding of ourselves and of others by the same route' (Crossley, 1995: 143). Put differently, how we act, behave, or per-form, as embodied and materially relational agents, takes place in and simultaneously constitutes / constructs the embodied societies in which we play a role. We 'belong to each other by belonging to a common world. This does not preempt the possibility of distinctions and conflicts between different groups, but it suggests such divisions are relational and thereby secondary to a prior unity' (Crossley, 1995: 143). Bodies and social orders feed back between one another as an incipient organism of activity.

Following Marcel Mauss, Crossley calls 'pre-reflexive' and embodied action 'body techniques' (Crossley, 1995: 144, 139). Body techniques follow social rules without mediation or thought. They are the movements we practice in and with society. We are a part of what constitutes accepted body techniques in the public order, but no such movements are ours alone. Here a body – its movement, affect, and sensation together – coordinates itself, but the '*exercise of body techniques* is directly and immediately governed by the rules and exigencies of their immediate situation' (Crossley, 1995: 138). Body techniques are learned, physical responses / actions that our affective and affecting bodies can adapt and apply. We have been habituated to our body techniques, but perform them without thought or reflection; to cite a more commonplace phrase, body techniques are 'second nature.'

'Intercorporeality' serves as the context for the exercise of body techniques. It 'revolves around the notion of relations between sentient-sensible bodies,' and is 'the public order in which body techniques are exercised' (Crossley, 1995: 144, 139). It is our embodied society. Vital to Crossley's thesis is that intercorporeality is constituted through the practice of body techniques - through our movements as social agents in space. Societies are always already intercorporeal, are 'hives of on-going, situated actions, and these actions constitute and reproduce those spaces and that world' (Crossley, 1995: 146). Society is made up of how bodies move and touch, and how bodies move and touch is based on that society. Body techniques take place within the social, intercorporeal order, which, at the same time, they constitute and organize. There is an interdependent and relational emergence of body techniques and intercorporeality, of our actions and our (social) world. They are reciprocally constitutional, and reliant on one another's formation: per-formed.

The social-anatomies thematic is used to study artworks that intervene in this mutual emergence of embodiment and the embodied social order. The phrase and sensible concept is itself purposefully ambiguous, alluding to the feedback loops Crossley suggests. 'Social-anatomies' can reference the socially per-formed body techniques of one active participant or several embodied agents within an artwork's frame; it might point to intercorporeality as a contextual network of organisms; or it may address all of these all at once. The social-anatomies thematic brings enhanced encounters with and understandings of art that intervenes in contact and difference, embodiment and society, body techniques and intercorporeality. The situation of the interactive artwork puts these various relationships in quotes, magnifying and interrupting their communal constitution.

Artworks that can be grouped under the social-anatomies thematic re-cite and re-situate bodiliness and society, opening them up to the kinds of ongoing discussions that we find in the interdisciplinary journal of *Body & Society*. In the introduction to the first issue in 1995, editors Mike Featherstone and Bryan S. Turner explain that the establishment of the journal is testament to an expanding interest in the body in the academy and in popular culture. The body, they state, 'as an overt and thematized issue now appears to be central to a good deal of contemporary thought and practice' (Turner and Featherstone, 1995: 1). The body as 'a sign and symbol of social and political processes,' as well as its physical presence, is ubiquitous (Turner and Featherstone, 1995: 1). They go on to map out four 'deep theoretical and interpretative' areas of inquiry, which they hope the journal, and the discourse it attempts to engage, will address (Turner and Featherstone, 1995: 6). I shall briefly summarize these in order to highlight them as parallel areas for investigation and intervention in the social-anatomies thematic.

Turner and Featherstone ask, 'What is the body and what is embodiment? A theory of the body requires a systematic and sophisticated understanding of the fundamental notions of body, body-image and embodiment' (Turner and Featherstone, 1995: 6). Here, the editors' aim is provoke discussion around not only what a body is, but how it is, and how it is that we (as bodies) are available to society, and vice versa. This approach is central to stagings of the implicit body, and experiences, practices, and examinations with the social-anatomies thematic.

The editors state, '[w]e need to develop an embodied notion of the human being as a social agent and of the functions of the body in social space' (Turner and Featherstone, 1995: 7). These functions, I am arguing, are equivalent to body techniques, the operational and per-formed body in society. Turner and Featherstone invite a context for understanding bodiliness within the social order, in the intercorporeal. Similarly, the social-anatomies thematic critically examines interactive artworks with a focus on the embodied activities of the inter-actor(s). It looks at society as always already in conjunction with the embodied public, who produce bodies-with-social space.

'We need a sociology of the body which will do more than give an account of the representational or cultural notion of the body.' In other words, 'we need to understand how embodiment is fundamental to the processes of reciprocity and exchange between humans' (Turner and Featherstone, 1995: 8). This area of inquiry is the context of social space, the situational and intercorporeal 'with' of (between) social-anatomies. The interactive artworks in this thematic implicitly interrogate 'embodiment and embodiment' through the specific relationships – the contact and difference between bodies – that they invite us to explore.

And finally, '[w]e also need a strong sense of the history of the body' (Turner and Featherstone, 1995: 8). This is intercorporeality's legacy, continuously feeding back between both the social order and our body techniques. It is inscription and signification. But, as alluded to by Crossley 's, and also Nancy's, notions of exscription, we must be careful not to see this history as static or merely as a social construct, as only representational. The history of the body must be understood as, itself, an emergent sensible concept.

These key areas of inquiry can be thought of as parallel to those posed by the implicit body framework I set up, but are more specific to the context of an embodied society. What is a body and how do we understand it, together? How does it move within society? How do bodies and society relate? What does this relationship imply (both historically and continuously)? These are the questions I ask about the work of Mathieu Briand and Scott Snibbe. Each artist intervenes in a processual intercorporeality by intervening in viewer–participants' body techniques (and vice versa). Second nature is denaturalized, so as to be virtually felt. Relationships between a collective and continuously differentiated embodiment are suspended, inviting an experience and practice of the body with society.

## Social Systems: Mathieu Briand

Mathieu Briand's ongoing body of work spans interactive and social environments, public performances that involve volunteers, long-term collaborative music projects that incorporate physically produced sounds by active participants, traditional media-based works of contemporary installation, video, prints, and more. It is an avowed investment in linking bodies, technology, and public space. His artworks form 'a continuing multimedia project that focuses on… the body – in both its sensory capacity and its political construction' (Gray, 2007: 16). For Briand, 'public space' is not a physical, architectural place, but a relationship best described as the locus of intercorporeality. It is the ongoing, cyclical, and emergent social context in which we practice body techniques, and where, in turn, body techniques produce that social context.

Briand's interest is in 'challenging our senses, disrupting our habits, bending rules, confounding our relationship to space and objects, turning viewpoints upside-down' (Jouanno and Briand, 2004: 115). His work 'distorts and disrupts' our 'ritual' behaviors (Art Review, 2005), while simultaneously making implicit the mutual emergence of body and society through the interactivity it engenders. This art is not something you 'look at,' he says, it *is* the participation, and it addresses plurality, always. How Briand approaches his pieces – he calls them 'systems' – resonates with his interrogation of the body in / as society. The artist states, 'I try to put the public in the center' (Dea, 2006). The systems he develops are themselves tweaked and changed over time, where he re-uses fragments, technologies, content, and concepts. They encompass a 'complex ensemble made up of different elements' (Jouanno and Briand, 2004: 115). This ongoing relationship between parts illustrates a linkage between his overall practice and the thematic of social-anatomies: there is a continual refiguring of the rules, exigencies, and formations that produce and emerge as his series of art.

Briand's work resonates with his understanding of '*individuum*: namely, individual, undivided' (Jouanno and Briand, 2004: 115). He believes that one must start with division to get to a whole. 'Conceptually, aesthetically, or even technically all the works,' just like all people and bodies, 'are connected to one another' (Jouanno and Briand, 2004: 115). Here Briand sets up a system of systems as an organic (social) anatomy itself. Each piece creates nodes of contact between his body of work and the body with/in society. Each intervenes in the undivided and working parts that are working together to form an ongoing and continuous system that is in excess of its individual parts. Each attunes us to a collaborative mode of making, and being made.

Briand states that he tries 'to conceive works within which the visitor becomes a receiver-emitter' (Jouanno and Briand, 2004: 115). His pieces 'don't lead the viewer to a truth or a response, but rather lead ... to oneself' (Jouanno and Briand, 2004: 115). That being said, this 'oneself' is only understood in relation to other receiver-emitters. One's body is always within a plurality, a social order. Such a complex collaboration between bodies manages to avoid a sense of instrumentalization. Every-thing 'evolves according to the connections' (Briand, 2006: 54), is an emergent system made up of relational bodies, matter, and matters that are always already implicated across one another.

Briand's continuous re-makings of his work mean case studies of specific pieces are difficult to write. His interactive video system, for example, has been developed and refigured at various points between the 1990s and 2000s. 'The work is never static. As an ongoing public project for the last 10 years, the installation has expanded with new forms of media that Briand adds while continuing his investigation' (Dea, 2006). It is best understood, then, as a series, precisely as 'an ongoing public project' that continues to develop through its various instantiations. Like society and like the body, each installment is a constructed stop-point, seen only in hindsight, along Zeno's arrow's path.

Briand's titles, which shift with every instance, are not descriptive or representative of meaning, but rather 'concise descriptions of their provenance' (Gray, 2007). He uses semiotic codes that relay idiosyncratic information about where the ideas came from, what past systems he is building on, or what music he was listening to at the time. The particular video installations written about here have been known as, for example, *SYS*05.ReE*03 / SE*1\ MoE*2–4* or *SYS*017.ReR*06 / PiG-EqN\ 5*8* or *SYS*017.ReR*06 / PiG-EqN\15*25* or *SYS*018 / PeN-InM*. And elements from these impossibly named works have also been used in other, dissimilar, systems and exhibitions Briand has produced over the last decade.

> This is not a title but a classification code. It is part of a unit composed of other SYS. The aim is not to replicate (mime) a gesture but simply to note its existence among the others. The gestures are autonomous but coordinated. Together they form a movement. It is a question of impermeable systems placed before bodies. (Briand, 2007)

Here, Briand's naming mechanisms could be said to parallel the social order, which both pre-exists, and is continuously transformed by, any given work. These moving relations and formations, the pieces that could themselves be seen to be agential bodies, are both autonomous and an incipient part of the larger system that helps to define them. With regards to Briand's names in practice, and for ease and sanity, the artwork (and art re-workings) discussed in this chapter will henceforth be called *Sys05* (pronounced 'sis oh five').

*Sys05* (Figure 19) uses the audiovisual perception of one subject to intervene in another's, and asks a question: How does this effect our affect? This is a situation where looking, and all it entails, is experientially shared, and collaboratively practiced. Here two people see and hear what the other is seeing and listening to simultaneously. Shared or swapped 'viewpoints' are exchanged among several individuals. The resultant plurality of overlapping visual and aural experience not only enables us to 'enter another's visual domain,' but also unsettles our own, 'requiring us to constantly confirm our compromised perceptions' (Hasegawa, 2006: 51). To achieve this, *Sys05* literally turns its participants into audiovisual transmitter-receivers, 'allowing them to switch from seeing straight ahead to witnessing what other people' see (Art Review, 2005). Participants are each outfitted with networked helmets that incorporate video cameras, microphones, video screens, and earphones, and each instantiation of *Sys05*, each slightly different system that came out of Briand's ongoing exploration, creates different encounters of connection and feed swaps with other device-wearing participants.[5]

Some installments have as few as five wireless helmets, where each viewer negotiates a large, garage-like room and is able to switch audiovisuals with the click of a button. Other versions are wired, where performers plug their wearable gear into up to 14 different jacks, which connect them not only to other helmets, but 16 stationary audiovisual feeds scattered throughout the museum or building. Briand's system might give us another helmet-bearing body's moving perceptual field, or furnish our eyes and ears with empty rooms from one of the many possible perspectives of the system itself. We might even catch a glimpse of ourselves from various stationary or animated camera views. Most often, participants are unaware of what or whose sound- and viewpoint they are experiencing.

In each *Sys*, Briand develops a kind of matrix combining fixed and dynamic sites or sightings, from humans and nonhumans, inside an architectural space. When participants plug their headset jack into

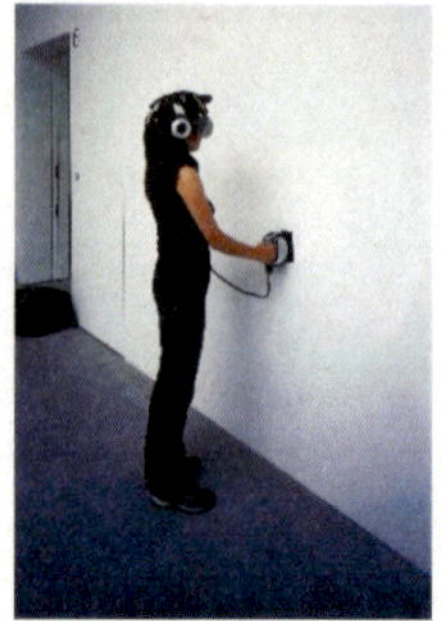
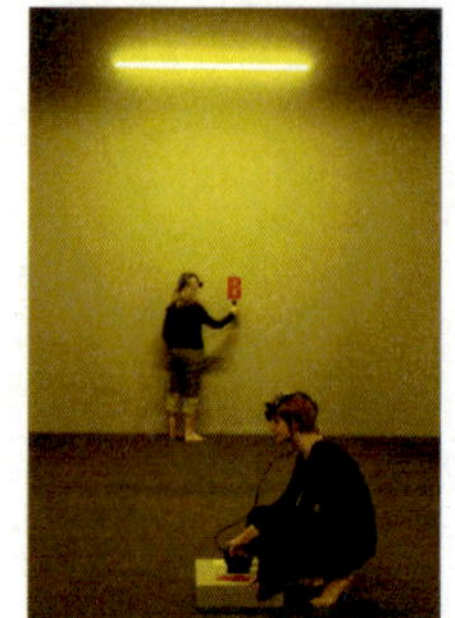
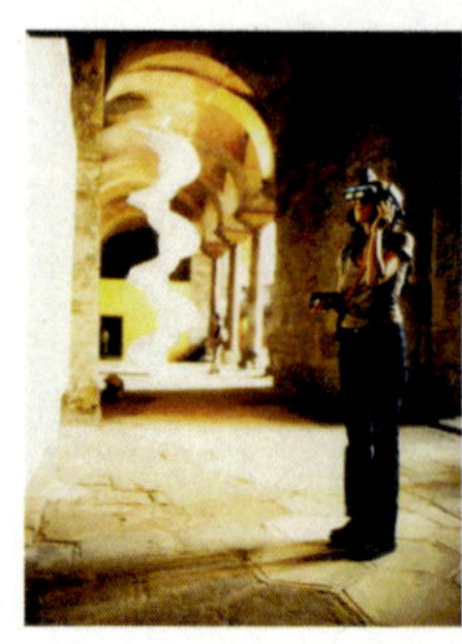
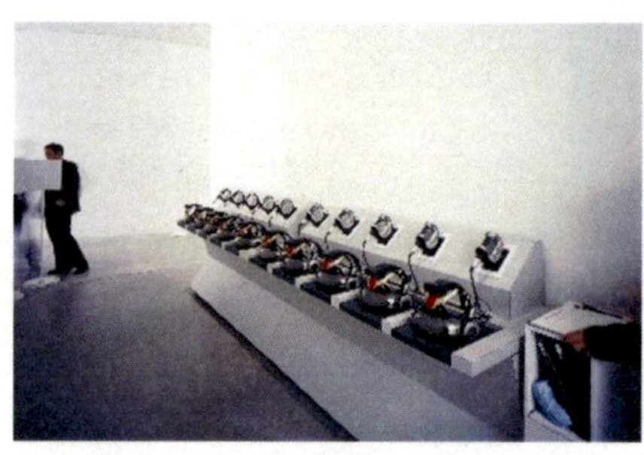
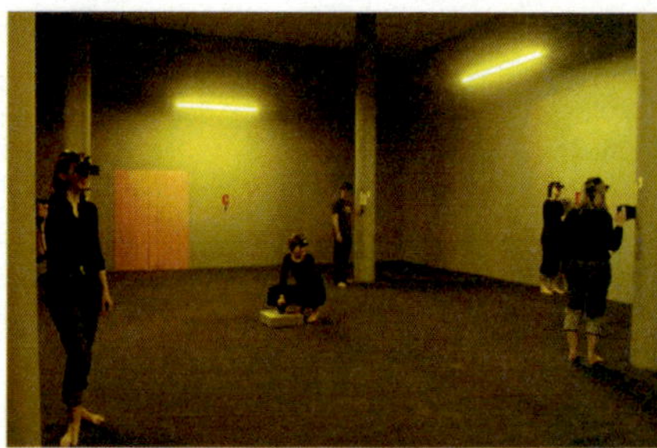
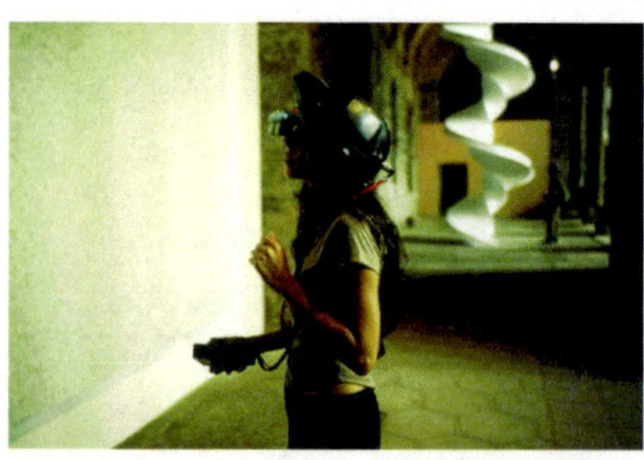
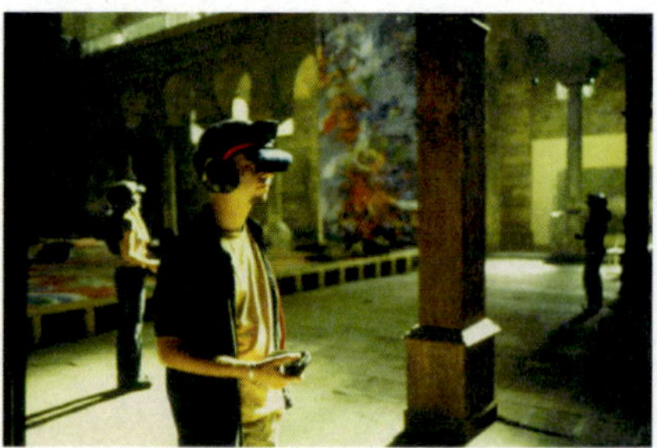
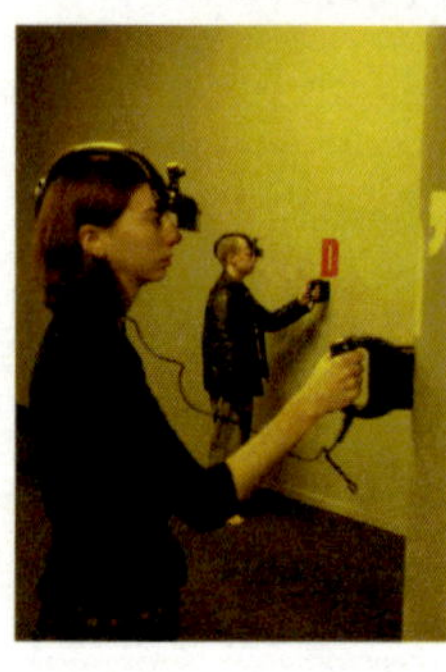
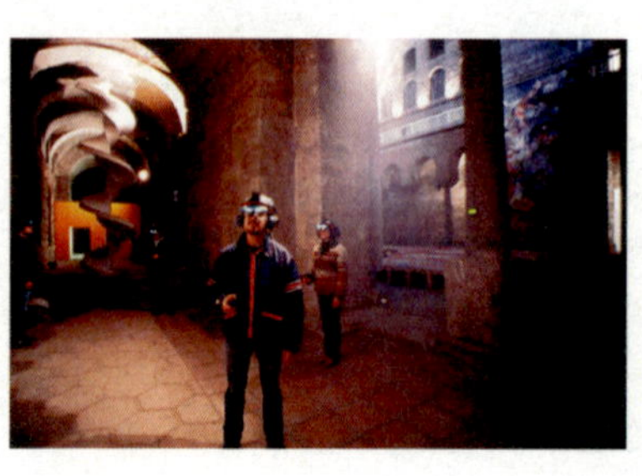
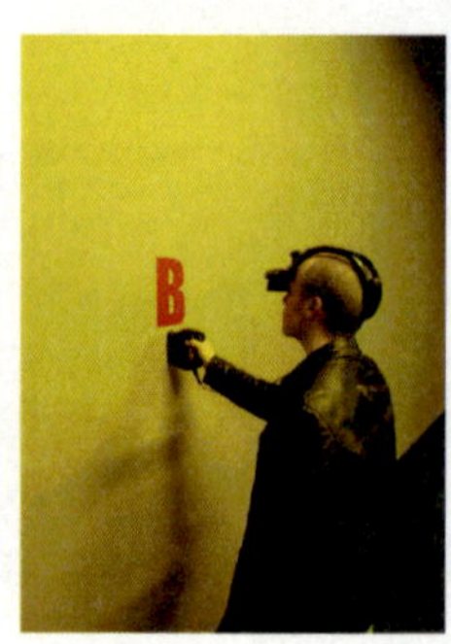

Figure 19. Mathieu Briand | *various 'Sys05' documentation*, 1996–2006

one of many outlets found throughout the building, they both offer up the audiovisual feed from their own helmets for others to encounter, and simultaneously get one of an / other participant's (or a static camera's) feed into their own helmet. The artist hangs his fixed cameras in spaces similar to where the jacks for the headsets are, and in positions that capture almost identical shots, creating an odd dis / connect between stasis and continuity in varying fields of vision. People and shapes and structures disappear and reappear from view in an instant. Although each helmet only offers sight and sound between parties, audience members' cross-modal senses are activated along with their mobile bodies in their immediately surrounding space. Each intervenes in the other, interrupts the system of perceived and perceiving, performed and performing, bodies at large.

As evidenced by the mostly still, and somewhat confused-looking, participants in the documented images, all our senses are perturbed. Walking almost always results in tripping and falling. And it is this 'destabilization that allows us to discover new things' (Jouanno and Briand, 2004: 116). As visitors move between viewer and performer, viewed and viewer, they fumble for stabilization. It is an overwhelmingly dislocating sensation of a body and its affect and connections and how they make sense (or don't), and one that each contributor gifts (positively or otherwise) back to others in the same system. We can plug or click into the system / matrix to gather experiences and perceive and conceive of its whole (intercorporeality), and / or practice and contribute interesting experiences with our own gestures and body techniques – intentionally or otherwise. Either way, we always already do both.

The constantly transforming, intimately complex, and always multiple perspectives highlight an embodiment and intercorporeality that 'superimpose, merge, slip, from one to another. It is in this way that they form and evolve' (Briand, 2006: 54). Here 'movements are driven by a will to share or not share' individual activities and sensual experiences, and also 'by the capacity of a group to organize itself in a way that they can all access all possibilities' (Briand, 2006: 55). Yuko Hasegawa contends that Briand's participants experience a 'dispersal of the subject' (Sensorium, 2006: 51). I argue that, more precisely, they practice embodiment as it is: continuously per-formed in, and as, its connections. Touched, and interrupted. *Sys05* is a situation that asks us to virtually feel and rehearse not only an embodied looking, but a *socially* constituted mode of affect. Any participant's movements in space – where they navigate their bodies or turn their heads to look, for example; when and where they click the button-swapping feeds or plug into the interconnecting audiovisual cables – contribute to the larger system and to other active participants, which guide their own performances, again.

In *Sys05*, our dynamic and embodied activities – body techniques – also make up the parts and rules and very being of a larger social system, the context and the backdrop of our activities – intercorporeality. 'We' are literally suspended: held to a spot that is saturated with a virtual feeling of where we are, but absent of any surety in that feeling. This is a potential rather than actual situatedness. It is a decontextualized re-situation, a quoting without quotation marks, a semblance, of 'me, you, and we.' *Sys05* highlights social functioning, where we are virtualized and virtualizing through each other's movements, and stasis. Here Briand has created a potentialized context that intervenes in the experience of 'body' as and with 'bodies.' Society and sensation are both materializing and emergent, processes and performances, sensible concepts that he re-sites within a technological rig that asks us to 'look,' again, together. *Sys05* uses interactive connections between its agents to highlight how those very connections govern our behavior, in turn shifting the connections themselves. We incorporate and practice how: a micro-society interrupts the process of embodiment; embodiment interrupts the constitution of said micro-society; and, these interruptions are precisely the relational emergence of each. Briand's perspective- and perception-swapping 'systems' make the stakes for mutually constitutive bodies and societies strange, and almost dangerous, in their intensive encounters. They invite us into an embodiment that is of the relation: between what we, as individuals and a collective, see and do and make in our moving–thinking–feeling.

## Interdependent Bodies: Scott Snibbe

Scott Snibbe believes that 'human mental structures and processes, including languages, ideas, memories, and preferences, all emerge from our interactions with other individuals and society,' and he hopes to 'portray this interdependence of individuals with their environments and with each other through bodily interactions' (Snibbe, 2006a). He holds views of relationality and emergence that have been argued throughout this book, and are now widely supported by emergence and complexity theory, network theory, and social psychology, among other fields. His work engages embodied cultural materializations of/with society as always implicitly emergent, and explicitly together. Snibbe states that his art explores how 'seemingly independent phenomena are, upon analysis, actually interdependent with their environments' (Snibbe, 2006a). No 'object,' whether 'physical or mental,' he asserts, can exist 'in isolation from the rest of reality' (Snibbe, 2006a). And so his artworks utilize sensors that invite us to actively engage, to touch or breathe or move. While cutting edge technologies make up what his art is and does, the artist insists that human-to-human interactions, embodied communication between peers, are at the heart of each experience. Linkages and breakages between bodies are the work of his works. They intervene in the relational feedback loops between a processual embodiment, and the emergence of societal norms.

Snibbe's practice is grounded in his training as an experimental filmmaker and animator. His interactive installations either create visual re-presentations of participants' relationships to other bodies in real time, and / or leave remnants of their movements for future interactors to encounter and explore. In accordance with 'how the body "thinks"' affectively, 'rather than through reason and language' alone, Snibbe attempts to give us 'at every moment a global, practical, and implicit notion of the relation between our body' and the matters of matter (Snibbe, 2006a). Here it should be clear that although he uses representations of the body in his work, Snibbe's interests lie in a sensation and relation to, and with, and as, those images. He believes, as I do, that the interactive process in interactive art is the 'work.' What you do 'is what you are creating – completely intertwined and inseparable' (Simanowski and Snibbe, 2006).

Snibbe sees the body and its parts as defined through their relations with social conventions, which are fed by both their activities, and our communal understandings of those activities. 'The line between you and someone else is the relationship, constantly changing' (Simanowski and Snibbe, 2006). He talks about a thought experiment he often played when he was young:

> if you look very closely it's impossible to find the border between the hand and the arm. You can't identify one cell that is 'hand' and one right next to it that is 'arm.' Since this is certainly so (I've asked many a biologist since then), it calls into question the very existence of the hand. If you can't say where it begins and ends, then can you really say it exists at all? Of course you do have a hand – it can pick things up, pat someone on the back, and so on. By its conventional function we can label it a hand – the word really refers to the functions performed by the hand, rather than any intrinsic 'hand-ness.' And of course the

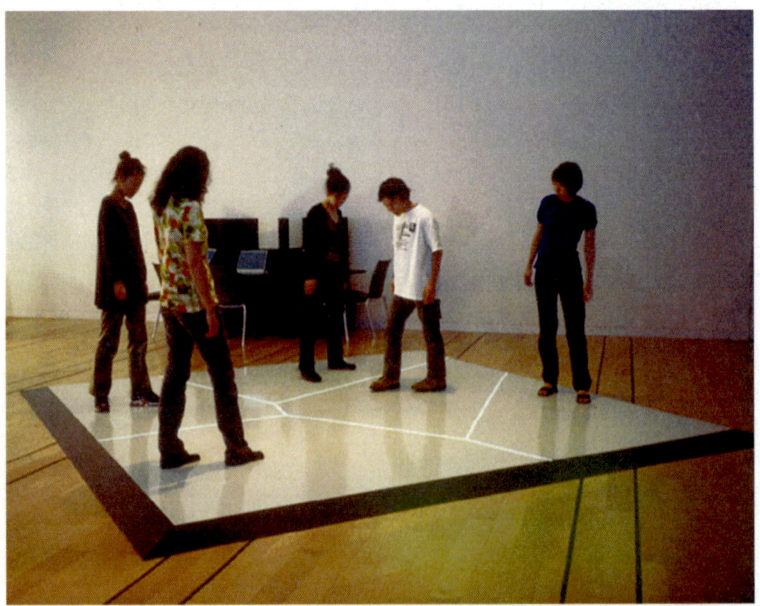

Figure 20. Scott Snibbe | *Boundary Functions*, 1998

> hand is only made of non-hand elements – skin, bones, blood, hair, etc. The hand isn't the sum of the parts, nor is it any single one of them. (Simanowski and Snibbe, 2006)

This understanding of a body in component parts which are not actually parts, a hand or body which can neither summarize the whole nor be represented by its modular pieces, is not dissimilar to Nancy's people. Our comprehension of both hand and people come from their relational activities with everything else: hand with body, body with bodies, and people with (other) people. Each is defined by its performative relations over time, its ongoing contact and differentiation.

Snibbe's first full-body interactive work, *Boundary Functions* (1998, Figure 20), is an exemplary intervention in the constitutive relationships between body and society. This piece literalizes the fine line between publicly constructed and personally constituted space, between 'you (plural)' and 'me.' Here Snibbe uses a bird's eye view camera and data projector above his participants, throwing animated lines onto the floor below them. As his audience members cross the threshold onto the interactive platform, the work draws and projects a real-time Voronoi diagram around them. No matter how many people are present (and moving) in the installation, each gets a partition of exactly the same size: mobile lines that continually separate them. If no one is on the platform, the projection is deactivated, and we see nothing. If one person strays into its clutches, again, we see nothing. But if two people are present, a line separates them equally, no matter where they both move – it dynamically changes to keep an even distance between them. Three people, and we begin to see complex shapes emerge, cellular in their structure; four people produce smaller and faster moving cells around them; and so on, with as many people as can fit inside his interaction area. The math here is such that all space within any given cell is closer to the person inside it than to any other person on the outside, all of them effecting, and affected by, how the piece, and its pieces, move.

With *Boundary Functions*, Snibbe intervenes in – puts in quotes – our emergent categories and understandings of 'personal space,' 'me and mine,' 'you and yours,' 'us and ours.' He literally puts an animated box (quoting without quotation marks) around our 'bodies.' The Voronoi diagram is continuously defined by where we move, together, and we then move in relation to that very same image, and more importantly, the bodies that move it – including our own. In fact, we move *the* relation. 'We and I and you and us' are intensely felt as performed, in the embodied relation between our playful interactions with one another.

Usually the first thing any interactor does is step on the lines. These immediately jump away from them, and that response 'adds energy to the space, creating a social stirring' (Simanowski and Snibbe, 2006). A dance begins. People chase each other and the lines that separate them; they move towards and away and choreograph. Here 'personal space' is 'only defined by others ... doesn't even exist without' collaboration. It is 'purely defined by an intertwined social relationship' (Simanowski and Snibbe, 2006). Snibbe states that his initial inspiration for *Boundary Functions* came out of a desire to reveal how we relate to one another, how we define ourselves and the physical space of our bodies through, and with, those around us. He wanted to turn the 'invisible relationships between individuals and the space between them... visible and dynamic,' to make the 'intangible notion of personal space and the line that always exists between you and another... concrete' (Snibbe, 1998). When the artist witnessed his audience's interactions in using *Boundary Functions,* however, his *revelation* of their relationships wound up *changing* the relationships: participants immediately work together to trap or destroy or trick the piece and what it re-presents. It was after seeing his own creation in action that Snibbe began referring to himself as a 'social artist' – given that he does not just reveal, but actually affects, social behavior.

Here, 'my body' is understood only through its activities in relation to other bodies, through its body techniques and intercorporeal connections. Snibbe intervenes in our activities and enfleshed understandings of all of the above, and invites us to engage, through passivity or aggression or playfulness, with how we play out our social and embodied relations. We relate with and through the movements of our own and others' bodies, incorporating and constructing a system that lives only through those very same movements. This social-anat-

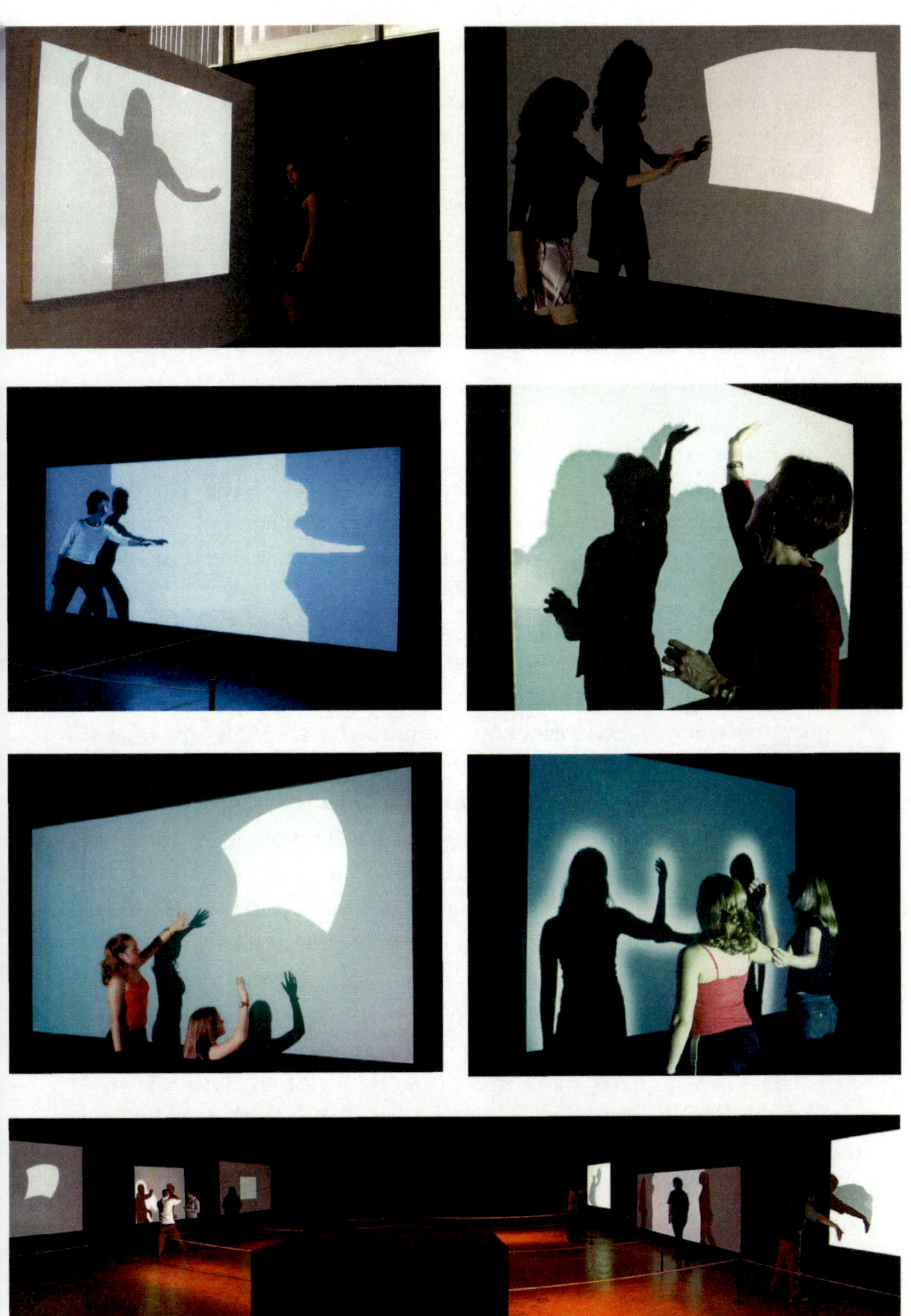

Figure 21. Scott Snibbe | *Screen Series*, 2002–3

omy couples embodiment with the emergence of a kind of actively produced and differentiating community, and community with the emergence of the body, in a way that amplifies each as not only relational, but a moving, sensible concept that we experience and practice, as it is formed.

Snibbe's later work is cinematically-inspired, and plays with the languages of film, animation, and shadow-puppets to create spaces for potential narratives, where social rules and bodies in motion inter-act with and influence one another over time. In each, we are staged as implicitly per-forming 'body and bodies,' while simultaneously substantiating communal rules as an amplification of societal structures. Many of these pieces were featured in Snibbe's 2005 solo exhibition *Shadow Play*, at the now defunct Art Interactive gallery in Cambridge, Massachusetts. I will specifically consider his *Screen Series* (2002–3, Figure 21) and *Deep Walls* (2003).

In all of the installations at *Shadow Play*, Snibbe encourages viewer–participants to use their animated shadows as flat and iconic re-presentations of the body. In a carnival-like environment with many interactors and onlookers, these shadows literally materialize as stories along with cartoon-like geometric shapes (re-presenting projected screens themselves), real-time drawings, as well as other people's shadow-selves that are being, or were previously, captured. In his *Screen Series*, viewers find themselves in seemingly simple and linear relationships with large images. Each work 'initially presents an identical premise: an empty rectangle of white light projected upon a screen' (Snibbe, 2003). Here the rectangular projection already has social implications: it references the filmic or computer screen and all each represents to us culturally and historically. When viewers move between the projector and the image, they cast shadows between them, and Snibbe captures these animated forms so that we may inter-act with screen and with cinema, with the underlying narratives, meanings, and histories that screen and cinema bring to bear.

In *Shadow* (2002), for example, the projector acts like a spot light, the shadows of any given viewer or viewers cast behind them. What each performer may be unaware of is that Snibbe's software begins recording as soon as they have entered its domain. When the viewer steps away, 'the screen replays the movements of their shadows over and over, so that their shadows are detached from their bodies.' These videos 'become a recorded performance for a larger audience, and the work is revealed as an instrument for composing cinema with one's own body' (Snibbe, 2003). In *Shadow,* our embodied performance in front of the screen is archived as a kind of mini narrative, an ongoing artifact, per-formed, then actively responded to by others, and thus per-formed again.

Snibbe's *Screen Series* continues, from here, to build on this basic premise of coupling body-as-performed with a public, and constantly transforming, artifact. In *Compliant* (2002), our shadows cause a small projected rectangle / screen 'to be distorted and pushed away, as if the screen were a rubber sheet' (Snibbe, 2005). Although inspired by Charlie Chaplin's hat in *The Tramp,* Snibbe gives his screen within a screen a sentience that more closely resembles Peter Pan's shadow running away from him. The rectangle's edges bend and ripple and slip away when our shadow-fingers push or grab its form. Snibbe sets up a quirky interplay that gestures – and asks us to gesture – towards the structures, forms, and games that bodies make, and the bodies that structures, forms, and games make. We and the social space of his screen are staged as entwined game-players and rule-makers, involved in a kind of narrative-driven (perhaps even body-language based) community, which is per-formed by multiple bodies over time and space.

There were six pieces in all to Snibbe's *Screen Series,* and the interactions ranged from leaving behind animated silhouettes or distorting screens, as in *Shadow* and *Compliant,*[6] to collaborative and moving shadow drawings between several participants (*Impression* and *Depletion,* both in 2003), and interactive games of tag, where projected light illuminates the shadows of the it-person, and is transferred between them when their shadows touch (*Concentration,* 2003).

Some viewers did not even realize the work's interactive potential, merely standing to the side and admiring the quality of light. One woman 'reflexively stepped back' when 'the screen pulled away from her body' at first encounter with *Compliant* (Simanowski and Snibbe,

2006). After understanding and acclimating to the rules of the experience, she engaged with it intimately,

> gracefully waving her fingers on the edges of the distorted rectangle, tickling the frame and, later, sticking out her tongue to make small dimpled impressions into … its edge. Long after she had departed, and the rectangle had returned to its initial form, a man quickly glanced at the piece, then, strode purposefully through the projection without looking back. Behind him, the luminous rectangle shuddered and jerked away, distorted from a clean rectangle into the warped form of a fallen tissue. (Simanowski and Snibbe, 2006)

Snibbe's work 'invites drama: one person might make wild gestures; two people could act out a pantomime' (McQuaid, 2005). Playful interactions by each individual in the space feed into how current and future interactors decidedly engage. Here implicated bodies experience and practice inscriptions and incorporations with other implicated bodies, as well as with Snibbe's body of work – which did, does, and will help to continuously per-form potential narratives and communities over the course of an exhibition.

Snibbe's *Deep Walls* (2003, Figure 22), the height of this type of work at the *Shadow Play* exhibition, invites viewers to interact directly with many bodies at once, and over time. This piece basically multiplies the interaction of *Shadow* into a grid of 16 individual boxes. When in between the installation's projector and its projection, viewer–participants cast their shadows over the grid, obscuring bodies and parts of the whole, while a camera captures their silhouetted movements in the square. Once they leave the frame of light and their shadows are no more, their recording is placed in one of the boxes, replacing an older film, looping indefinitely alongside other clips of body-outlined actions in adjacent boxes. Every active performance snippet in front of this cinematic narrative is thus suspended, stored, and re-involved in one of its comic book-like squares. Each supplants an animation that was there before, put alongside 15 others similar to, but different from, it.

*Deep Walls* invites an even more intensive experience and practice of a 'social-anatomy' than any of its predecessors. Here each shadow-

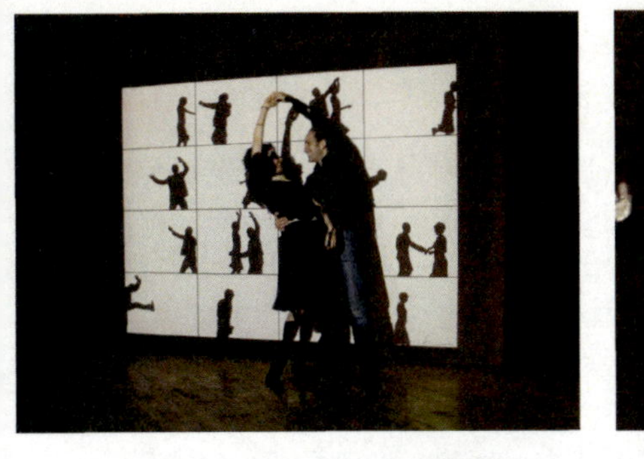
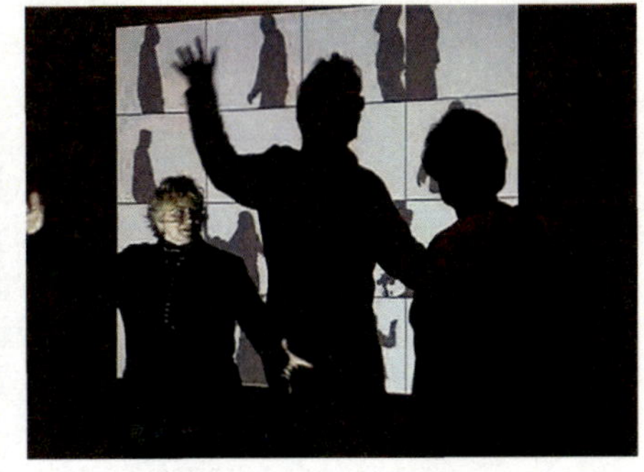
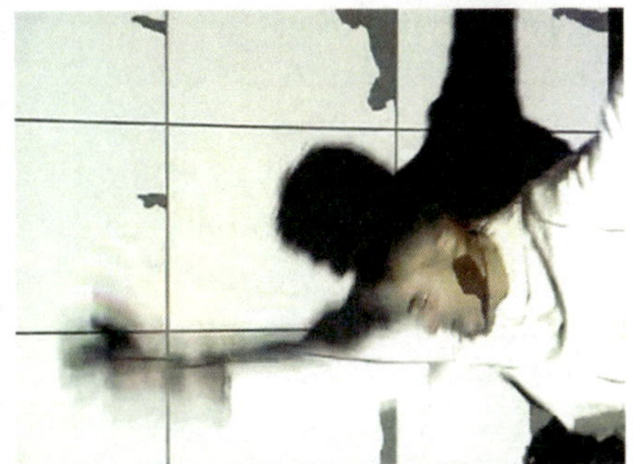
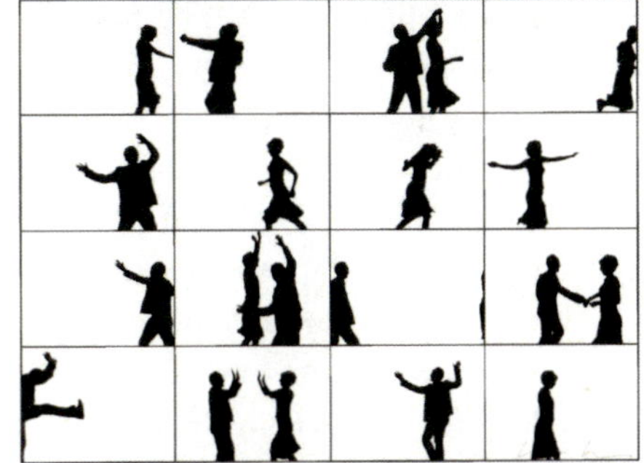
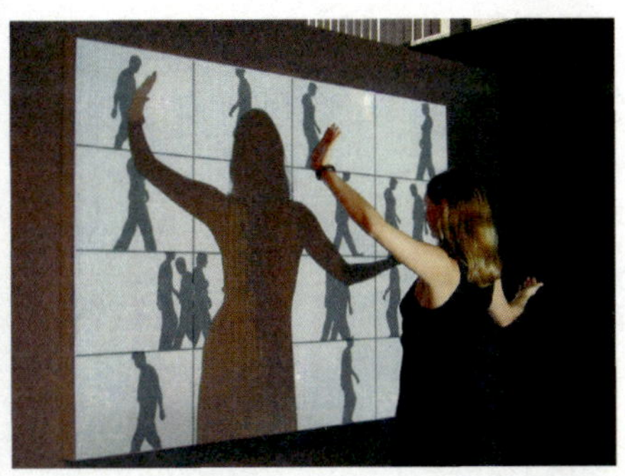
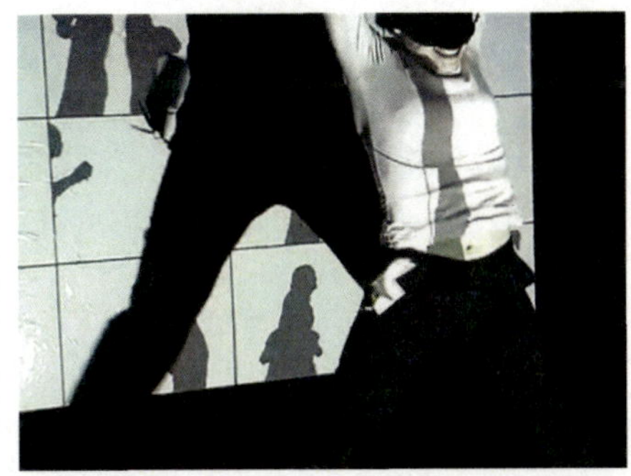
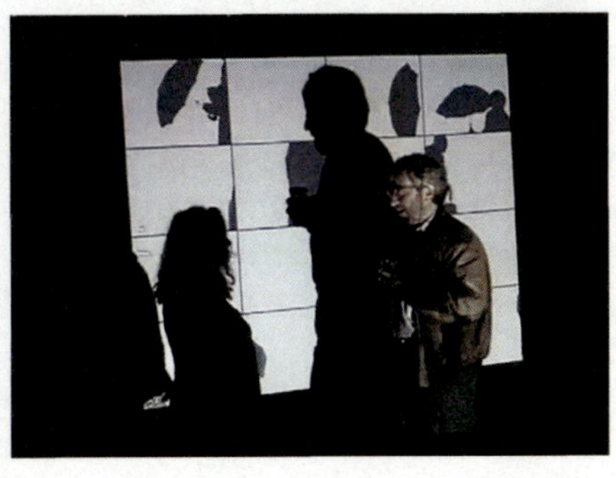
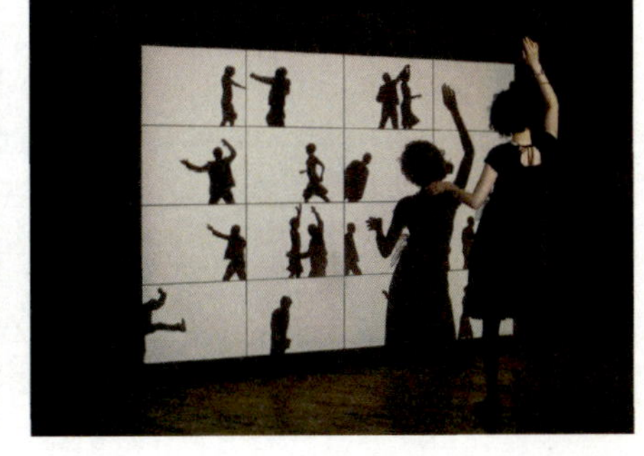

Figure 22. Scott Snibbe | *Deep Walls*, 2003

body has more than a dozen collaborators in its grid (which can include groups of people working together on one cinematic snippet). These performers often try to outdo each other, throwing their children in the air before catching them, kissing or dancing or interacting with one another or other boxes on screens, doing cartwheels or whipping their hair or sometimes even playing out familiar scenes from movies of old (I saw attempts at *Indiana Jones* and *Casablanca* at the Milwaukee Art Museum). The accompanying images might intimate iconic iPod advertisements with its stark silhouettes, or allude to graphic novels – but ones that can move through time and space. We see a complexity of narrative imagery that emerges in a mobile, physical, and non-linear fashion, as each individual interaction feeds into the whole, and into future performances. Some inter-actors glide past, others run or dance and shake their heads and tresses, still more try to work together within a frame and perform deeper meanings into the micro-narratives of a given square – which may or may not contribute to the whole in the ways they initially intended. Here the artifact of the screen is a small society made of embodied collaboration.

I am arguing that, given the open space of the gallery, the performances in Snibbe's work are always shared. Once the first audience member participates in *Shadow*, for example, we each watch the films by previous inter-actors before playing our own role, and then build on or respond to them; and we are fully aware that current and future gallery-goers will see and engage with the animations we ourselves leave behind. We interrupt an ongoing body-film, and that interruption magnifies the productive transformation of both our bodies and the social structures (always) asking us to perform. The artifactual screen story is what we, as bodies, contribute to, relate with, and change, but also informs what and how and why we contribute and interact. In our interaction, as we produce the work with our shadows, our body techniques are preconsciously aware of the cultural ways our shadow-movies might be read. We pass on traces of our bodies as part of an ongoing intercorporeal narrative.

This is most evident in *Deep Walls*. *Shadow Play*'s curator, Mary Polk, explains that in this piece the 'pictures of our shadows remain

– copies that, though reduced in size, otherwise bear a precise resemblance to the original' (*Shadow Play*, 2005). Despite this resemblance, they are completely removed from the body – a semblance, perhaps. They no longer work 'indexically – as imprints of the body, a mark of presence, but iconically – as products of artifice, an indication of absence' (Polk, 2005). While artifacts of the past, of those who have passed through the space, the shadows are a part of our present, and our presence, as we engage with them, again. The grid of the screen encompasses many frames without itself having a frame (other than the live shadow-body of the current player). As such, each frame extends into and is a part of the other, becomes an action and reaction and inter-action 'with.' The situation creates a partnering between body and screen (as a cultural artifact), body and bodies, body and society – all virtually felt.

*Deep Walls'* performers move and re-move, participate and remember, their own bodies along with the organizing, re-moving and re-membering bodies on screen. This loop of action and reaction, participation and social production / constitution, continuously feeds into what any interactor does, which is then captured and fed into the larger organization (both as noun and as verb), again. The audience, both implicitly and explicitly, constitutes a people or community, a (micro) culture or society, through its en- and unfolding structure. This structure – whether artifice or edifice – is an intercorporeal backdrop to our interactions, to our body techniques, which in turn makes up the structure itself. In *Deep Walls*, and Snibbe's work at large, we are creating an embodied and dynamic relational community within our greater, collaborative community; we experience and practice the development of social reciprocity, with and through body and bodies.

The plurality of bodies in *Shadow Play* is staged as both social artifact and relational diagramming of that artifact. The piece re-situates a mutually immanent and multiply embodied society and / with / as cultural artifact. Snibbe, in other words, intervenes in 'we': the past, present, and future of a continuous and embodied 'us.' Our inter-activities, how and what and why they are, and how they themselves govern how and what and why they are, are put in quotes. Snibbe asks us to encounter not only what a body is, but how it is, and how it is in relation to others, to society, to culture. He asks us to question 'social,' 'anatomy,' how our anatomies are social, and how society is, itself, a processual and performed anatomy. And in this, he implicitly argues that we could – he in fact explicitly provides spaces where we can – learn to do better in how we perform them.

## Notes

1 See 5050ltd.com for another arts collaborative working with similar wearable technologies and www.whitney.org/www/2008biennial/www/?section=artists&page=artist_dragons for Luke Fischbeck's *Make a Baby*, a project that generates real-time sound based on skin contact between audience members.

2 What is at stake for Nancy in this is far ranging and paramount: 'The body, as an expression of meaning by virtue of its singularity or alterity, is the site where both ethics and community take place' (Sorial, 2004: 4). 'We' is, for Nancy, the expression of a plurality. It expresses '"our" being divided and entangled: "one" is not "with" in some general sort of way ... a "we", even one that is not articulated, is the condition for the possibility of each "I"' (Sorial, 2004: 3). While the subject is always singular, s/he is not isolated in her difference, but is rather exposed to, affected and touched by, the other. The central point here is that 'we' are always in relation, we are always 'I' as something shared with others, not as a fused collective or a collection of autonomous individuals. This is an ethical mode of being that seeks out and affirms otherness. It is a tactful, rather than tactical response, 'the testimony of a fracture, of the opening onto the other,' rather than 'an experience conducted by an I in the quest for self-knowledge' (Lyotard, 1988: 113). Touch then, for Nancy, opens up space's strangeness. An ethics that is tactful recognizes the need to maintain the space between self and other, and to make contact.

3 Is this problematic for bodies that have not had the privilege of being seen as self-identical and whole? Jean-Luc Nancy, as so many, pays scant attention to gender. But, argues Perpich, his account addresses 'those bodies considered borderline without having to position them at the outer limits (or, for that matter, at the center)' (Perpich, 2005: 7). His work also augments the work of feminist philosophers such as Judith Butler in its movement beyond the *a priori* instantiation of social constructionism – the sexed body that is prior to the social inscription of gender.

4 It is worth noting that Crossley's main thesis ties the work of Erving Goffman to the writings of philosopher Maurice Merleau-Ponty. The former is an oft-cited source in performance studies, while the latter is one of the progenitors of phenomenology. Given these foundations, Crossley centers many of his ideas on structure and human perception, where I am more interested in sensible concepts and bare activities.

5 Kazuhiko Hachiya's *Inter Dis-communication Machine* (1993) is similar in its application of video headgear with swapping views; it invites (only) two viewer-participants to interact with one another through the other's eyes. See http://www.petworks.co.jp/~hachiya/works/IDCM.html and http://www.we-make-money-not-art.com/archives/2005/05/through-the-dev.php

6 *Shy* (2003), also shown, is a work very similar to *Compliant,* but Snibbe creates a more animated, anthropomorphized character in the moving screen – in addition to manipulation, it quickly jumps, shirks, and cowers away from real-time shadows (Snibbe, 2006c).

# Chapter 6

## 'Flesh-Space'

### The Potential to Spatialize

Pioneering creative technologist David Rokeby believes that rather 'than creating finished works, the interactive artist creates relationships' between viewer–participants and an ongoing work and space (Rokeby, 1995: 152). Rokeby avowedly produces systems that we must experience and practice with our bodies. In his artist statement for the groundbreaking *Very Nervous System* (1986–2004, Figure 23), he asserts his desire to be contrary. Since computers are 'purely logical, the language of interaction should strive to be intuitive.' Because computers remove 'you from your body, the body should be strongly engaged.' Since the activity of digital media 'takes place on the tiny playing fields of integrated circuits, the encounter with the computer should take place in human-scaled physical space. Because the computer is objective and disinterested, the experience should be intimate' (Rokeby, 1990). In other words, Rokeby hopes to employ digital interactions in order to intensify analogical relations.

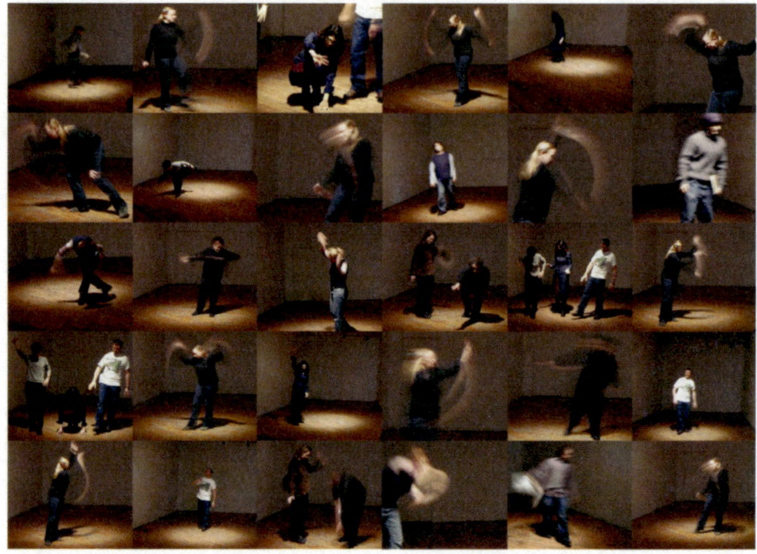

Figure 23. David Rokeby | *Very Nervous System*, 1986–2004 | video camera, digitizer, computer, custom software, sound synthesizer, amplifier and speakers | dimensions variable | installation views at ace art inc, Winnipeg | photos by William Eakin, Liz Garlicki and Risa Horowitz | image arrray design Mike Carroll

One of the first artworks to utilize complex computer vision,[1] *Very Nervous System* puts together sensors, cameras, computer processing, synthesizers and a complete sound system in order to make a space where the moving body creates music. Rokeby's interactors might at first look to outsiders like they are dancing to a strange sonic composition, but they are actually creating sounds in a real-time, response-driven environment, which uses generative feedback loops in order to guarantee both a non-repeatable experience and non-repeating musical scores. He explains that *Very Nervous System* asks us to remember that the body responds to its environment more quickly than consciousness does. Rokeby highlights embodiment as always improvised: we are both participant in, and creator of, body, work, and space.

*Very Nervous System* alters our experience of how bodies and spaces occur, together. After prolonged interactions, we expect every relational encounter to move as we move. Rokeby explains, 'I'll put on a CD, and when I make a sudden movement, I feel cheated that the music on the disc hasn't changed to mirror my gesture. So, yeah: It does alter you. You expect the whole world to be interactive' (Cooper and Rokeby, 2003). The piece inaugurates and magnifies a richly embodied exploration of space, and a sensuously spatial exploration of our own bodies.

In an interview with *WIRED* magazine, Rokeby describes how he

> once demonstrated the work to a 5-year-old blind child.... Walking into the space through silence and then hitting the edge where he was visible to the camera: suddenly he was making noise. It was quite startling.... The edges of the active area were like physical walls for him. He literally bounced off them the first time he ran into them.

Here Rokeby's embodied 'wall' is relationally carved out through movement and stasis, while his software quite literally 'amplifies' a (sonic) interaction that, along with its interactors, takes account of flesh-space relations. Rokeby's work has us move–think–feel, and make, a large expanse into a confined 'room' – as sensible concept. His system 'frames' how our conceptually sensed relations produce space (and bodies) at large.

In a series of questions surrounding Liebniz's understandings of flux and matter, Anna Munster asks 'how the capacities of different substances force their unfolding, their production of a particular kind of spatiality ... Not what *occupies* space, but what twists and folds of substance can occupy space, and therefore *spatialize,* in different ways?' What, she goes on, 'relations are made compossible by the simultaneous folding/unfolding of different substances?' (Munster, 2006: 45). How do matter, bodies, and space make one another possible?

The potential to spatialize, and in particular the potential of bodies that relate-and-spatialize, has in recent years preoccupied many philosophers of dance. I turn to José Gil and Erin Manning's analyses of dance as parallel to my examination of interactive art and the flesh-space thematic, and study works that suspend, amplify, and intervene in the relational emergence of embodiment and spatialization. Rafael Lozano-Hemmer's process, and the eloquent language he uses to describe it, is remarkably congruous with the approach this book advocates for, and Norah Zuniga Shaw directly ties the experience and practice of dance to the experience and practice of interactive art. She additionally foreshadows possibilities for the 'non-interactive,' 'potentialized' art outlined in the following chapter.

## Paradoxical Body / Paradoxical Space

Like myself, José Gil imagines the body – more specifically the dancer's body – as as a continuous and reversible Möbius strip, forever opening and closing itself to other spaces and bodies. He asserts that the body's openness is neither metonymy nor metaphor, but 'really the interior space that reveals itself once it returns to the exterior, transforming the latter into the space of the body' (Gil, 2006: 29). Here, as with Ridgway's argument that we as relational becoming-beings are not 'in' the between but rather 'of' the relation, Gil avers that the body is not 'in' space but 'of' it. Bodies and space are made *of* their relation.

Gil initially turns to phenomenology to consider the body as a sensing, perceiving, and living exploration of meaning but then explicitly departs from phenomenology by saying that its 'body' does not understand either the 'energy' or 'space-time' of a dancer. He rejects Cartesian space and phenomenon 'as a visible and concrete perception,' and rather asks us 'to consider the body as a meta-phenomenon, simultaneously visible and virtual, a cluster of forces, a transformer of space and time, both emitter of signs and trans-semiotic, endowed by an organic interior ready to be dissolved as soon as it reaches the surface' (Gil, 2006: 28). This body is a 'paradoxical body' that is open and shut, emptied and connected, traversed and traversing in and around other moving forces, bodies, spaces. Here the body 'can become animal, become mineral, plant, become atmosphere, hole, ocean, become pure movement' (Gil, 2006: 28). Echoing some of the distinguishing terms of phenomenology, Gil differentiates what he calls 'objective space' from 'the space of the body' – the latter is a 'new space' that 'emerges,' is actualized and secreted from movement (Gil, 2006: 21).

The dancer, Gil explains, learns to adapt to the rhythms and imperatives of dance, and thus 'to tightly imbricate interior space and external space, the inside of the body invested with energy, and the outside where gestures of the dance unfold' (Gil, 2006: 23). Movement across depth and dimension (and over time) 'allows the dancer to mold space, to expand it, or to restrict it, to make it acquire the most paradoxical forms ... because the space of the dancer's body is riddled with virtual vacuoles he can make it into an eminently plastic matter' (Gil, 2006: 26). Following Deleuze and Guattari, Gil says that bodies and space are emptied of organs and organization, making all of matter reversible and topological surfaces, surface energies that continuously affect and (re-)materialize, together. The paradoxical body and its paradoxical space become an interior–exterior space and body producing multiple architectural and porous formations, matter and matters that are *of* space and *becoming* space, embodied and *becoming* body.

Gil specifically privileges the dancing body because of how it intensifies the continuity between interior / exterior, body / space. A ballet dancer must learn techniques of movement – they position themselves in front of a mirror, acquiring embodied knowledge of the kinesthetic tensions their gestures make. Through experience and practice, those passages and positions of movement become a map of body and space, of interior and exterior. A dancer's learned and living body in movement can then 'prolong the body's limits beyond its visible contours' (Gil, 2006: 22). Gil likens the experience of the dancer to that of a subject in a full tub of still water, where a spider is dropped on the surface. The performer will feel the spider's contact with the water all across their skin, will feel the constant transductions between and transformations of body–water–spider–space. Gil calls this prosthetic, but not in the way that Erin Manning criticizes technology as prosthetic – an extension that she states subjects the participant's body to specific parameters. In Gil's case, emphasis is on the quality of feeling and movement between body and water and spider and space. This is 'an intensified space, when compared with the habitual tactility of the skin' (Gil, 2006: 22). To dance in and of this space, the space of the body, is to assemble the body and assemble space, and to see and feel those assembling assemblages as they come into being. The dancer senses their dancing as both virtual and actualizing flesh and space.

Manning too speaks of how a dancer creates new spacetimes in how they move with the world. Here the 'ground' – not necessarily a literal ground (the floor beneath us), but that space where we dance, that space of the body – dances with the dancer. Ground and dancer are always entering into movement, as incipient action and novel reconstitution. The dancing ground is technogenetic: a 'technique of composition, the ground becomes a condition of emergence for the ontogenetic body' (Manning, 2009: 70). A dancer doesn't align to an exact position or person, but rather to the movement of bodies and space around them. A dancer aligns to the dance, to the environment that is itself moving with the bodies within it.[2]

Dancers, Manning writes, 'preaccelerate' – they express 'movement's capacity for invention' (Manning, 2009: 19). I believe this is a particularly pointed coinage. Remember that acceleration is not merely movement. Movement is change or continuity. Acceleration is a change in speed for that movement: changing change, or *moving movement*. Acceleration is the movement of (the already moving) moving–thinking–feeling, and *pre*acceleration virtualizes and intensifies that moving movement, makes it *felt*. It is a doubled force. Manning's preacceleration is similar to Gil's felt intensity – the virtual and moving movement *before* its movement, about to actualize – and her grounding techniques can be said to parallel his dancer's learned but continuous mappings of inside / outside. Manning asserts that dancers breathe space, walk space, sound space – they create occasions of experience where 'the sensing body in movement alters experiential spacetime such that spacetime is felt in its emergence' (Manning, 2009: 71) – a topological formation.

Gil explains that it is not just the dancer who produces the space of the body. 'In theatre, or on other stages and in other scenes,' the actor 'transforms the scenic space; the gymnast prolongs the space that surrounds his skin – he weaves with bars, mats, or simply with the ground he steps on' producing 'relations of complicity as intimate as the ones he has with his own body' (Gil, 2006: 21). In fact the space of the body is everywhere, a reality that is born whenever there is an embodied, affective investment, and continuously reborn in every eventful and affective moment, in the interval of preacceleration. In the language of this book, sets or stages, rigs or prosceniums, create situations that amplify the relation and emergence of the flesh and space both Gil and Manning refer to. And interactive art, I am arguing, has the potential to create a semblance of such situations – to put in quotes and suspend 'flesh-space.'

In some of her criticisms of interactive art, more specifically her assessment of gesture-tracking software used by dancers, Manning asserts that digital technologies are not technogenetic (at least not yet). 'Technogenesis cannot be premapped' to specific gestures or behaviors, and too rare are the nuanced software systems that make a 'technological recomposition' that is emergent *with* a 'body system' (Manning, 2009: 74–5). She asks, 'Can technology *play* the virtual?' (Manning, 2009: 71), and answers that while technology might never 'ground,' it can – and in the very best of cases does – make grounding *virtually felt*. I pick up on Manning's suggestions for digital art and argue that if the software creates a semblance of a situation, it asks us not to look at a pre-coded screen-space, not to move to a prefigured located space, and not to enact a pre-scripted gestural space. It rather introduces and amplifies spatialization, asking us to concern ourselves with the quality of our own movements in / with / as space. Rokeby's blind 'wall' is a wonderfully successful example of virtually feeling a 'ground.' Here we-and-technology intervene in an emergent flesh-space as we-and-it, together, move–think–feel. If, as is the case in *Very Nervous System*, the technology helps to focus us on qualities of movement, then we, like dancers, inaugurate, experience, practice, and analyze the intensity that is preacceleration. We feel ourselves as 'in and around'; we are the space of the body.

Gil reminds us that 'the space of the body does not come about except by the projection-secretion of interior space on exterior space' (Gil, 2006: 26). In this way, interactive art provides a unique opportunity to implicate the body of space, and space of the body. It can attune us to the relation of inside and outside by staging an implicit body as per-formed with and as space. Like a learned dance, successful interactive art may make a potentialized context where we move–think–feel the assemblages of flesh and space as they are: continuously actualized and actualizing. Here the dancing ground and dancing body might be re-cited and re-situated as incipient and dynamic mappings of one another.

In the work of Rafael Lozano-Hemmer and Norah Zuniga Shaw, movement and architecture, body and ground, virtual and actual, are conceptually sensed. These two artists were chosen not only because of the flesh-spaces they introduce, but also because they answer some of the more critical commentary on interactive art visited earlier the book. Brian Massumi has cited Lozano-Hemmer's relational architectures as successfully 'staging ... aesthetic events that speculate on life, emanating a lived quality that might resonate elsewhere, to unpredictable affect and effect' (Massumi, 2007: 90). And Zuniga Shaw's *Synchronous Objects, reproduced* premiered in productive dialogue with Erin Manning at the International Symposium on Electronic Art (ISEA) 2010 in Germany. It re-moves, re-mediates, re-thinks, and re-feels dance and the dancing ground in William Forsythe's choreography as a multichannel, multimedia, and interactive installation. Both artists stage a body that is per-formed and implicated with space.

## Relational Architectures: Rafael Lozano-Hemmer

Rafael Lozano-Hemmer is a Canadian-Mexican artist who develops large-scale, public, interactive installations that attempt to 'transform urban spaces and create connective environments' (Lozano-Hemmer, 2003). In the artist's own words, 'Using robotics, projections, sound, internet and cell-phone links, sensors and other devices, his installations aim to provide "temporary antimonuments for alien agency"' (Lozano-Hemmer, 2006). Here, the adjective 'temporary' refers to the ephemeral nature of his technological and performative installations; and Lozano-Hemmer uses the term 'antimonument' because, while the works' scale is often monumental, the installations *are* an event, rather than a monument that commemorates one. Interactive art, he says, is not time-based – does not have a predefined start and end – but event-based.

Lozano-Hemmer explains that when he uses the word 'alien,' he means something:

> that's foreign, that's non-contextual, that comes from a disparate plane of experience. Many times I use the word 'alien' to replace the word 'new' as an acknowledgement of the impossibility of originality. When I work in a public space, I don't try to address the 'essential' qualities of the site, as site-specific installations do; rather, I emphasize artificial connections that may emerge from people interacting with alien memories. (Sullivan and Lozano-Hemmer, 2002)

So when Lozano-Hemmer uses the phrase 'alien agency,' it should be read to mean that we still have agency, the ability to affect and feel affect, but are placed in a citation without context, in a re-situated activity that is out of the ordinary and out of place. Participants move–think–feel as foreign and potentialized bodies and spaces, as insides and outsides, as intensified and incipient action. In other words, Lozano-Hemmer aims to suspend and intervene in embodiment and place-making.

Dubbing one of his ongoing series of works 'relational architectures,' Lozano-Hemmer claims to focus on the relationships that 'emerge from the artificial situation' of his site-conditioned installations (Sullivan and Lozano-Hemmer, 2002). Relational architecture sets out to transform the narratives of specific buildings by adding and / or subtracting audiovisual elements and de- / re-contextualizing them via audience participation (for example, through hyperlinked and projected images to other times and spaces). The 'alien memories' in these artificial situations may include other buildings, peoples, and histories, which are conveyed through the political or aesthetic circumstances in the images. The motivation behind the special effects and plasticity of the work is a situation where 'the building, the urban context and the participants relate in new, "alien" ways' (Lozano-Hemmer, 2001b).

For Lozano-Hemmer, a given intervention succeeds when the work 'interrupts and points to our standard action and reaction circuits, amplifies and potentially changes how we move and relate in public space.' Central to his practice is the uncertainty of the outcome. While there can be a range of 'causal, chaotic, telepresent, predetermined, or emergent behaviours programmed' into his software (Lozano-Hemmer, 2001b), each instantiation provokes and highlights interactions and relations between bodies and space. Emphasis is placed on architecture and flesh as per-formed through their reciprocal relation.

One excellent example of a relational architecture is Lozano-Hemmer's award-winning work circa 2001, *Body Movies* (Figure 24). Here he projects an archive of thousands of photographs, one by one, onto large buildings around a square. Each image in this collection was taken on the streets of cities all over the world, and they are shown using powerful, robotically-controlled data projectors from above. From the centre of the square below, huge floodlights wash out these images. The photographs can only be seen when passersby on the square block out the lights and, with their shadows, reveal the overhead projections underneath them. The shadows range in size from 2 to 25 meters, depending on a visitor's distance from the light, and they are tracked in real-time with Lozano-Hemmer's custom software; if the participants on the 'live' square align their shadows in such a way as to reveal all the bodies in the image beneath, the program triggers the next image in the sequence.

All of us have played with shadows – particularly our own – and *Body Movies* relies on the sophisticated vocabularies we have developed with them, since childhood. But while interactors immediately understand this interface, the experience and practice of performing their shadows is new, 'alien,' because of how the sheer size of their shadows changes the architecture, the images, and the atmosphere around them. The revelation of other bodies and spaces in the images actively unveiled from beneath these shadows – a play on presence that Lozano-Hemmer ironically calls 'tele-absence' – and all the other bodies working together on the square add layers of complexity to the interaction. Viewers can reveal all, part, or parts of the artist's photographs of people and places, bodies and spaces, from around the world, and they often try to tell a physical story by playing around the image's contents, engaging shadows across each other and bodies in the image, and / or triggering the next photo.

With regards to how participants physically interact with *Body Movies*, Lozano-Hemmer takes into account the large field between the lights and building, begging for players to make quirky two-dimensional movies out of, and projected onto, three-dimensional space. As evidenced in the included images, the artist's often dancing and collaborating participants become active agents in an unfolding and enfolding narrative of bodies and space, whose flesh – depending on where they individually move – might collectively span several stories high, remain close to their actual size, and everything in between. Together, they create complex shapes, animations, and architectures through experimental and repetitive movements.

Would-be static viewers run back and forth between the buildings and lights, shifting their individual sizes relative to other bodies, the architecture, and the photographs of the other architectures and bodies that they are revealing in Lozano-Hemmer's database of images. They use these tele-absent and projected forms in relation to each other, to the constructions around the square, and to the partially broadcast images in order to perform. I have watched participants use shadows and images to shadowbox a giant, swallow a dwarf, smash a building, or carry a friend or foe to safety. They move between intimate and exaggerated flows, hand shadow-puppets and sweeping and running formations. They produce animated rabbits and dogs, pour drinks from on high and eat arms of others down low, ride bicycles or run or skateboard. They pull and push each other and across each other and across times and spaces – and all across the surface of a large building, rallying back and forth in size as they move toward or away from the light. The more creative performers play out complex scenes in the previously photographed international cities, their shadows enabling them to bicycle through Madrid, use real-world umbrellas to protect virtual Italians from the rain, or create multi-armed beasts that grow and shrink as they scale building walls or invade foreign lands. They can corporeally and incorporeally align themselves with

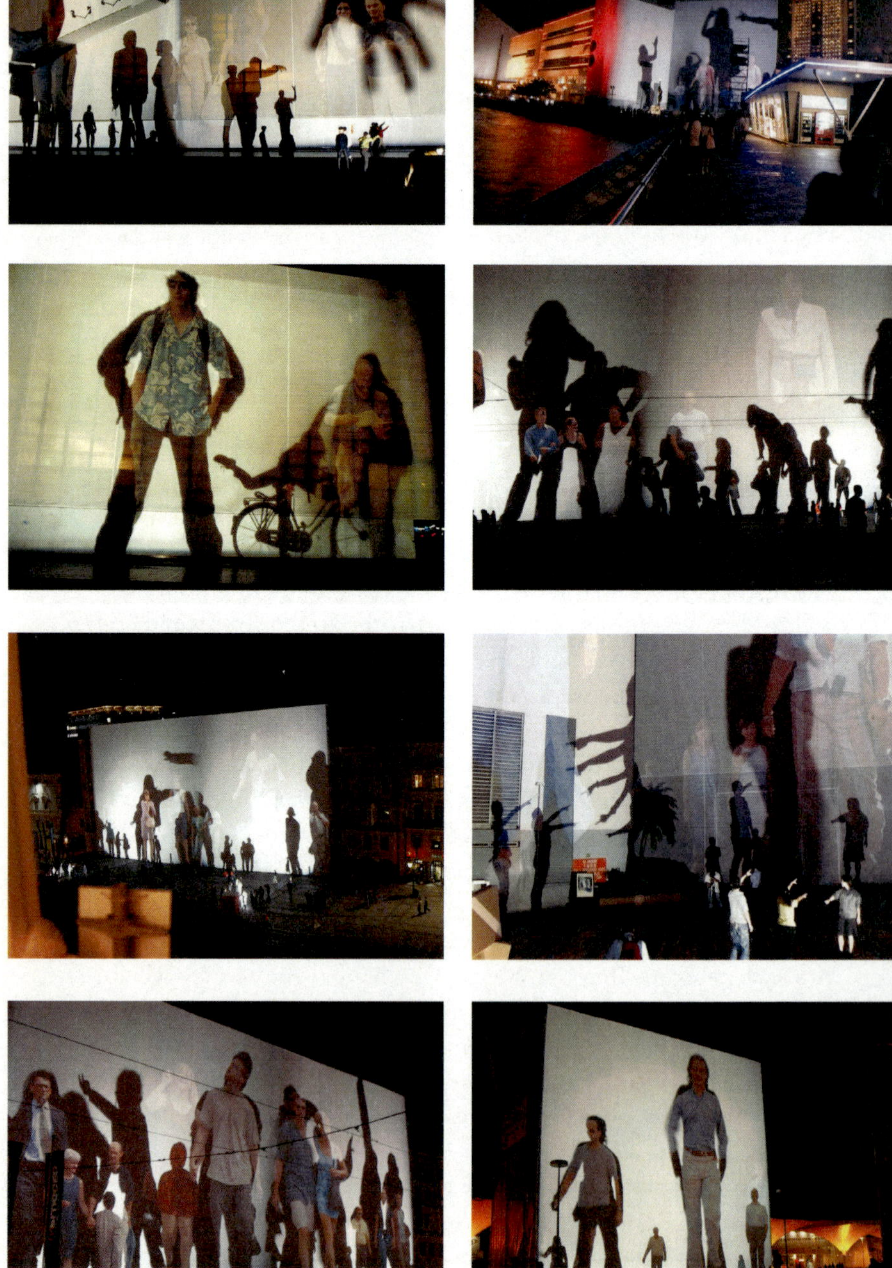

Figure 24. Rafael Lozano-Hemmer | *Body Movies, Relational Architecture 6*, 2001 | Four 7kW Xenon projectors with robotic rollers, 1,200 Duraclear transparencies, computerized tracking system, plasma screen and mirrors. Dimensions variable | see endnote for full image credits.[3]

strangers and friends alike, with others present and absent, in the plural singularity of their communally shared space.

*Body Movies* invites us to rehearse public, embodied, and communal space. The 'people on the square,' writes Lozano-Hemmer, 'embody different representational narratives,' creating 'a collective experience that nonetheless allows discrete individual participation' (Lozano-Hemmer, 2001a). While each active participant understands a per-formed body through their shadow play, they also encounter per-forming the square and buildings and people around them, the shaping of this space and its continuous relationship to their own flesh as well as to other spaces and bodies and matter – in their immediate environment and (in images) around the world. In *Body Movies,* participants' interactions– all of which they may or may not be consciously aware of – intervene in the mutual emergence of a broadly defined and engaged embodiment and a broadly defined and engaged space. It stages drawn-out and implicit bodies and spaces that we simultaneously activate and experience, through movement. *Body Movies* productively confuses processual embodiment and architectural space-making, asking us to practice the relation of inside and outside, personal and public, actual and virtual. It inaugurates a complex and creative dance, where inter-activities make space virtually and actually felt.

Lozano-Hemmer's work attunes us to our body's preacceleration, in space – personal and public space, architectural and virtual space. *Body Movies* emphasizes the space of the body that cannot be reduced to the boundaries of our skin, the limited image we see on screen, or even our present movements around the square. Here our moving, affected, and affective bodies evince stories and alien histories that are made sensible in and as space; they are incarnated, together, but fleetingly, as something shared and yet not. This sharing and not, present but not, body and bodies, space and spaces becomes, like a topological figure, more than what it is. Both space and bodiliness are potentialized, are accented as susceptible to folding, division, and reshaping, open to continual negotiation. Participants shrink and grow, live and transform and shift with the spaces and stories they move with and in and as their environment. Body and space, here and elsewhere, are implicated in one another, and each presence (or absence) is an incipient action that we *feel* as instantiated through movement and relation. *Body Movies* effectively and affectively intensifies our incorporating practices, our moving, interrelating bodies and spaces as they come to matter, as matter, performed. *Body Movies* is a complex layering of bodies and space that frames the performance of embodiment and spatialization. Here we conceptually sense, we move–think–feel and practice 'flesh-space.'[4]

Lozano-Hemmer's interests in place-making and embodiment are explored further in his later series of *subsculptures*. For example, *standards and double standards (subsculpture 3)* (2004, Figure 25) sees fifty individual belts suspended at waist height from the ceiling of the exhibition room. Each is fastened at the front, appearing to hold up an invisible being's pants, and attached to stepper motors that seem to turn this person in a full 360 degrees. When the space is empty of people, the belts slowly ripple back and forth in a circular fashion, appearing to be floating would-be bodies that are scanning the room and looking for someone or something to focus on. The dynamic movements are determined by cellular automata equations similar to those used by Simon Penny in *Traces*' active trace. When there are people in the space, however, these almost-absent forms are controlled by a digital video tracking system, whereby the twisting belt buckles make it look as if their absent bodies are turning to face passersby.

As the first body enters the empty space of *standards and double standards*, the belt they are closest to turns its buckle to face them. After several seconds, belts further from his or her position follow suit. This movement continues undulating outward, the participant 'triggering a wave-like chain reaction and creating a force field' (Perron, 2004). As more people enter the installation 'numerous force fields are generated and much like weather disturbances provoke unpredictable movement among the belts' (Perron, 2004). Each individual's presence and movement creates patterns of interference in the room. Organic life-like behaviors rotate the belts in relation to each other, the space, and everyone moving in and around both.

Lozano-Hemmer again plays with notions of presence and absence in this piece, but instead of using large-scale shadows as in *Body*

*Movies,* he gives visible and tangible life to many non-bodies, while also relating them to our own, through their relative movements and installation at waist height. The sum of the contraptions is an 'absent crowd' any participant can walk around or through (Lozano-Hemmer, 2007). The artist turns inanimate objects into animate forms, in a doubled gesture that performatively presents space and matter as inextricably linked. In the first gesture, Lozano-Hemmer produces an absent body by giving movement and life to a belt; in the second, he makes a sea of absent bodies respond to our presence and movement.

Lozano-Hemmer avows that he has created an 'unpredictable connective system,' one that can 'visualize complex dynamics' (Lozano-Hemmer, 2007); but perhaps more notably, the system actually catalyzes such dynamics, in and of the relation between bodies, non-bodies, and space. Contrary to the other works thus far written about in this book, *standards and double standards* is a very slow-moving interaction; its lightly swinging and creeping belts ('never losing sight of the symbolic association between the belt and paternal authority'

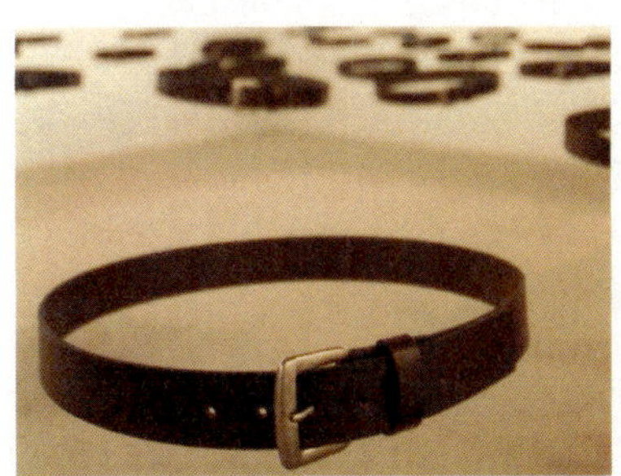
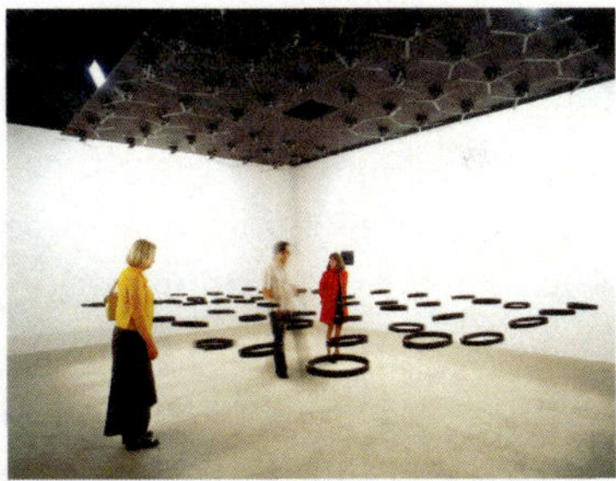
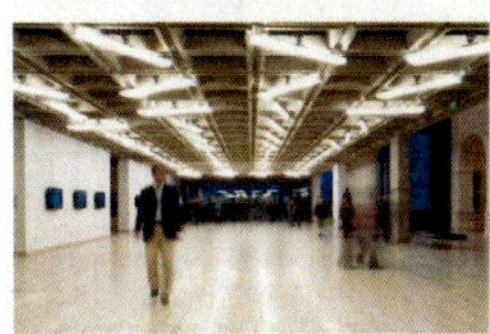
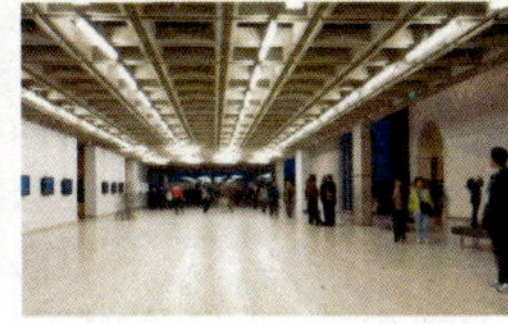
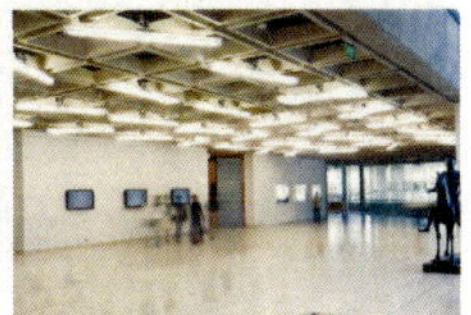

Figure 25. Rafael Lozano-Hemmer I Top: *Standards and double standards, Subsculpture 3,* 2004 I Leather belts, stepper motors, surveillance camera, tracking system. Dimensions variable I Bottom: *Homographies, Subsculpture 7,* 2006 I Motorized fluorescent light tubes, computerized surveillance tracking systems, custom software. Dimensions variable I see endnote for full image credits[5]

[Perron, 2004]) can be perceived as either frivolous or ominous, and our navigation, and thus creation, of space is found in how we experience and practice with and around it.

Viewer–participants tip-toe carefully under and around its edges; they sway lightly back and forth in place, consciously and physically trying to elicit, while unconsciously and affectively mimicking, a response; they run to a singular spot and then crouch and remain completely still, waiting to see how the piece will catch up, catch them. They continuously engage with the inter-acting space, amplified as creative and transformed. They dance to and with the cyclical and circular motion of the belts, a creeping rhythm, a crawling and running, a hiding and seeking, an emergence of flesh (and space) *as* and *with* space (and flesh), in yet another complex interaction that intervenes in embodiment and space, disembodiment and vacancy, public and private.

Lozano-Hemmer's *subsculpture 7, homographies* (2006, Figure 25), uses one-hundred and forty-four robotic and fluorescent light fixtures, controlled by a networked computerized surveillance system. As visitors meander and explore under the installation, its glowing tubes of light rotate from the centre, in a circular and fan-like fashion, to 'create labyrinthine patterns of light' (Lozano-Hemmer, 2007). The overall emerging shapes of these mobile structures are reminiscent of paths or corridors, spaces of passage that beg for participants to move between, as they simultaneously transform, them. Lozano-Hemmer says that *homographies*' 'vanishing point,' the point where its lines converge, is 'not architectural, but rather connective' (Lozano-Hemmer, 2007). In other words, the space and how we see and interact with it is determined relationally, by who is there and where they stand or move at any given moment. It is thus a 'reconfigurable light-space that is based on flow, on motion, on lines of sight' (Lozano-Hemmer, 2007).

*homographies*' 'light-space' not only shifts in relation to each individual person's presence and movement, but also to how many people are present and where they are in relation to one another and the space. According to the video documentation online, the light fixtures respond to the presence of a single person as if they were producing a magnetic field of influence; when two or more people are detected, the system rotates its lighting so that 'light corridors' are made between them; and, as more people move in and around the space, the lights reflect the influence of all of them, creating complex patterns similar to isobars.[6] This is all occasionally interspersed with cellular automata algorithms that choreograph the lighting in a programmed sequence, in order to complexify and introduce a level of randomness or outside influence in our interactive experience.

In *homographies*, Lozano-Hemmer transforms not just the light fixtures and the light they make, but also the physical space of the room. It feels and moves with us, as we feel and move with it. The connective tissues or forces between our bodies and their environment influence how we see, experience and move in, as well as change, the space around us; and the dynamic light structures pirouette to create new shapes, influencing the very movements that they are responding to as we try to choreograph their course. Performers might walk as they normally would through any passage, but with their necks craned upward to watch the rippling effects / affects of that walk; they sometimes, and again, mirror the piece's reactions, standing in one spot and pirouetting around like the fixtures above; they run around the circumference, to the corners, chase the lights and lighting, sometimes jumping up into, or leaping through, the air, in a futile but no less fertile attempt to catch the invisible space they feel themselves transforming; they watch each other as they move, the movement of others that changes their own inter-actions, and vice versa, in an ever-transforming and dynamic flux of bodies and space. And all of this amplifies the inside / outside of the technogenetic 'ground' – not just beneath their feet, but as the space of the body.

Lozano-Hemmer's works create potentialized contexts, semblances of situations, where embodiment and spatialization are intensified as relational mappings rather than pre-mapped and quantifiable configurations. Here complex and emergent forms are literally and figuratively suspended – as image, as belt, as light fixture, as body – so that we may take account of our ongoing, environmental, and bodily formations. At stake is how we make and mediate, understand and practice, space – for ourselves and for each other.

## Synchronous Objects, reproduced: Norah Zuniga Shaw

Trained as a dancer and environmental scientist, Norah Zuniga Shaw is acutely attuned to bodies and the territories they traverse and create. Her work is 'at the intersection of dance research and digital media and concerned with the re-articulation and transmission of bodily knowledge in contemporary dance practices' (Zuniga Shaw, 2010a). It has spanned traditional performance, interdisciplinary composition and improvisation, and a variety of digital formats, including a series of locative media projects that foreground bodily activity and experience in lived places, where 'mapping represents and creates spaces' and thus frames 'new ways of understanding our bodies (center) in our environments (periphery)' (Zuniga Shaw, 2007: 247–9). The project I analyze in this section went, first, from an original dance piece that explored space – and body – and matter-making through relational movement, second, to a mediated series of web-based formations that empowered explorations of the moving–thinking–feeling in dance with other, information-based structures, and, third, through another re-mediation into a three-room installation where interactors physically encounter the interference, counterpoint, and suspended potential of dance and the space of the body.

Zuniga Shaw's collaborative installation *Synchronous Objects, reproduced* (2010)[7] initially began as William Forsythe's controversial *One Flat Thing, reproduced* at the Pacific Northwest Ballet in Seattle (2008),[8] where fourteen dancers performed on, around, through, and under twenty metal tables – and each other – for seventeen minutes, to startling affects. They drag in the tables, arrange them in a grid, curve 'in and around the hard surfaces, reading each other, moving with liquid control and slicing through the space in abrupt waves of activity' (deLahunta and Zuniga Shaw, 2006: 59). They fly, slide, and twist, appear and disappear, move and freeze, in a combination of fixed movement and structured improvisation. In Forsythe's tightly choreographed work, twenty-five themes are remixed, repeated, and recombined so that bodies, themes, tables, matter, and spaces are all in counterpoint to one another, through their three interwoven systems of organization: movement material, cueing, and alignments. Here counterpoint – a critical term for Zuniga Shaw and her collaborators – should be understood as an intense interruption and amplification, a movement, constitution, and differentiation through the dance. It is a kind of grounding, a spatialization and embodiment, with other bodies and matter (and matters). The dancers rarely do exactly the same thing, but are always in relation, 'constructing a... cacophonous structure' (Zuniga Shaw, 2009) of connection, interference, and reversibility. Manning states that, the moving materials, cues, and alignments 'activate a field of relation rather than starting or stopping at one particular human body' or table or ground. 'What emerges is an intensive diagram – a mobile architecture – that in turn dances the bodies of the dancers' (Manning and Massumi, 2011). Here slaps and jumps, sweeps and ripples of motion, bodies and tables and their parts, perform inside / outside movements across all the audience's senses. It is an ecosystem, a complex interplay, a community of practice, a flesh-space.

Zuniga Shaw, along with Forsythe and Maria Palazzi, studied *One Flat Thing, reproduced* and its successes and began to ask, 'What else might this dance look like?' They wanted to explore 'possibilities for communicating choreographic thinking' (Graham and Zuniga Shaw, 2011), or more elaborately, the moving–thinking–feeling of the space of the body, but outside of live performance – not as a replacement for such work, but as a parallel mode of making-material. As with any incorporating practice, these producers recognize that the 'materiality of dance is inextricably bound up with its own immaterial dimension' (deLahunta and Zuniga Shaw, 2006: 53), but perhaps a 'choreographic object' could serve as 'an alternative site for the understanding of potential instigation and organization of action' (Forsythe, 2011). This started the team on research for *Synchronous Objects* (2009), a 'choreographic visualization project' that combines camera work, animated and static graphics, and generative software towards new experiences of dance.

*Synchronous Objects* is a series of web-based videos, interfaces, annotations, and representations that 'tell a story of the radical mobility of moving ideas wherein all movement phenomena can be considered choreographically' (Graham and Zuniga Shaw, 2011). Forsythe's original performance was transformed into a dance for camera, re-staged – with seventeen people and twenty tables, over fifteen and a half minutes – at a train station in Frankfurt Germany. This version was shot from multiple angles with pans and zooms, long, bird's-eye, and close-up views, which give it an/other quality through technological mediation. Zuniga Shaw and her team worked diligently to interpret, transform, and concentrate the video, sound, and dance – as it was recorded, and as it appeared/ was felt – into twenty web-based 'choreographic objects.'[9] More than mere communication, all objects are framed with a magnification of movement and space-making in order to intensify our and the dancer's affective moving–thinking–feeling, experience, and practice.

Describing all twenty objects here would take up a lot of space, and do little to communicate exactly how it feels to encounter the site. I will briefly unpack the five gridded columns in the figure shown (Figure 26) – as I understand them through my own interactions – and then go into more detail with just a handful of the objects as they relate to the flesh-space thematic. The first, blue column on the left contains four videos that reveal the most didactic understandings of *One Flat Thing, reproduced,* by highlighting explicit patterns of counterpoint. It contains a beautifully edited video of the dance, where the moving camera perspective, stereo sound, and jump cuts make the space and dance and ground and tables feel *alive.* This is followed by three indexical and annotated videos, each exhibiting one of the three elements of counterpoint: movement material, cues, and alignment. And perhaps in direct counterpoint to *these* objects, the second, green column houses the most interactive devices, allowing participants to explore choreographic thinking with varying degrees of code and control over animation, visualization, drawing, and dancing widgets.

The middle, orange column performs the most interpretive threads of the dance, through three-dimensional textual forms, counterpoint statistics, a geographical diagram of movement density, and a visualization of the continuously constituted architectural shapes surrounding movement – not of the dancers, but of the space and 'furniture' dancing them. The fourth, purple column of objects has an intense choreographic feel, where cues, body centers, three-dimen-

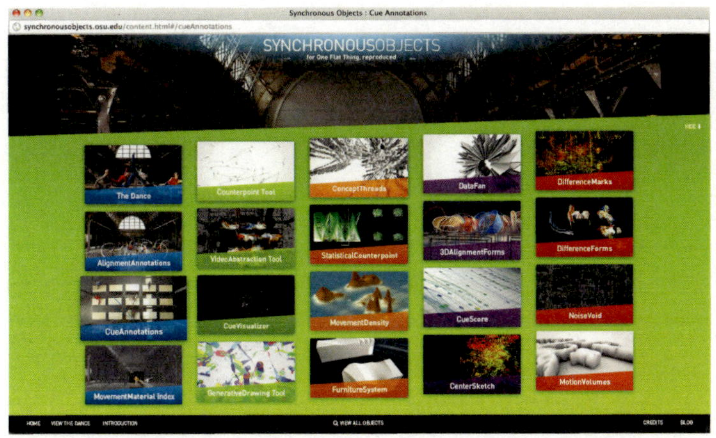


Figure 26. Norah Zuniga Shaw et al. | *Synchronous Objects interface*, 2010

sional shapes of the synchronized bodies in space, and a sculptural formation of the movement 'data' are all re-presented as emergent with the dance. And finally the fifth, red column utilizes the most explicit trajectory from dance to data to object. Here computer vision analyzes movement to create difference marks, difference forms, spaces of noise and stasis, and volumes of body-space occurrence.

As a whole, the choreographic objects 'are closely linked to the dance, they issue forth from it (as does any translation) but they also step out' and make 'parallel virtual incarnations or transformations' (Zuniga Shaw, 2010a). Like any occurrent art, movement's potentials are made *apparent* by being held to visual form, where they *virtually appear*. With the *MotionVolumes* object, for example, we 'see the dancers carve out their own three-dimensional spaces; it looks kind of like an envelope of behavior, as an architect might say' (Zuniga Shaw, 2009). The *FurnitureSystem* configures the shape of the body along with the shape of the tables, showing how they are relationally per-formed. With the *GenerativeDrawing Tool,* we control a balance between structured movement and improvisation as somewhat autonomous brushes of varying colors, thickness, and vibration work in productive tension with one another, and with us, to generatively and collaboratively create a tangible vision of dancing implication.

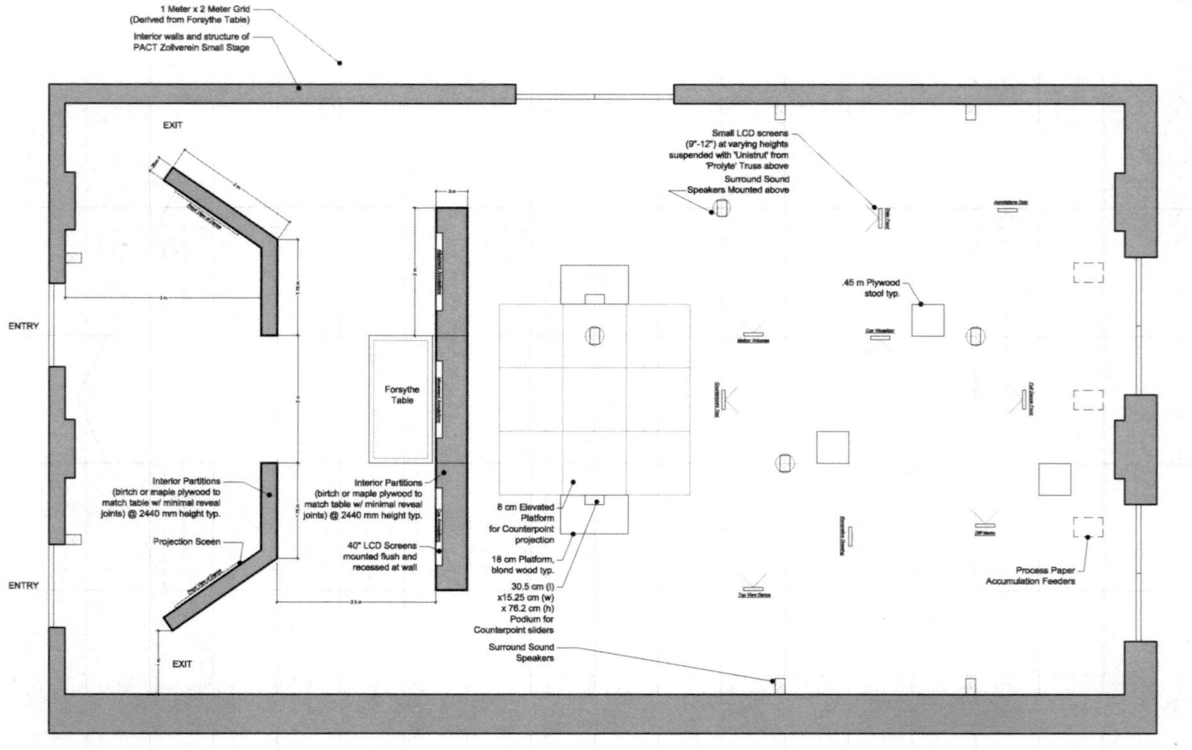


Figure 27. Norah Zuniga Shaw et al. | *Synchronous Objects, reproduced floor plan*, 2010

In *Synchronous Objects*, counterpoint – grounding, inside / outside mappings – is mediated and materialized in / as / with other formations. Here space and movement and their qualities are recomposed as lines drawn and fading over time, diagrams of space that show acceleration and articulation. And these diagrams all virtually gesture towards preacceleration (and prearticulation) of the space of the body. 'Liveness,' says Zuniga Shaw, 'returns when the viewer then moves back into the world and sees (live) patterns in other performances and experiences based on the perspectives afforded through technological mediation' (Manning, 2010b: Zuniga Shaw blog comment). More vividly, I argue (along with Manning) that in our chairs, with our screens, mice and keyboards, on and with the web, we move, cue and align, virtually and actually move–think–feel and make, in counterpoint to and with an 'interface-in-the-making' (Manning, 2010b). We and our bodies and space are always in material and conceptual relation with our computers and what they show to and with us – the 'window' we look both at and through (Mondloch, 2010). Homebound spectators of *Synchronous Objects* are affected, inside and outside, by the space of the body, and the space of the computer, and the space of the dance, and data-space, and more, all in contrapuntal emergence with the others' tele-actions and material movements.

This site was then transformed, again – re-cited and re-situated as an inter-active encounter that stages our own bodies as implicated and per-forming with 'real' space (and other bodies and matter). Here the artist moves between materials and media to create an/other kind of engagement, a different experience and practice for choreographic thinking. Zuniga Shaw's ISEA2010 project 'stays close to the conceptual foundations of the original while extending them into the architectural and experiential possibilities of an installation' (Zuniga Shaw, 2010b). As shown in the floor plan provided (Figure 27), upon entering *Synchronous Objects, reproduced,* audiences first view two high definition projections of the camera-dance itself: 'hitting the tables, breathing, speaking cues to each other, sliding, running etc' (Zuniga Shaw, 2012). The first 'room' is actually two free-standing and hinged wall-corners open to the entrances, with a large space between them.

The videos are shown as a diptych across the two, and are diagonally facing both the viewers in the entrance, and each other.

The second room is already visible through the framed 'doorway' threshold that the floating walls from the first room make. We see one of the metal tables used in the dance – making very real the virtual space of the bodies in the dance – framed by a back wall containing a triptych of three *Synchronous Objects*: 'analytical perspectives' of 'the cueing, alignments, and thematic recombinations / movement material' that, according to Zuniga Shaw, 'primes' viewers (Zuniga Shaw, 2012) for the exploratory, interactive, and participatory experience of the final room. These are each from the blue column online.

Visitors enter the third room from the corners around the video wall, breaking the theatrical 'front.[10] The final room has four elements that all activate and relate to each other and us across the space of the installation. Just behind the wall is the interactive *Counterpoint Tool,* adapted from the web to real space, which I will discuss in greater detail in the following paragraphs. Beyond that is a 'video forest' of eight more *Synchronous Objects,* plus a ninth video that reflects back interactions from the *Counterpoint Tool.* Interwoven with these nine videos is an eight-channel sound installation, synchronized with the diptych at the very entrance of the entire installation, which 'moves' – by panning and playing with amplitude across the speakers – the moving sounds of the dancers in and with bodies and tables as well as Forsythe's sung instructions. And finally is the artist's *Wikimill,* where a robotic feeder continuously drops to the floor print-outs (fifteen hundred pages per day) about choreographic thinking, authored by all thirty producers of the piece via their collaborative website.

The installation version of the *Counterpoint Tool* (Figure 28) is made up of a large projection on a small dance floor, where participants might interact. On the two ends of its interaction area sit wood and metal stations where viewers can use physical dials and sliders to create and choreograph virtual dancers and their movements, which are projected on the floor below. In this bird's-eye view, dancers are represented by graphical heads and arms that swing around one another, and move in space. As is also the case in the online version, visitors can decide on the number of widgets, their color, whether or not they leave a trace of their motions, and 'how they move (more or less in unison / counterpoint, i.e. with more or less difference between their speed, motion pathways, shape relationships and so on)' (Zuniga Shaw, 2012). Here with sliders – which could all be moved at once, unlike with the online tool – we control the difference and correspondence between, and speed and acceleration of, how each 'widget' moves their arms in relation to their bodies (and the other widgets), how they move across space and each other, and how much of their movement materials, alignment, and cues are revealed in this generative and interactive animation. Participants can additionally step onto this 'stage' themselves – an overhead computer vision system tracks their movements, and projects their own spot-lighted widget on top of them. These 'live' performers are connected to the 'generated' widgets as part of the software, and real-time lines and trails are drawn between them. All the dancing widgets respond to our stasis and movement through 'an attraction and repelling algorithm (clustering near or avoiding the space occupied by the user)' (Zuniga Shaw, 2012). The counterpoint and grounding between space, software, and bodies are revealed and amplified, moving and changing a relation just as it en- and unfolds. We feel the incipient formation of space and bodies.

It is difficult to describe the intensity that is counterpoint and how these dancer / choreographers make bodies and space felt with and through movement and stasis. While at ISEA, I attended a discussion between Zuniga Shaw and Manning, where Christopher Roman – part of The Forsythe Company and one of the dancers in *One Flat Thing, reproduced* – demonstrated movement materials, cueing, and alignments with the artist and audience at large. As Roman wandered the room, stopped, started, and stuttered, screamed, whispered, and performed silences across bodies and space, I felt stranded, suspended, and potently alive in my seat. The space of his body and its action and my guesses of how he might move, then does move, and then my previous, present, and virtual moving–thinking–feeling in relation to its, and our, possibilities were extraordinary.

*Synchronous Objects, reproduced* attempts to create exactly this kind of intensity. In some ways it is more intimate – we explore media and movement ourselves. In others, it is more public – we may be asked

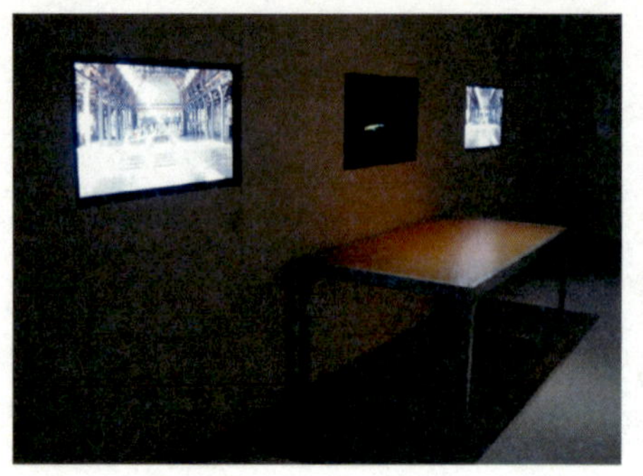

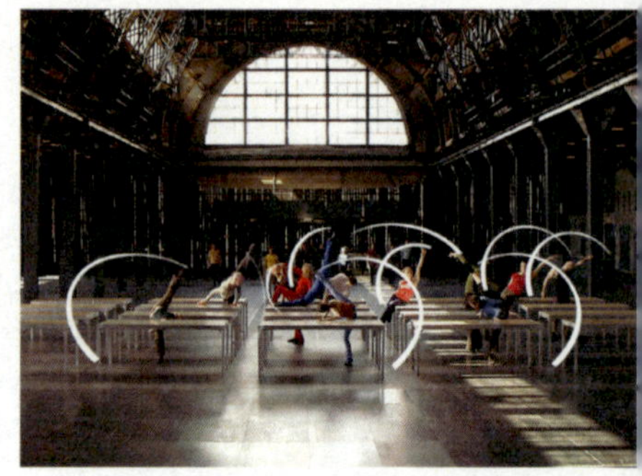

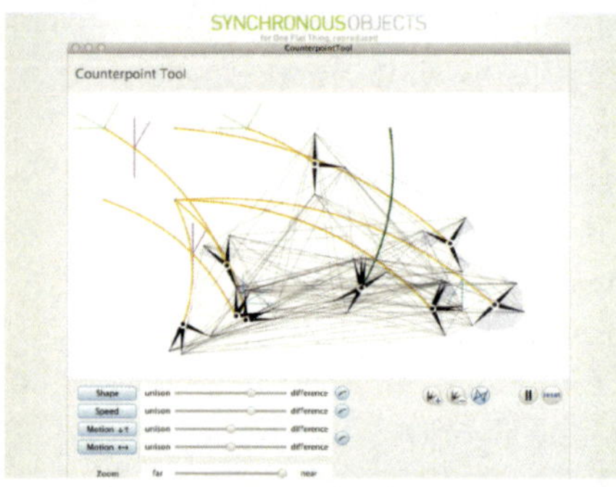


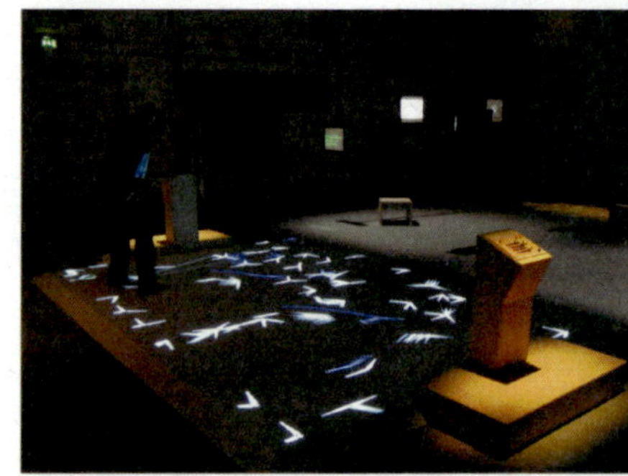

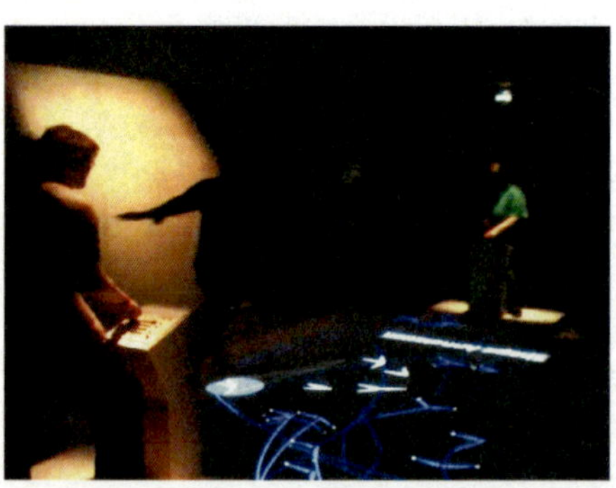

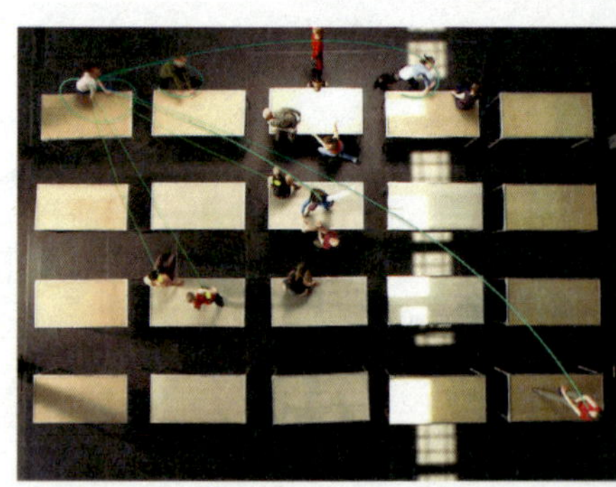

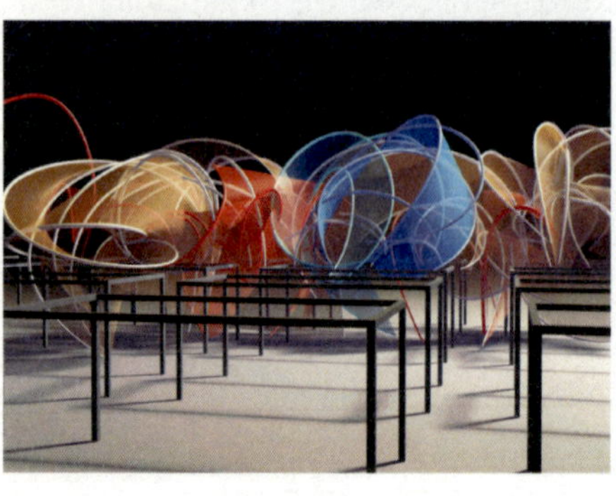

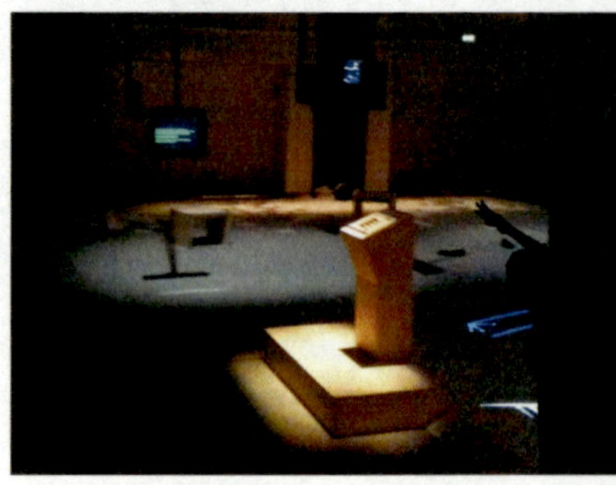

Figure 28. Norah Zuniga Shaw et al. | *Synchronous Objects, reproduced*, PACT Zollverein 2010

to move in front of and with other dancing dancers, computers and media, and the spaces of their bodies. Visitors are drawn through appearances of video and sound and movement, active texts, paradoxical bodies, and inter-active kiosks. One loudspeaker might amplify a dancer's breath to the point where your very skin vibrates, another whispers or sings, reversing course around piles of paper, pushing you in and around other videos and speakers and into the implicit body stage itself. Counterpoint is not only revealed but per-formed by the installation – for example in how various videos and sounds are synchronized while others are not – and then by us, the participants, in how we move–think–feel, in and around.

Zuniga Shaw wrote in an email to me:

> The clearest moment of synchronization is when the dancers drag the tables on and off the 'stage' at the opening and ending of the piece. It is loud and very visually evident and often was an 'aha' moment for viewers of the work that everything was synchronized. I loved watching people's discovery of relationships between things ... one of the deepest 'stories' in [the work is] that forms [of] knowledge are related in unexpected ways, that ideas are mobile and can leap from one domain / discipline into another with rigorous attention to their specificity, that deep structures of relationship are evident around us all the time if we hone our attention to them. (Zuniga Shaw, 2012)

Here multi-modal affect, perception, interaction, and relation feed back in to each other, complex and confused, different and the same, potentialized with a generative and ever-shifting movement. This is the space of the body, in quotes: 'flesh-space.'

In one encounter Zuniga Shaw described to me, an elderly German woman spent more than thirty minutes meandering across the three rooms of *Synchronous Objects, reproduced*. She was a bit startled in the *Counterpoint Tool* when the simulated dancers flew away from where she walked and again when she looked back at a screen to see what her presence had done. As she watched, the widgets behaved differently again; they flocked around her, like butterflies. She eventually squatted 'amidst the paper piles and started sorting through them,' picking some up to join her for a ride as she explored the audiovisual forest 'looking closely, walking from screen to screen, standing near a speaker and listening, walking back to previous screens, kind of like a detective.' This participant later approached the artist and explained that 'dance was becoming other things, that the other things were becoming other things too and that it all showed motion,' discovery, and space (Zuniga Shaw, 2012).

I too spent a long time moving-through and thinking-with this space. I felt most encouraged to interact – and Zuniga Shaw says this is not uncommon – after watching children play with the *Counterpoint Tool,* trying to imitate the dance and movements, trying to direct and misdirect the widgets and space in and around them. I would run and sweep my arms and legs, push and pull the lines and forms, spin and twist along with the widgets but also try to move them, move space, move bodies, move the *relation*. When I needed a rest, I would wander through the forest, let papers pile around me, read for a bit, perhaps sit down, close my eyes and listen, walk back around to watch the dance out front in full, then dance and spatialize, again.

Zuniga Shaw and her collaborators invite us to play between dance, interaction, and occurrence, between looking and feeling, between transformation and acceleration. By 'flowing from dance to data to objects, and back around again' (Zuniga Shaw, 2009), and inviting interaction and intervention between them, I argue that *Synchronous Objects, reproduced* is an encounter with how we spatialize – materially, conceptually, and politically. In this, it frames what I am calling *prespatialization*. Here we preaccelerate specifically towards the making of potential material, conceptual, and political *spaces*.

Zuniga Shaw says, 'I am a dancer and choreographer trying to excite' the audience 'about choreographic knowledge... through animation and visual media' (Zuniga Shaw, 2009). With *Synchronous Objects,* we confront both concept and action, a re-siting and refiguring of each. She grants us different modes of attention and distraction, mobilizes choreographic thinking in varying domains. With *Synchronous Objects, reproduced,* she provides spaces to spatialize in and with and as the space of the body. She potentializes and makes us virtually feel what is possible. Like Gil's ballet dancer in front of the mirror, we learn about interior and exterior through virtual appearance, and then are invited to virtually move, highlight, and frame, to move–think–feel and make-space-with. It is anticipated and incipient action folded with inchoate space.

Spaces and bodies are suspended in a loop of past and future could-have-becomes, as they *are* and *become,* again. Here we experience and practice, we conceptually sense, we virtually feel, how we might otherwise make space for ourselves and each other. At stake are both the research creation surrounding spatialization at large, and the implicit and explicit politics lying just beneath the surface. We are not pre-formed spaces and bodies, either in construction or constitution. There are always multiple forces pushing and pulling, folding and unraveling, on and about and *as* body and space. Zuniga Shaw opens a space of the body for occurrence, is excited about difference and disagreement, wants us to 'heighten our attention to the deep structures, the deep sets of relationships [and] degrees of alignment… that are percolating under the surfaces of our lives all the time' (Zuniga Shaw, 2009). *Synchronous Objects, reproduced* opens rather than closes spaces for moving–thinking–feeling–spatializing. Here possibility frames intensity, which frames potential, and each gifts us with understandings of, and practice spaces for, both potential and agency in how we act.

What Lozano-Hemmer and Zuniga Shaw give us are stages to rehearse in and around the various forces, both present and non-present, in the making of bodies and spaces – as moving–thinking–feeling and political relations. These artists not only frame what we do as we do it, but also make very real the affects of art and bodies, space and culture, even when they are not directly in front of us. Lozano-Hemmer brings to the fore our relations to other, tele-absent, times and spaces and bodies, while Zuniga Shaw remediates and reforms the forces of an 'original' danced body-space most viewers have never actually seen. In each, as we carve out and enact embodiment and spatialization, we are asked to take account of the implications of the past, as well as our own affects and effects on the future. We prespatialize, are asked to feel and transform the differences and differencing we make, in how we move.

## Notes

1 Myron Krueger utilized machine vision in computer art before Rokeby, and both have been extremely influential on present-day interactive artists.

2 Here what Manning calls 'technicity' brings 'into alignment the more-than-human that is the intersection of the human and technology' (Manning, 2010b).

3 Image credits from left to right, top to bottom:
A. Rafael Lozano-Hemmer, Body Movies, Relational Architecture 6, 2001. Schouwburgplein, V2 Cultural Capital of Europe, Rotterdam, The Netherlands. Photo: Arie Kievit.
B. Rafael Lozano-Hemmer, Body Movies, Relational Architecture 6, 2006. Museum of Art, Hong Kong, China. Photo: Antimodular Research.
C. Rafael Lozano-Hemmer, Body Movies, Relational Architecture 6, 2001. Schouwburgplein, V2 Cultural Capital of Europe, Rotterdam, The Netherlands. Photo: Jan Sprij.
D. Rafael Lozano-Hemmer, Body Movies, Relational Architecture 6, 2002. Hauptplatz, Ars Electronica Festival, Linz, Austria. Photo: Antimodular Research.
E. Rafael Lozano-Hemmer, Body Movies, Relational Architecture 6, 2002. Hauptplatz, Ars Electronica Festival, Linz, Austria. Photo: Antimodular Research.
F. Rafael Lozano-Hemmer, Body Movies, Relational Architecture 6, 2006. Museum of Art, Hong Kong, China. Photo: Antimodular Research.
G. Rafael Lozano-Hemmer, Body Movies, Relational Architecture 6, 2002. Hauptplatz, Ars Electronica Festival, Linz, Austria. Photo: Antimodular Research.
H. Rafael Lozano-Hemmer, Body Movies, Relational Architecture 6, 2006. Atlantico Pavillion, Lisbon, Portugal. Photo: Antimodular Research.

4 For similar work, see also Lozano-Hemmer's *Under Scan* (2005), http://www.lozano-hemmer.com/under_scan.php, Kelly Dobson's *scream body* (1998–2004; this project has additional similarities to *Front*), http://web.media.mit.edu/~monster/screambody/, and Luisa Paragui Donati's *vestis* (2003), http://luisaparaguai.art.br/web/?page_id=38

5 Image credits from left to right, top to bottom:

A. Rafael Lozano-Hemmer, Standards and Double Standards, Subsculpture 3, 2004. OMR Gallery, Art Basel 35 Unlimited, Basel, Switzerland. Photo: Antimodular Research.
B. Rafael Lozano-Hemmer, Standards and Double Standards, Subsculpture 3, 2004. OMR Gallery, Art Basel 35 Unlimited, Basel, Switzerland. Photo: Peter Hauck.
C. Rafael Lozano-Hemmer, Homographies, Subsculpture 7, 2006. Art Gallery of New South Wales, Sydney Biennale, Sydney, Australia. Photo: Antimodular Research.
D. Rafael Lozano-Hemmer, Homographies, Subsculpture 7, 2006. Art Gallery of New South Wales, Sydney Biennale, Sydney, Australia. Photo: Antimodular Research.
E. Rafael Lozano-Hemmer, Homographies, Subsculpture 7, 2006. Art Gallery of New South Wales, Sydney Biennale, Sydney, Australia. Photo: Antimodular Research.

6 In both meteorology and physics, isobars refer to lines or curves that map or represent pressurized systems.

7 With Marc Ainger, Shawn Hove, Joshua Penrose, Julian Richter, Petra Roggel (Goethe Institute München), Benjamin Schroeder, Lily Skove, and Stephen Turk.

8 Choreography: William Forsythe. Music: Thom Willems. Staging: Ayman Harper, Jill Johnson, and Richard Siegal. Scenic and Lighting Design: William Forsythe. Costume Design: Stephen Galloway.

9 Creative Directors: William Forsythe, Maria Palazzi, and Norah Zuniga Shaw. Generative Designer: Matthew Lewis. Ohio State Graduate Research Associates: Beth Albright, Michael Andereck, Sucheta Bhatawadekar, Hyowon Ban, Andrew Calhoun, Jane Drozd, Joshua Fry, Melissa Quintanilha, Anna Reed, Benjamin Schroeder, Lily Skove, Ashley Thorndike, and Mary Twohig. Ohio State Faculty Researchers: Ola Ahlqvist, Peter Chan, Noel Cressie, Stephen Turk. Forsythe Company Dance Research Collaborators: Jill Johnson, Prue Lang, Amy Raymond, Christopher Roman, and Elizabeth Waterhouse. International Collaborators: Scott deLahunta, Patrick Haggard, and Alva Noë.

10 'Breaking the front' is a strategy used by architects so as not to privilege any specific part of the space – designed here with collaborator Stephen Turk.

# Chapter 7

## Implicating Art Works

### Potentialized Art

This book argues that embodiment is performed of the relation, and that interactive installations suspend, amplify, and intervene in that relation. It puts forward an approach for practically and critically encountering such art as a situation where we intensively experience and practice being and becoming, opening new , or other, possibilities in how we, and the world around us, mutually emerge. With the implicit body framework, each piece is explored and analyzed not only through the artist's inquiry and artwork description, but also through how we literally inter-act, alongside a rehearsal and examination of the embodied relationships in, and of, said interaction. Here relational categories are applied to an ongoing list of sensible concepts – called thematics when utilized within the implicit body framework – that emerge with and as the body that matters. Sensible concepts are not only emerging, but emerging emergences: continuously constructed and constituted, re-constructed and re-constituted, through relationships with each other, the body, materiality, and more. Any interactive artwork, I maintain, could benefit from multiple relational readings, where each iteration focuses on a different thematic implication. This approach remembers that the body is active and incipient, not blank matter on which society inscribes itself. It calls for a critical and productive investment in art where we might rehearse the formation of bodies of all kinds, along with meaning, communities, architectures, and so on. Intensively practicing and studying how we interact, relate, and reciprocally emerge with both concepts and matter can deepen our understandings of not only interactive art and embodiment, but also what is at stake in the multiple agencies, potentials, and limitations surrounding each.

There are, of course, other categories of art with the power to imply and implicate. What else might implicit art look like? How can we invest in continuity and relation through other art formations? The work I am calling *potentialized art* falls within the expansive rubric of new media art, and has in common with interactive art its use of technology to amplify action, affect, embodiment, performativity, transformation, and / or materiality. Where they differ is that rather than being interactive, in the sense that the viewer's embodied participation in the gallery is integral to the *work* of the work, potentialized art is performative and / or relational, in and through the artist's production, and / or it is processually formed through some kind of technologically mediated performance. It intensifies experience and viewership through mediation, anticipation, and imagination around that which is per-formed and implicated. Here I broaden the scope of what can be understood as a staged and amplified 'body,' in order to critically analyze, and more consequentially practice, materialization and articulation in and through contemporary art. I hope to show, as the title of this chapter expresses, (how) implicating art *works*.

One excellent example of a potentialized artwork is William Kentridge's series of stereoscopic and performative prints / light sculptures (Chapter 1). The viewer's participation is not 'the work' in the same way as with interactive art, but nor are Kentridge's prints 'complete' and explicit objects in themselves; the entire series is, rather, an ongoing iteration of movement. As in Massumi's 'occurrent' arts, Kentridge's work *appears* – is virtually seen – *as* movement and time and space, materializing and mattering. Another example of potentialized art is Stelarc's previously discussed *Ping Body* (also Chapter 1), where network activity transforms the piece over time. Audience members do not *make* the work directly through their interactions; it is transformed indirectly, through Internet activity itself.

I again want to shift emphasis, towards making and thinking (non-interactive) digital works that highlight the entwinement of materiality and a (specific) sensible concept ('embodiment – or materialization – and x'). Potentialized artworks such as these are manifest as a kind of living activity, an ontogenetic and per-formed relation. In Kentridge's case we experience them as a continuous set of prints, and with Stelarc, as a performance (and its performed documentation online). These are, I argue, *doubly* per-formed. First, in their continuous and performative creation (with the artist, space, light, Internet, electricity, ideas, and more), and second, in their ongoing and performative occurrence – how we experience and practice (with) them, online or in the gallery. Although potentialized art differs greatly from interactive art's direct (human) bodily contact, here *matter* is staged and implicated; we *see* and feel it as performed in and with (non-human) bodies and concepts. Human and non-human matters are always present, moving, and implicated in such formations, and I suggest we can better take account of embodiment, interactivity, media, and how art relates (and relates to) all three.

My catalog-like examples feature digital art that stages three implicated and implicating sensible concepts: vestigial-vision, tangible-temporality, and virtual-performance. The works were chosen because of their diversity in when, where, why, and how they creatively explore, to paraphrase Anna Munster, materializing media. I begin to visit some of my own potentialized artworks in this chapter as well, to show how the implicit body approach can and does feed back between affection and reflection, how frameworks for experience and practice might move between and transform both studio and gallery spaces.[1] By attempting to examine 'non-interactive' work with the implicit body approach, I gesture towards a discourse and corpus larger than this book, to an art philosophy where matter matters, however mediated. I look ahead in new media criticism and production by signaling how implicit body thinking may inform, perform, and transform how we incorporate and implicate interactivity and embodiment across the many disciplines that constitute contemporary digital cultural practices.

## Implications

Gordan Savičić, who lives and works between Vienna and Rotterdam, is a self-proclaimed games developer, electronic practitioner, and social-circuit-bender. His work tends to critically interrogate our relationships to technologies, our communications media, and each other. Savičić's *Constraint City* (2007 and ongoing, Figure 29) is a continuous performance that, in many ways, inverts Theodore Watson's *audio space,* the interactive artwork that encourages moving and noise-generating viewers to simultaneously explore and produce an aurally resonant and physical space (Chapter 1). Where Watson invites his participants into the pleasure of play, Savičić's work generates pain and bruising. While Watson uses the sounds and bodies of his performers to create and shape space, Savičić harnesses alternative spatial interactions outside of his control in order to inflict pain upon, and distort, his own body.[2]

Subtitled 'the pain of everyday life,' in *Constraint City* Savičić adorns himself with a corset whose straps can be activated to painfully tighten around his bodice with a simple electronic command to high torque servomotors. He uses a hacked gaming console to detect any enclosed and encrypted wireless networks in close proximity, as he wanders the streets of the city. The higher the strength of a given signal, the tighter his jacket becomes. Thus, says the artist, 'Everyday walks between home, work and leisure are recompiled into a schizogeographic pain-map' (Savičić, 2007). It is not a participant viewer framed as a relational body; the outside world intervenes on the performance of the artist's flesh. The 'intangible reality' of the telecommunications-activated urban space is mapped to Savičić's skin, forcing him to physically experience 'the codes of the new digital architectures' (Canonico, 2007). The outcomes of his city walks provoke 'an emergence of a city-shaped body' (Savičić, 2007).

Savičić also records his own movements in the city as a result of this dynamic relationship. He uses a Geographic Information System to keep track of how his routes change both over time and on individual days, depending on his moods, desires, and plans in relation to the encrypted networks he has become aware of in the landscape around him. In other words, while the invisible electromagnetic city is imposed upon Savičić's body, he adjusts his ongoing performance of, and in, the city in response, and the two, together, create new formations from, and of, their relation. The city is mapped to his flesh, and his body and movements re-map the city in kind. They are diagrammed, in continuous and reciprocal development.

Savičić's *Constraint City* is clearly not an interactive artwork; it does not stage an implicit body performed by the viewer. It is also not explicit body art. In historic pain performance pieces like Chris Burden's *Doorway to Heaven* and *Trans-fixed,* where Burden electrocuted himself and nailed himself to a car, respectively, the artist used shock to performatively unfold and challenge taken for granted cultural constructions such as personal danger, death, desire, or the body itself. *Constraint City,* on the other hand, is an intervention in the relation of body and the technologized world, a concentration on how each is a map and a mapping of and with the other. The body of the artist is staged as a locus of digital experience, practice, and perfor-

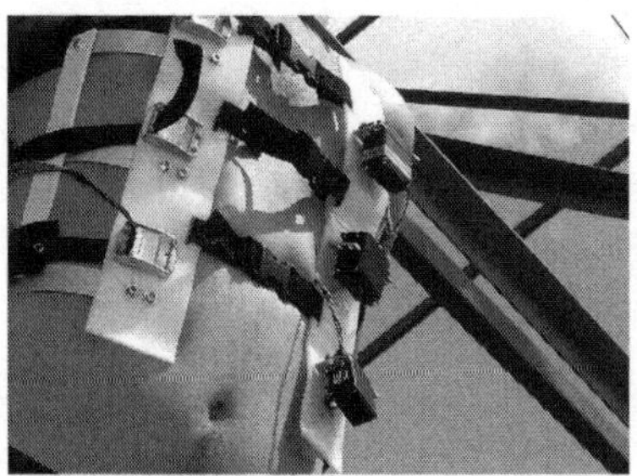
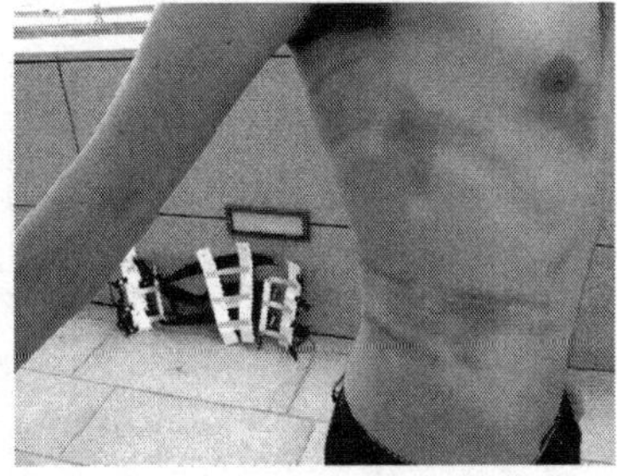

Figure 29. Gordan Savičić | *Constrain City*, 2007 and ongoing | photos by Julia Staudach and Luc Gross

mance. Savičić's flesh and its invisible but very real surroundings are not pre-formed 'things,' but a per-formed event. And we, as viewers and bodies and part of the city – digital and otherwise – are implicated across such work.

I contend that interactive artworks set up situations, use technology to rig stages open to an event, to create potentialized contexts where we experience and practice styles of being and becoming. They de- and re-contextualize (quote without quotation marks), and thus intervene in, some of the body and world's continuous and emergent relations. This chapter goes on to argue that while non-interactive pieces such as *Constraint City* do not accomplish this same amplification for an individual interactor, they similarly intensify an ongoing process of transformation, revealing an event's emergent properties through ontogenesis and iteration. They do what Forsythe's choreographic objects do for choreographic thinking. They add to the discussions of interactivity, relationality, materialization, and performance that this book is invested in. They suspend matter, and our relation to it, in such a way as to implicate – to unfold and enfold – moving–thinking–feeling.

In *Constraint City*, Savičić exhibits his per-formed body in photographic images, and in relation to a local mapping of encrypted wireless signals. Another potentialized artwork might, for example, see: the birthing of digital prints through performances in the landscape; the iterative and temporal transformation of electronic music, based on how we listen over time; or, the chronicling and remaking of new media-based relationships between the Internet and real world – all examples of work which will be discussed later in this chapter. In each case, the artist or artists do not create a potentialized context, but rather, potentialized matter that exists in images, video, audio, installation, or other forms. These 'objects' are precisely *not* objects in the sense of complete and standalone works of art. They are, rather, continuous substantiation: traces of a performance, of an (ongoing) event of emergence, potentialized through their accent on the past and future of a substanceless and durationless moment. The continuity of an event is implicit in the object (which is not an object) of potentialized art. The 'work' exists as twice more than the matter in front of the viewer: as a relation in excess of what was 'made' by the artist, and as a relation in excess of the embodied viewer for whom it virtually appears. It is, in other words and to allude to another formation discussed earlier in the book, a topological figure. Perhaps it is more than that: an incipiently active, topological *figuring*.

The potentialized artworks discussed in this chapter have been birthed through performance, transformed over time, and/or remade in the network. They are full of potent potential because of the per-formed and relational processes in which they are made and continue to be remade. If, as discussed in Chapter 2, explicit body art puts Zeno's stop points in quotes, and implicit body art does the same to our movement, then potentialized art could be considered an/other citation – a recital – of matter and bodies. Potentialized art is the implied body's quotation – out of context, staged via another form, but nonetheless per-formed and full of potential. It is not a static body in quotes that is interrogated explicitly, not a continuous body in quotes intervened in implicitly, but occurring 'quotations' *of* moving and implicated bodies and materials. Interactive art asks us to *feel* performed relations, and potentialized art invites us to *look* – including all that looking is – at the ongoing being and becoming of performance. It is the citation that comes from a re-situation – the quotable quote, the implicit body passage – substantiated as a *work* of art. Potentialized art may thus be actual or virtual, static or variable, matter or energy. Like this book itself, it is an attempt to qualify the forces of movement, sensation, materialization, and experience.

It could perhaps be argued that Fluxus performance, the happenings of the 1960s, butted up against the impossibility of documenting an ineffable art event similar to those described in this chapter. But potentialized art is not documentation; it does not attempt to capture the essence of an interaction in the frozen time of stale images or video. Rather, potentialized art is an ongoing work, where staged and implicated 'matter' contains traces of its own performance, includes elements of potentiality through hints of past and future enactments, which appear to us. Potentialized art uses technology to show movement, with a difference – to not only reveal, but also embody, transformation. Potentialized art is a manifestation, several manifestations, of that which is implicit.

## 'Vestigial-Vision'

The vestigial-vision thematic examines artworks that stage the emergent relation of embodiment and looking. Pieces such as David Rokeby's *San Marco Flow* (2004) and Erwin Driessens and Maria Verstappen's *Tickle Salon* (2002), I argue, re-present the vestigial traces of movement either with or over the body to continuously map ways of seeing cities and bodies, respectively. Maria Bolivar's *Within and Between* (2010) layers projections and reflections of a dancer's body across curved and moving surfaces, to make vision a part of matter. And in my own series of performative digital prints, which I affectionately refer to as *Compressionism* (2005 and ongoing), I birth images in and of the relation between my body, technology, and the landscape. These potentialized artworks each develop and distill their own framework for experience and practice.

Rokeby was first introduced in the last chapter, along with his interactive installation, *Very Nervous System*. His *San Marco Flow* (Figure 30) uses a high-resolution digital video camera to capture the ongoing movements of participants on a piazza. His software only redraws what has changed from one video frame to the next, visualizing continuous, alternative views, in the form of two slowly shifting projections. These videos are, 'in effect, lit by animate presence; things that are not moving are invisible' (Rokeby, 2004). Slowly mov-

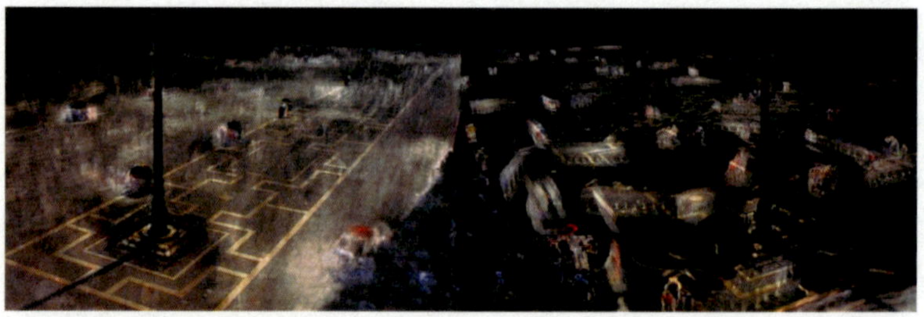

Figure 30. David Rokeby | *San Marco Flow*, 2005 | 2 channel video work | dimensions variable | edition of 7 | screen capture of the two channels | image courtesy of the artist

ing bodies generate saturated and pixilated artifacts, and rapid motion causes sharp trails like a multitude of lines in the sand. The artist writes, 'Walking pigeons leave worm-like traces. Gathered people abstract themselves through their shifting motions. Tour groups flow across the image like a river' (Rokeby, 2004). The diptych is thus a diagrammatic figuring of recent activity.

The left-hand projection leaves longer-lasting trails behind each movement, and so acts like a slowly developing polaroid photo, its moving elements made visible over minutes, rather than seconds. This video image captures and develops only the accumulate activities on the piazza, and broadcasts a ghost-like rendering of San Marco's happenings. In the right-hand projection, the gestural markings fade more rapidly, revealing a rhythmic flow of life in Venice. These video projections are mirrored in the centre, and are 'different readings of the same unfolding source material providing a kind of stereoscopy into the dimension of time' (Rokeby, 2004). How we move and how we look, and the relation of the two, emerge in and as an ongoing potentialized work of art. The artist's motion-tracking software continuously suspends and amplifies the embodied, abstracted and inter-active viewers in the space-time of the piazza. It traces the remnants of what they do and experience in their three-dimensional environment, but on a two-dimensional image plane. Rokeby then exhibits this dynamic video to the artwork's other viewers, watching from elsewhere, showing how we *see* not only through our own movement, affect, and sensation, but with and through those of others as well.

Rokeby's accomplishment is inverted in Erwin Driessens and Maria Verstappen's *Tickle Salon* (Figure 31). Instead of viewers seeing the urban landscape through the lens of others' movements, in this piece an exploring 'tickle-bot' rapidly traverses the contours of our skin, its movements dynamically plotting the body as if it were a landscape. Here, a map of flesh emerges through and as the physical relationship between body and robot.

Driessens and Verstappen have a declared interest in the concepts found throughout this book: complexity, dynamism, and transformation, to name a few. They are also among the earliest investigators with computer generative systems, and assert they use simple rules, encourage spontaneous interactions and operations, in order to give rise to art that might be beyond human or even biological conception. The work is performed. The stated goal of *Tickle Salon* is to be an inexhaustible pleasure machine for those who love to be tickled (something both creators admit to). Participants lie, completely still, on a bed in the gallery, and allow themselves to be stroked and teased. There were two technical – and conceptual – innovations that needed to be achieved towards this end. First, Driessens and Verstappen had to create their own machine vision system in three-dimensional space, one that allowed their tickle-bot to 'see' where it should lightly maneuver around its charge. Second, they needed a mechanical system for said activities.

Driessens and Verstappen eventually produced a feedback structure that accomplishes both of these feats at the same time, a generative mechatronic program whereby their bot's exploratory tickling movements simultaneously diagram those very movements as a body in real time. A suspended feeler – a large steel marble with yarn skirting around it – is fastened to four monofiber lines. Each of these lines is in turn controlled by stepper motors, which wind and unwind to adjust the lengths of the strings, and coordinate the feeler's movements in space. The artists call this their 'inverted pyramid' suspension system (Driessens and Verstappen, 2004). The feeler can reach any position between the bed and ceiling.

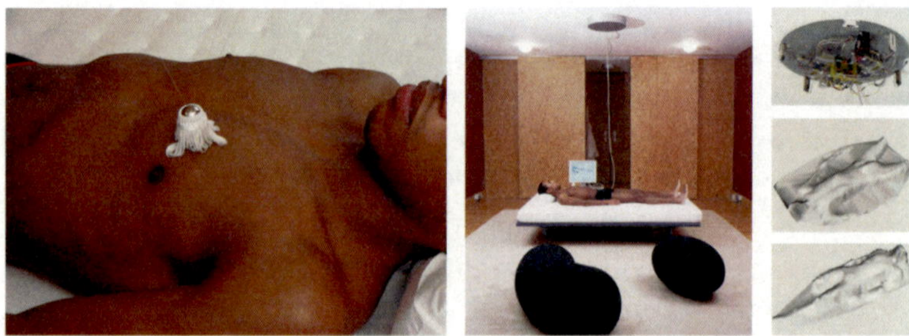

Figure 31. Driessens & Verstappen | *Tickle Salon*, 2002 | Photos: Erwin Driessens

The tickler always knows exactly where it is, by performing a geometrical computation based on the length of each suspension line. Whenever it touches the body, sensors detect a slight loss of tension in one or more of the lines. In response, the bot both records the collision position in an ongoing virtual map, and also halts its downward movement, rather trailing across the surface of the skin. So while creating, updating, and displaying a representative body shape, the exploring sensorimotor robot also gently strokes the participants' skin.

*Tickle Salon*'s mechanism both moves the probe *and* serves as a touch sensor. It collects information by touching and feeling its way around, simultaneously adapting its trajectory to whatever it encounters. It is a 'blind' robot, yet it per-forms an ongoing map it can use to plan its own motion over time (Driessens and Verstappen, 2004). *Tickle Salon* 'sees' the body through its interactions with it, mapping skin-as-landscape. It prods and probes, leaving tickles and drawings in its wake; it finds embodiment – for both itself and the participant – through the vestigial traces of its continuous contact.

Like Norah Zuniga Shaw's work, Milwaukee-based Venezuelan artist Maria Bolivar's *Within and Between* (Figure 32) is a mediation of a dance piece – though one that was itself mediated by and in relation to sight and technology. Bolivar's collaborative *Residual Moment* saw solo dancer Liz Zastrow repeat steps and silent gestures alongside projected videos of those just-completed movements, creating a call and response between dance and looking and back to dance again, a 'disconnection that arises between present experience and the virtual imprint of that experience' (Bolivar, 2011). *Within and Between*, then, takes videos of this layered performance and layers them again, across vision, space, and movement.

The artist produced a miniature architectural space of curved, Plexiglas walls that catch, reflect, and pass through now distorted videos from three separate projectors. These small walls themselves move and rotate via servomotors, once more moving the relation. Through projection, reflection, and refraction, the entire room is illuminated with moving images, parts, bodies, and materials. 'Within this makeshift world of moving walls and transparent reflections, the recorded memory of a dance leaves dancer and viewer both present

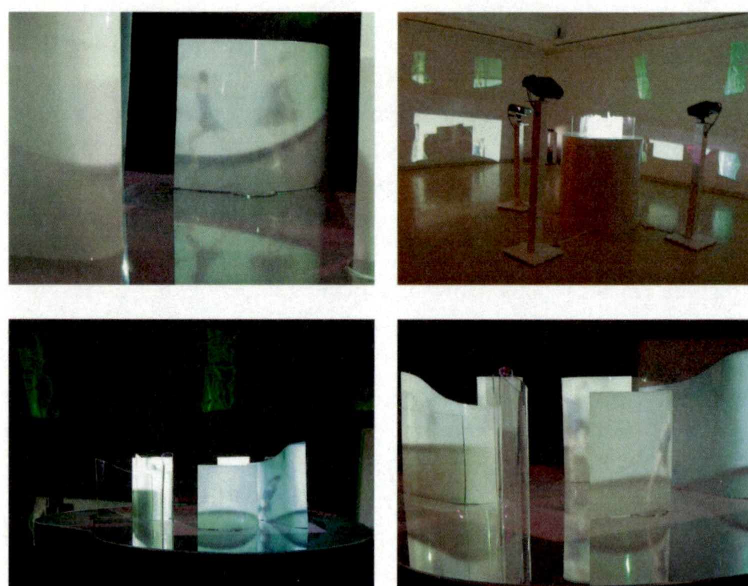

Figure 32. Maria Bolivar | *Within and Between*, 2010

and absent, dimensional yet sensational, trapped in the space yet released as light escapes beyond the installation's walls' (Bolivar, 2011). Although according to Bolivar *Within and Between* is a prototype for a larger space with human-scale moving walls, the result of this prototype is itself that of vestigial vision. Here traces within traces of what we look *at* and *with* can perform and reflect, affect and re-make, how we ourselves make and move and see. Within and between, we map a mapping of related and material images, in movement.

My own artistic practice since the late 1990s – which informed, and is informed by, my research and writing around the implicit body – seeks to interrogate the relationships between embodiment and other emergent categories, including but not limited to the thematics presented in this book: language, society, space, vision, time, and networks. I try to amplify and challenge that which is often presupposed in contemporary culture, in order to foster greater dialogue around these complex systems and their relationships to affect and meaning-making. This art exists as digitally interactive installations like those examined in earlier chapters – expanded on in the free companion chapter at http://stern.networkedbook.org – as well as site-conditioned and participatory performance, generative video works, mixed reality installations, and relational art in the vein of that which Bourriaud and Bishop write about. In the mid-2000s, I also began working on several series that combine new and traditional media to create unfamiliar encounters with multiple materials, concepts, affects, and agencies. Here what I call 'multidimensional images,' or per-formed Internet artworks, for example, suspend potential and intervene in relation.

In my playfully titled *Compressionism* series (Figure 33), I create archival prints that invest in affect, movement, and material and technological agency. I attempt to wrap the tensions between performance and pre-formism into serialized artworks: pieces that intensify the emergent categories of embodiment and vision. I strap a desktop scanner, laptop, and custom-made battery pack to my body, and birth images into existence. I might scan in straight, long lines across tables, tie the scanner around my neck and swing over flowers, do pogo-like gestures over bricks, or just follow the wind over water lilies in a pond. The dynamism between my body, technology, and the landscape is transformed into beautiful and quirky renderings. I have very little control over what any given image will look like. I cannot see it in the making, cannot see the landscape below the scanner face, can only move and make and reciprocally create 'looking' and 'image' and 'matter.' These performed computer files are then turned into archival prints using photographic or inkjet processes. I also often take details from the digital images and iteratively remake them, again, as traditional prints: lithographs, etchings, engravings, and woodcuts, among others. I like to think that *Compressionism* follows the trajectory of Impressionist painting, through Surrealism and beyond Postmodernism, but rather than citing crises of representation, reality, or simulation, I focus on engaging the relations between and around them (Stern, 2005).[3]

The Johannesburg Art Gallery's former museum director, Clive Kellner, writes that I traverse 'the material landscape in search of, and simultaneously birthing, images ... in a series of poetic gestures often

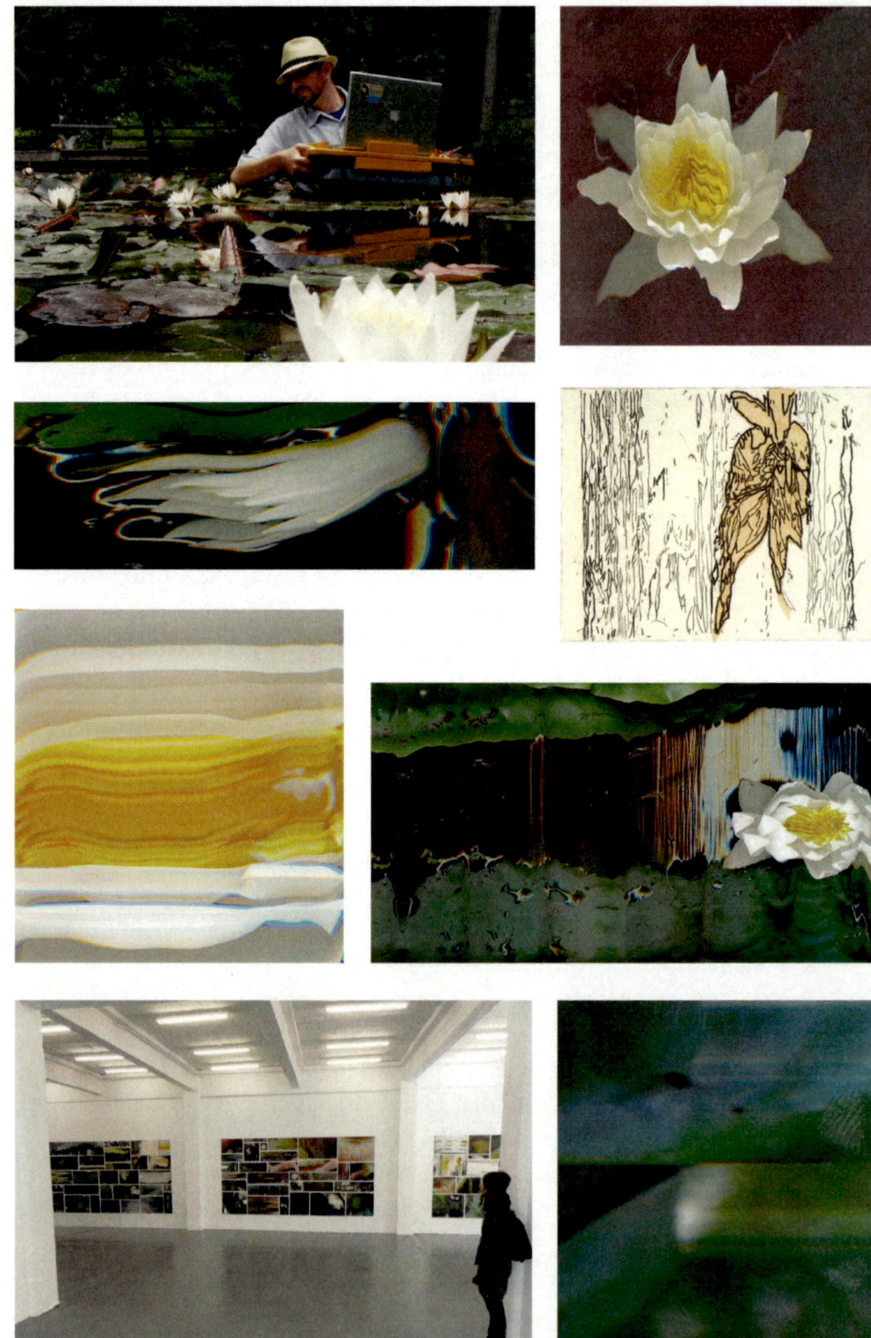

Figure 33. Nathaniel Stern | performative print series, 2005 and ongoing | photos by Jim Charles and Jesse Egan

likened to that of Jackson Pollock's topographical painting' (Kellner, 2007). I would argue the prints are less me / mine / gestural and more body / technology / landscape relational. *Art South Africa*'s Brenton Maart supports this with how he experiences viewership:

> The result is a series of zones that make up each image: bands that discern between adjacent times and successive views. At first the works seem abstract, but in moving closer the viewer is able to discern, in each band, elements of ... matter – ripples of water, flower petals, bricks, plastic bags, the sky – each rendered in a sequence that is both cubist and impressionistic. And within each band, and within the series of bands that make up each image, is an incredible and almost overwhelming sense of beauty; that almost religious feeling you get when you view an awesome artwork. (Maart, 2006)

Maart goes on to compare his affective experience to that of viewing a Rothko painting, where sense and sense-making are more apparent than the artist's hand, as in Pollock's work. My reworking many of these digital images into more traditional printmaking forms is another play on material relationships, time, iteration, and how performance can change the ways we look and see. *Giverny of the Midwest* (2011) went so far as to juxtapose ninety-three individual performative prints of varying size and shape, proximity and distance, in a Mondrian-like fashion across twenty-four square meters, where, writes arts critic Mary Corrigall, the 'scene cannot be relayed in its entirety. Stern doesn't order the visual world; he casts his garden pond scene as an indeterminate one that exists beyond the boundaries of any frame,' he 'amplifies the physical and sensual' (Corrigall, 2011).

Kellner argues that the implicit lesson of *Compressionism* is a performance and emergence of landscape / vision / work of art. 'What we see or experience ... is a mediated outcome in the form of an image or print, which grew out of a performance in the physical world.' He goes on, 'One of the most interesting things about the work is the vestigial traces it carries of the various performances through which it arose' (Kellner, 2007). This passage – which was a result of discussions between myself, Kellner, and Nicole Ridgway, who edited the catalog – is in fact where the vestigial-vision implicit art thematic received its name. The per-formance between body and landscape (and technology) leaves behind relational traces, and viewers affectively incorporate them. My multidimensional images are occurrences between a moving body, a dynamic landscape / ground, technology and technique, and a continuously sensing audience.[4]

These examples by Rokeby, Driessens and Verstappen, Bolivar, and myself all intervene in the continuous relations between embodiment and vision. As Mark B. N. Hansen might say, they go beyond the aesthetic perception of the object and have us encounter the image as 'image to the power of image', a 'topology where image infinitely exceeds object' (Hansen, 2004: 205).[5] Vestigial-vision artworks no longer belong only to the visual order of representation. They rather perform and visualize some of the various forces that act upon how we look and see. In other words, the ongoing constitution of art, viewer, vision, and matter, both are, and point to, more than the sum of their parts.

## 'Tangible-Temporality'

The tangible-temporality thematic places emphasis on the relational and mutual immanence of embodiment and time. After all, bodies are not only *present,* but *potent,* in and of time. They are coincidental with the potentials of past and future. If time is understood merely as many '"presents" in succession,' writes Massumi, then 'nothing exists outside of the march of the boxed-in' (Massumi, 2002: 200). The past and future always 'resonate in the present,' are in continuity with one another, smudging one another, where a body dissolves out of 'what it is just ceasing to be, into what it will already have become by the time it registers something has happened' (Massumi, 2002: 200). Bodies and matter *are* change, and a tangible-temporality reading of a given work of art gives primacy to the transitional and potentialized smudgings between past and future matters. This thematic is intended to help unpack art that asks us to investigate, perhaps amongst other things, the continuous and relational feedback loops between time and material per-formance. It will be utilized to concisely look at Brandon Labelle's *Death of the Composer, or All Tongues Are Mothers* (2001), David Rokeby's *Machine for Taking Time (Boul. Saint-Laurent)* (2007), Jessica Meuninck-Ganger's *Position / Opposition* (2010) alongside her and my collaborative *Distill Life* series (2009 and ongoing), and John F. Simon Jr.'s *Every Icon* (1997) alongside Arthur Ganson's *Machine with Concrete* (1992).

Brandon Labelle understands and works with sound because it is 'inherently and unignorably relational' (Labelle, 2007a). He writes that it 'emanates, propagates, communicates, vibrates, and agitates; it leaves a body and enters others; it binds and unhinges, harmonizes and traumatizes; it sends the body moving, the mind dreaming, and the air oscillating' (Labelle, 2007a). Here Labelle is dedicated to action, affect, embodiment, materiality, and, most of all, relationality. He argues that sound is always spatial, temporal, and relational, and describes it as a force that makes and unmakes, passes through and between. As an artist, he shows interest in both the social aspects of relational aesthetics that Nicolas Bourriaud puts forward, and the embodied and material relationality 'in excess' that this book considers foundational for approaches to media art.

Labelle's seven minute and twenty-nine second audio piece *Death of the Composer, or All Tongues are Mothers,* which could just as easily be read with the social-anatomies thematic, was created as part of his *Social Music* radio series in 2001. The program attempted to 'create a conceptual framework' that allowed for, in fact explicitly invited, 'outside influence or social input in determining sound production' (Labelle, 2007b). *Social Music,* as a series and project, aimed to generate 'musical and sonic activities that sought out public space, social interaction, spatial discoveries – found sounds, phenomenological tests, conversations between friends' (Labelle, 2007b). It was itself a social and participatory project that spawned several potentialized works of art.

I choose to analyze *Death of the Composer* because of how it exemplifies transformation over and with time, and to offer an alternative to Labelle's social reading of his own work. For this piece, Labelle first read aloud – and recorded – his curatorial statement for *Social Music,* some of which is in the previous paragraph. Following this, he had five different volunteers individually listen to his reading and try to simultaneously repeat what they heard as it played back for them. He then remixed the recordings as an accumulation, and repeated the process of listening, speaking, and layering until 'a chorus of misreadings, mishearings and misspeakings appeared' as a per-formed audio track (Labelle, 2007b). In other words, Labelle's embodied speaker–listeners perform his track's continuous potential while quite literally on the cusp of the virtual present. This is then made to virtually appear (to become aurally apparent) to his listeners.

Labelle argues that with *Death of the Composer*, the artwork, its context, and its audience, all emerge in and around 'the random interplay of phenomena' and towards 'the formation of what we could call a "public"' (Labelle, 2007b). I would say, further, that in *Death of the Composer*'s performative creation, the speaker–listener, as body and time, is introduced to and as a continuous but moving loop, between the pre-formed recordings of the audio files' past participants, and the per-formed, new recording by its 'current' (or rather, future) ones. Here we are engaged as physical beings and becomings, simultaneously listening and stuttering over that which we attempt to repeat, preaccelerating to the next moment of materialization. Labelle writes that the piece 'shows how communication is never direct or without faults but always influenced by factors outside' (Labelle, 2005). The same might be said about what it reveals, unravels, and disrupts in both time and bodies. Neither is direct or without faults; they influence one another and the outside, continuous smudgings of past and future affects, potentially present bodily and material moving–thinking–feelings.

David Rokeby's sculpture and installation, *Machine for Taking Time (Boul. St-Laurent)*,[6] commissioned for the Langlois Foundation in Montréal, algorithmically explores a database of over 750,000 images in real time. The artist initially used two high-resolution cameras on motorized pan-tilt mounts to capture 1024 images off each of the east and west sides of the Foundation building every day for an entire year. These sequential images encapsulate both the movements of the sky in relation to the earth, and the landscape in relation to the camera. For the installation, two computers randomly but fluidly concatenate pans over the landscape of the city, but from different times. In other words, while we see a smooth movement of the camera in relation to its surroundings as if it were a single, continuous shot, each frame actually jumps to a completely different time of day and year, making an uncanny traversal of human space, with non-human time. Rokeby explains that sometimes the software and compiled moving image follow a standard trajectory, allowing viewers to follow the scanning eye of the camera easily, but at other moments they slip across several days in very quick succession, while only moving from one position to the next.

Rokeby's mechatronic cameras capture successive and mobile moments in the emergence of time, to illuminate the impossibility of a static material-temporality. The piece plays on how our re-memberings always traverse and jump around in time as our bodies relate to the past and our actions in it. But here, we see and feel those jumps. We follow the movement of the camera's pan as if it were in the present, a live and uncut image. We mistake the changes in time as a play of the light. And finally, we are open to, experience, and practice, an / other form of time unfolding. What any description or still image fails to convey is how the artist's stitched together video sequences have a wondrous and pulsating glow about them, a visceral throbbing of light and shadow that reflects the flux and movements of time in and as and with space and an embodied landscape.

We move between seasons, see leaves and snow and bodies and objects appear and disappear, watch sunrise and sunset at different times of day, all in the span of seconds. We experience the temporal city through its transitioning clouds and sun overhead, the changing of the seasons, the ongoing but disrupted and intermingled gestures of the earth and sky and their inhabitants. One critic argues that the 'present does not tick away with the seconds on the clock; it is instead a moment where images of the past are fused into a reconstructed memory. From the deconstruction of time is built a present where expectation is enriched with illusion' (Gagnon, 2007). I do not believe this work is about the 'construction' or deconstruction of time as enriched with 'illusion.' It is, rather, time and its corporeal and incorporeal matters and mattering made visible in all their potential,

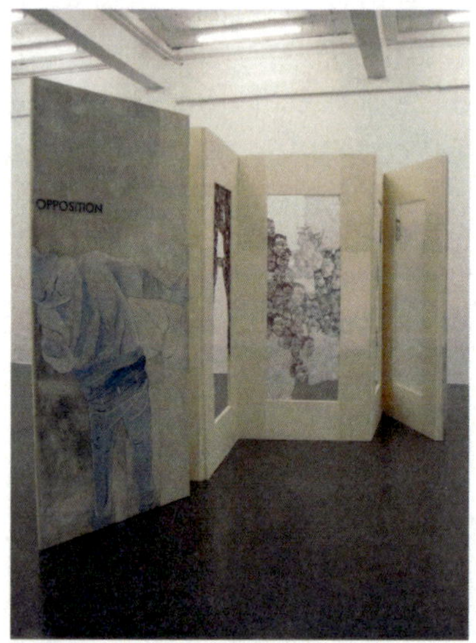


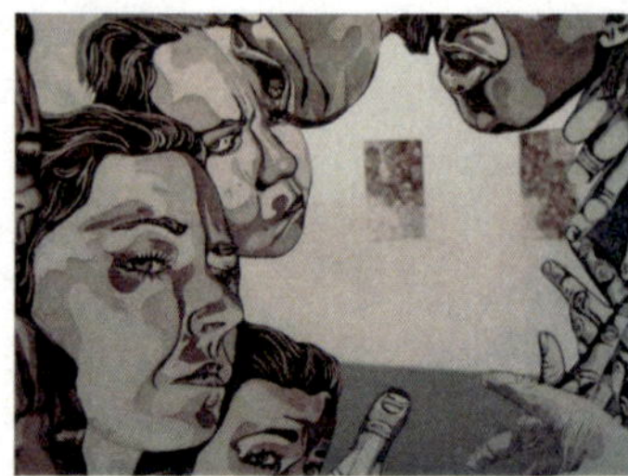

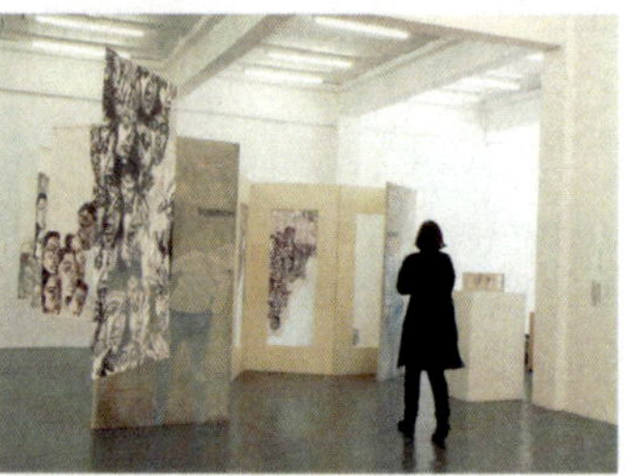

Figure 34 | Jessica Meuninck-Ganger | *Position / Opposition*, 2011 | artist book installation, 2.2 m high x 1.2m x 10m

intervened in as a continuously constituting and relational sensible concept. The video we see flows linearly in *our* time–body–space, all the while accenting its undirected traversals through *its* time-body-space. Here the smudgings of time and the landscape are composed as neither object nor concept, neither material nor category; both / and: a relation that is of both object and concept, both material and category. Watching a slow pan over an hour can feel like minutes or months or years in any given 'moment,' an en- and unfolding of the potential of time found in the seemingly subtle movements of the camera and its surroundings. The work shows continuity between body and time, and like a topological figure, coincides with its own transformation.

Jessica Meuninck-Ganger produces works on paper and participatory installations, all with narrative components, and with an understanding of narrative, storytelling, and memoir as inherently time-based. Her large-scale book art installation at GALLERY AOP in Johannesburg, South Africa, plays with the book as a material and temporal medium that asks us to move through time and space and matter as always embodied in relation. Although trained as a traditional printmaker – the first of mass media technologies co-opted by artists for interventionist means – Meuninck-Ganger, writes Max Yela, 'is not drawn to that medium in order to edition images. Rather, she prefers printmaking as an organizing process for the investigation of experiences' (Yela, 2011). More than that, I would argue that she invites us to experience and practice time and narrative as non-linear and bodily.

Over two meters high and ten meters long when open, Meuninck-Ganger's *Position / Opposition* (Figure 34) is an accordion book that we walk in and around, and are invited to fold and open and look *through* – since each of the prints is both translucent and cut apart, so as to reveal the space and people around it, the rest of the book, and the spacetimes each re-presents. Most fascinating about Meuninck-Ganger's process is that each fragmented 'print' in her installation is actually made of many, stitched-together editions from the same copper plate. The images break apart with each inking up and pressing down through the printing press, making time apparent: every smaller print in the installation's huge and porous sheets of paper is lighter and more degraded than the last. Time materializes by leaving its traces in the print, while printing manifests as something time-based. The result is that we can see and feel in each large 'page,' and the book as a whole, how time comes to matter, and how materials age, in relation to each other. And we encounter those temporal substances through and with and as each other's bodies and times in the gallery space.

My collaborations with Meuninck-Ganger combine her interests in embodied and participatory narratives, along with my approach to multidimensional and time-based images. In our *Distill Life* series, Meuninck-Ganger and I work with both old and new media as continuously mediated, conceptual–material formations. In short, we permanently mount translucent prints and drawings directly on top of video screens, creating 'moving images on paper.' We incorporate technologies and aesthetics from traditional printmaking – including woodblock, silk screen, etching, lithography, photogravure, and so on – with the technologies and aesthetics of contemporary digital, video, and networked art, to amplify images as *always* potentialized. Poten-

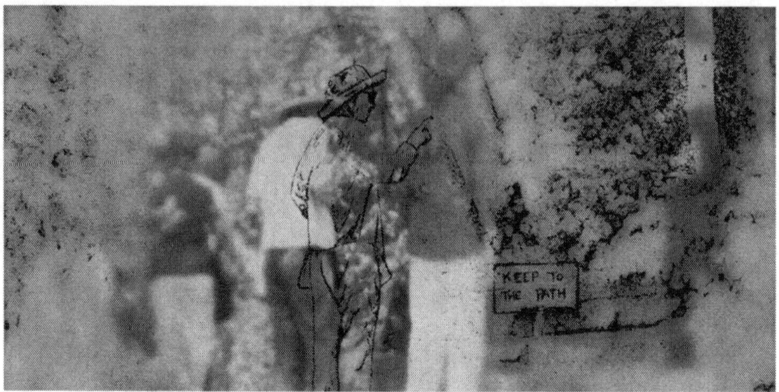


Figure 35. Jessica Meuninck-Ganger and Nathaniel Stern | *Keep to the Path*, 2009 | 11 x 14 inches, photo etching + LCD with video

tialized images re-member along with us; they embody more than we see in their frame; they potently activate cross-modal sensation, past memories, and future possibilities. While the paper prints in our work are made with stones, silk screens, inks, and copper plates, the LCD (Liquid Crystal Display) screens are store-bought and hacked digital photo frames used as assisted ready-mades to display animation, machinima, and live-captured video footage.[7] Here potentialization is doubly performed: forever looping images are overlaid with the suspension of time and space in that very same image.

Meuninck-Ganger and I use strategies from print and video to speak back to their own histories, narratives, timelines, and matters. Print artists have always been technological and referential, as well as somewhat anachronistic in their continual re-appropriation of 'dead' (what some call 'zombie') editioning tools. Many video artists, too, have a fascination with 'extendedness and repetition,' but 'change it; the phenomenology shifts from the artist to the viewer who becomes the locus of extension' (Ridgway, 2010: 2). Our juxtaposition of these disparate methods, materials, and content enables novel approaches to understanding each. Nicole Ridgway writes, the work expands 'our conception of printmaking and digital image making, while nimbly reminding us that art is always made in the margins of other art' (Ridgway, 2010: 14). In the context of the tangible-temporality thematic, I refer to a discussion I had with Erin Manning about the work.

She said these pieces emphasize the uneasiness of images with respect to this or that time and place, this or that event. The focus on the 'multidimensionality of the image gives the viewer a sense of an uncanny doubling that is always more than two – a multiplicity in the viewing' (Manning, 2010a). Manning gives *Keep to the Path* (Figure 35) – where Red Hat Society ladies continuously loop and overlap one another beneath a static black and white etching – as a case in point. 'There is a background / foregrounding of ephemerality (the trees as muted as the characters), overlaid by the drawing of a character who trembles between different layerings. This trembling gives a sense that the image cannot hold still' (Manning, 2010a), and neither can *our* sense of time and place *with* it. *Keep to the Path* is an intervention into the space-time of a straight and narrow 'path.' It literally blurs matter and time and space, and our experience and practice thereof.

Finally, inspired by conceptual and minimalist artists such as Sol LeWitt and Lawrence Wiener, new media practitioner John F. Simon, Jr. gained prominence in the late 1990s for his unlimited edition Java applet, *Every Icon* (Figure 36). In a 1999 interview, the artist calls his piece an 'activated idea' (Baumgaertel and Simon, 1999). *Every Icon* begins as a simple grid of 32 x 32 small white squares. In animated sequence, from left to right, top to bottom, each square slowly fills with every digital gradation of white-through-grey-through-black until it shows every single black and white combination of 'images' possible within its frame. It begins as an empty grid, and then at a speed of 100 variations per second, fills in the first square, then the second square, then displays all possible combinations with these two squares, and so on. Here we see white, then 253 different grays, then black, in the first square with white in the second; then white, then 253 different grays, then black, in the first square with the first level of grey in the second square; and so on, until we have every combination in the first two squares, then three squares, up until every combination of 1024 squares has been shown, each with 255 colors. In other words, Simon's artwork is a computer icon that 'basically counts forward, from 0 to 10 to the 308th power,' which, he says, is significantly larger than 'the number of atoms in the universe' (Baumgaertel and Simon, 1999). It takes about one year simply to show all possible variations on *Every*

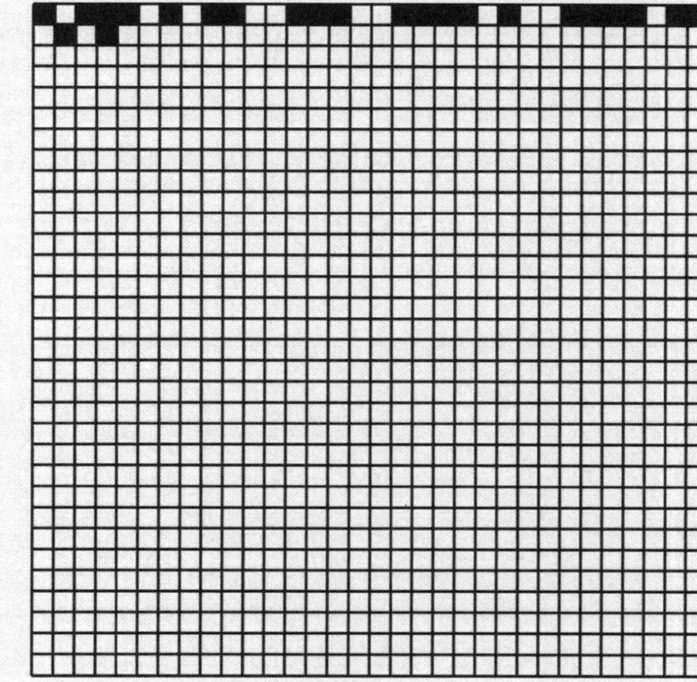


Figure 36. John F. Simon, Jr. | *Every Icon*, 1997 | Image courtesy of numeral.com

*Icon*'s first line of thirty-two squares. Simon estimates that exhibiting all combinations on the first two lines alone would take approximately six billion years. By his calculations, it would likely take several trillion years before a recognizable image emerges from the grid, and several hundred trillion years before every possible black and white icon within his confined square has been exhausted, and the icon goes completely black.

Simon's work could conceivably (and sensibly) be described as a digital manifestation of mechanical artist Arthur Ganson's kinetic sculpture, *Machine with Concrete* (1992). Ganson uses the simple engineering-based rules of gearing down from faster rotating toothed discs to slower and stronger ones in order to produce a machine that will drive a steel drill bit into a concrete block more than two trillion years in the future. In the case of both *Every Icon* and *Machine with Concrete*, the works live as their present *and* future (and past) selves, in a constant state of nearly invisible, yet extremely potent, transformation.

Simon's work, however, also lives as a potential sign – both of itself, and for everything else. At several points in time, the pixels of its grid will emerge as a legible image, for instance, the folder or hard drive icons we see on every desktop computer. At various times we might see recognizable alphanumerical characters in *Every Icon*'s matrix, or perhaps even a short text. The piece, by its very generation, references so much more than itself, both literally and metaphorically. 'In contrast to presenting a single image as an intentional sign,' Simon argues, '*Every Icon* presents all possibilities' (Simon, 1996). It presents what Troy Rhoades calls the 'Transduction of Images' from 'Representation to Sensation' (Rhoades, 2011). Here is an 'aesthetic composition of sensations', which 'generates a seeing that exceeds the limits established on the plane of reference' (Rhoades, 2011). We experience the image's potential and passage, as virtually felt rather than actually seen.

Where Ganson's sculpture presents physical time as grinding onwards, Simon's software is without physicality; it exists on a network of many machines, is performed, transformed, and sustained *only* through its image-based yet tangible movement in time. Ron Wakkary tells us that *Every Icon*'s 'value lies in the theoretical understanding of its existence to the point when it has defined its every limit and exhausted its every combination' (Wakkary, 1997). Although we will never experience that time, we can *feel* it, feel that potency of several hundred trillion years. The piece promises more than it could ever deliver – can you imagine a computer server running that long? – but we experience the work in the space of that 'more than.' In other words, *Every Icon* performatively creates a life and a body; it gives both the corporeal and incorporeal a present and future presence as time and sign, by continuously living in the potential of what they might become. It also foreshadows the final thematic of the book, which studies networked art as substantiating.

The works presented in this section all intervene in the mutual immanence of time and body / materiality. They call attention to both the sensual and conceptual experience of temporality, and bring to bear how we, as matter and as bodies, perform with, generate, and are in some ways generated by, 'timing' as smudged, rhythmic, and syncopated.

## 'Virtual-Performance'

The virtual-performance thematic puns on and refers to the more everyday usage of the word virtual than that used in the rest of this book. It is intended for art that is on, or makes use of, the Internet. It examines interactive and / or potentialized works which intervene in the relational emergence of bodies and / or materiality along with telecommunications systems.[8] This section briefly describes and unpacks artist collaborative MTAA's *1 year performance video* (2004), Hans Gindlesberger's *Westering* (2009), Scott Kildall and Victoria Scott's *No Matter* (2008), and my collaborative project with Scott Kildall, *Wikipedia Art* (2009). I close with my own *Given Time* (2010). Each of these artworks is produced, transformed, and / or remade via implicit and explicit connections in the virtual space of the Internet.

The Brooklyn, New York-based collaborative art duo, MTAA, was founded with some early network-based art in 1996. While the art-

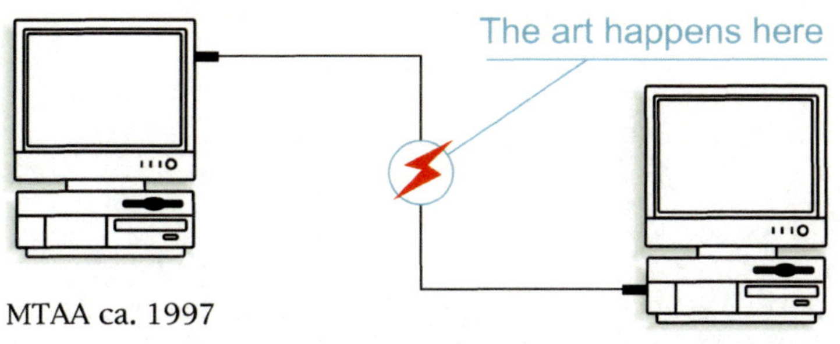


Figure 37. MTAA | *Simple Net Art Diagram*, 1997

ists' real names are Michael Sarff and Tim Whidden, their aliases and naming mechanisms – M.River & T.Whid Art Associates, or MTAA – reveal the tongue-in-cheek attitude with which they approach art's conceptual and commercial frames. The associates produce works that perform and examine the culture, materials, economics, and politics of art and the digital, through networked and real-world prints, sculptures, performances, and installations. MTAA is part of both the first generation of artists working with code online in the late 1990s and early 2000s, as well as in consistent dialogue with – and extremely influential on – the sometimes referred to as 'Post-net art' or 'Net Art 2.0' (Whidden, 2008) artists that now use online tools such as YouTube, Tumblr, Google, Twitter and / or Facebook towards artistic ends. One of their most well-known pieces is *Simple Net Art Diagram* (1997, Figure 37), which literalizes the connectivity-based existence of networked art. Here the art 'happens,' as a flashing red lightning bolt, between / with computers, bodies, systems, electronics, ideas, and networks of networks. It is a corpus. This piece has been referenced and re-mixed as part of many other artworks, and in the title of several press pieces and shows, throughout the world for more than a decade and half. In many ways, it represents not only MTAA's practice, but the fundamental ideas behind virtual-performance as well. Ultimately, Internet art, like embodiment and the network itself, is of the relation.

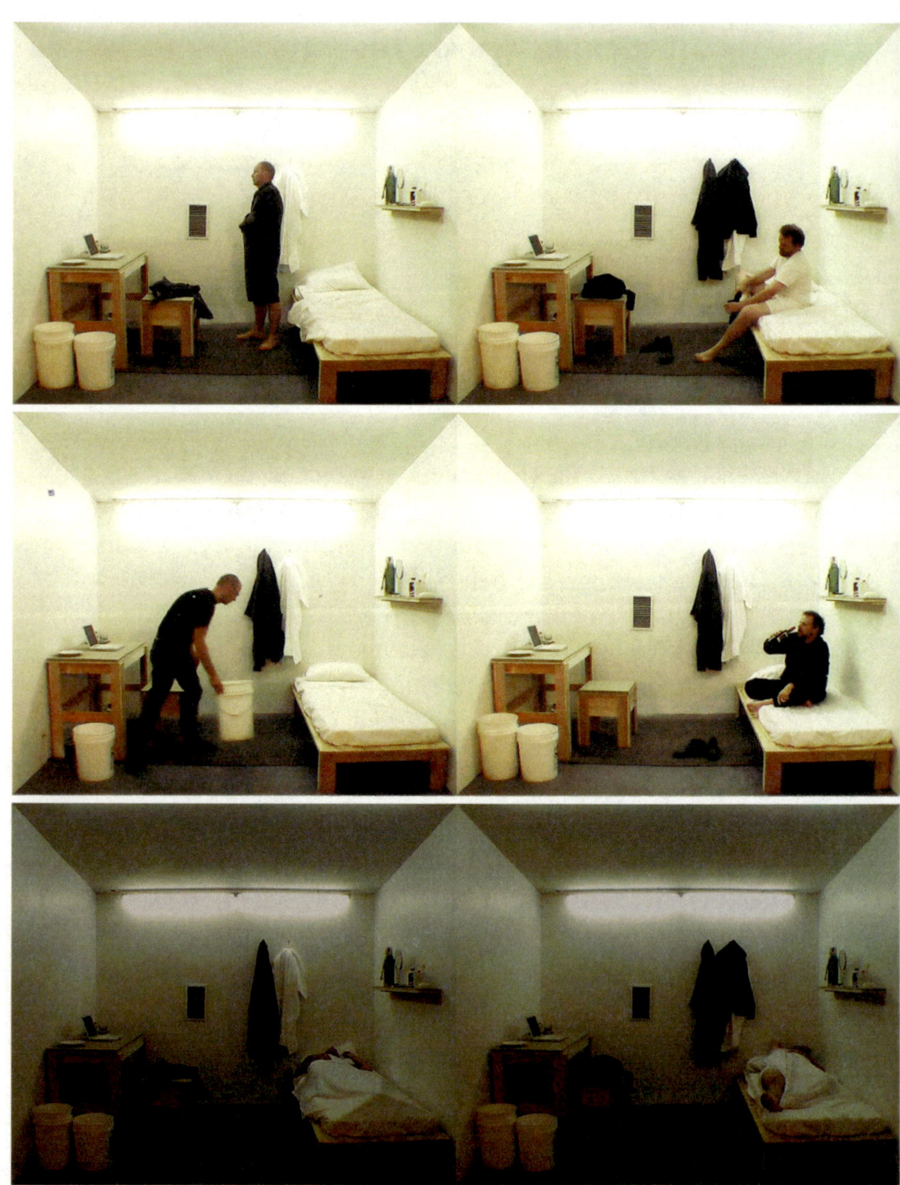

Figure 38. MTAA | *1 year performance video (aka samHsiehUpdate)*, 2004 | commissioned by *Turbulence.org*

Within MTAA's long list of works are several ongoing themes and trajectories, a number of which are explored in their continuing *Updates Series*. MTAA's *Updates* re-make pioneering performance artworks from the 1960s and 1970s, but use computer programs to replace much of the human activity from the originals. For example, since 1966, Japanese conceptual artist On Kawara has made a series of 'date paintings' (called the *Today* series), each of which sees Kawara paint the date of execution – the date he makes the painting – in simplistic white lettering over a solid black background. MTAA's *onKawaraUpdate (v2)* (2007) replaces Kawara's decades-long devotion with an automated script: software that simply writes the date, white on black, in your web browser. Time and material are re-membered first as relational by Kawara, and then as generative via MTAA.

MTAA's 2004 *Turbulence.org* commission, *1 year performance video (aka samHsiehUpdate)* (Figure 38) resounds Tehching 'Sam' Hsieh's *One Year Performance 1978–1979* (also known simply as *The Cage Piece*) in a similar way. In the original work, Hsieh first shaved his head, then locked himself in an 11.5 by nine by eight foot barred cell in his studio on September 30, 1978. He disallowed himself from talking, reading, writing, listening to the radio, or watching TV for an entire year. He wore a simple, white uniform with his name and the dates of the performance on it, and had his food, water, and clothing brought to the cage, his waste removed. Hsieh invited an audience into the piece through open viewings of his cell and ongoing, daily photographs that documented his actions. These photographs showed the artist relaxing in bed or going to the bathroom, and had the tangential benefit of serially showing him go from completely hairless to bearded and long-haired.

> After three months of contemplating his existence, Hsieh began to look for faces in shadows, watch insects with intense fascination and pace the length of the cage. Thinking became the art. He imagined his bed in the corner as the confines of the cage and the rest of the enclosed space as outdoors. A daily scratch on the wall marked the time he had survived and the days remaining. (Laster, 2008)

Hsieh performs time with his own body, and turns it into a conceptual work – a framework for conceptually sensing the world.

In MTAA's *Update,* they do not actually live in a cell, but rather created a database of video images where they perform themselves living in a cell (their studio). When viewers call up the *1 year performance video* website, these pre-made clips are dynamically pulled from the server and edited together within their Internet browser window, so each sees a slightly different portrayal of the life of MTAA. The clips are organized in the database by time of day, and so the clock on any individual viewer's computer will tell the art software to grab video of a time-appropriate activity: at night they may be sleeping; in the morning, they could be tapping their feet or making their beds, etc. Viewers become ongoing participants in the work by signing up for a username and password, and the work /website will log all the time they have spent actually watching M.River and T.Whid in their studio. After one year of viewing time by the participant has been logged – not one year from their first log in – dedicated watchers are rewarded: they get to view a final video only seen by those who have watched for one year (perhaps someone unlocking MTAA from their cells? I have no idea), as well as a downloadable copy of their unique, one-year, online viewing data in XML format (Extensible Markup Language). This data is simply a playlist, in order, of the video files watched by the viewer in question. It looks something like this (only much longer):

```
<playlist>
<video url='vid/twhid/anytime/exercise/twhid_exercise03.flv'/>
<video url='vid/twhid/anytime/bed_stare/twhid_bedstare01.flv'/>
<video url='vid/twhid/2afternoon/lunch/twhid_lunch02.flv'/>
<video url='vid/twhid/anytime/randomfill/twhid_randomfill03.flv'/>
</playlist>
```

According to the artists, this data serves as a collectible companion artwork, where each is numbered as if it were a limited edition object, based on the number of one-year viewers that came before.

MTAA assert that with *1 year performance video* they are asking viewers to commit one year of their life, rather than sacrificing themselves. And they in fact publicly doubted anyone would do so. The artists thus 'mimic endurance without doing the labor,' speaking back to 'how our society, culture, and the creative process has changed since [Hsieh's] original was created' (MTAA, 2004). Whereas Hsieh's original 'was notarized by a lawyer to give it authenticity,' MTAA are completely transparent about the fact that their *Update* is a total fabrication (Navas, 2005). Even the determined audience member, who is now responsible for the *1 year performance,* can log in, leave their browser running, and walk away. As M.River puts it, 'No one needs to suffer on this one. The failure is built-in at the front end' (MTAA, 2004). Interestingly, and despite this 'failure,' MTAA underestimated either the fascination people would have with their work, or the commitment of the general viewing public itself; as of July 2013, 28 audience members had logged watching the MTAA videos for over one year, and several others are very close.

Most readings of *1 Year Performance Video,* such as the one by Eduardo Navas of *netartreview.net,* concentrate on the how much the art world, and arts production, have changed since Hsieh's initial work. In Hsieh's time, the art object was in question, and performance and conceptual artists were instead attributing value to cultural production and ideas. While MTAA's practice also places value on the conceptual frame of their work, Hsieh had to give up his life for an entire year. Even if not considered 'suffering' per se, Navas points out that this would be nearly impossible in most present-day economies, where an artist's studio practice is not considered 'work.' Navas argues that there are very few artists, if any, who could make this kind of monetary / temporal commitment even once, much less several times, as Hsieh has done.

Navas' sociopolitical reading says that MTAA point to, and flip over, the monetary and temporal commitment of a one-year performance. Online 'users' are asked to perform that which is virtually implausible (pun intended), 'not passively but actively' – at least in their decision to use their network and computer – and this inversion 'exposes the role of the audience in any work of art' (Navas, 2005). *1 year performance video* might also be read through the body-language thematic, with a focus on the emergent signs performed through MTAA's dynamic video clips; through tangible-temporality, where the work and

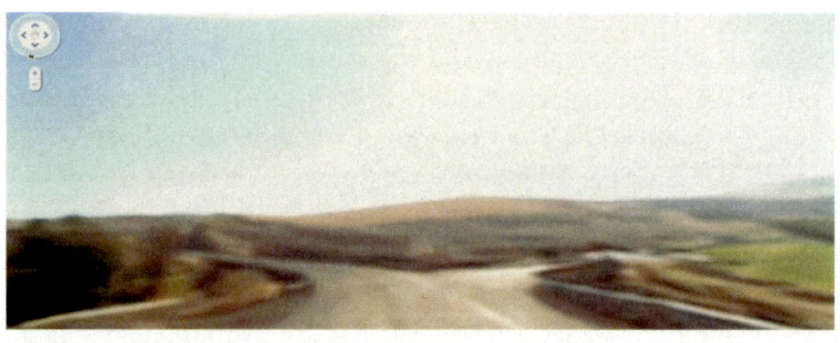

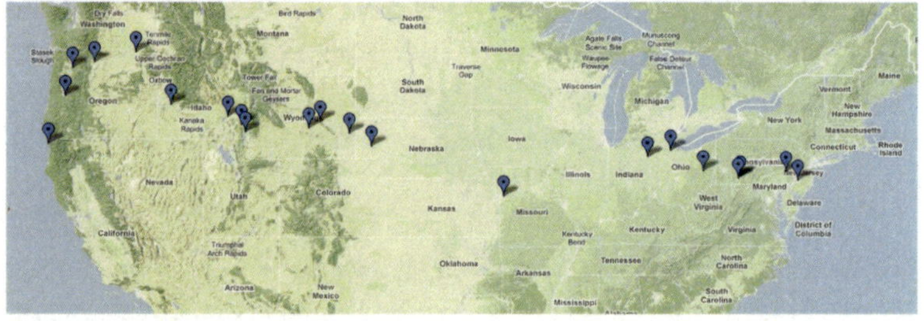


Figure 39. Hans Gindlesberger I *Westering*, 2009 I Still frame excerpt and Google Map with markers outlining the cross-country route

audience and artists are refigured as continuously embodied through the time they spend inaugurating a kind of mutual immanence; or, as is done here, a virtual-performance thematic, which suggests that the work of the artists and audience (whether time- or Internet-based) are continuously embodying and transforming one another, through a relationship that exists both on and of the network, as well as in the physical world.

Here *1 year performance video* shifts in its instantiation both as any given viewer watches the dynamically compiled videos, and as more audience members complete the one year time frame. Said viewers' embodied relationships to their computer and the Internet continuously move the relation: as they leave their computers running over time, no longer shutting down or putting them to sleep as part of their daily routine; as they regularly sneak glances at the slowly incrementing clock crawling towards one year; as they sit back and watch their computers at a distance rather than utilizing them as productive work tools. With *1 year performance video,* the online and fragmented connection *is* the per-formance, *is* the potential, and *is* the improbable and unnecessary and – in the vast majority of cases – unfulfilled time it takes to complete itself. The piece ironically strips the artwork's world of bodies: gone are the artists whose software generatively resounds Hsieh's original, and gone are the viewers who log on to the site, then go off to work, or to watch television, or to have a beer. And so it is the network, the virtual relationship between these tele-absent entities, the potency of uploading Flash files (MTAA) or logging in to the site (the audience) and performatively committing to exactly nothing, that gives the work its matter. Here there is no 'explicit body' in the everyday sense of the word; the work exists only through its implications. *1 year performance video* becomes a topological figure of disembodied relationships, network activity, and time – an absent yet implicit body made only of connections, of its relationality.

Hans Gindlesberger's *Westering* (Figure 39), too, potentializes actual space while giving a virtual intensity to the network and networked relations. Here the artist mapped out his own family's migration 'from the Port of Philadelphia to the American Midwest, continuing westward on the original coast-to-coast roadway, the Old Lincoln Highway, following on to parts of the pioneering Oregon Trail, and extending to the Pacific Ocean in California' (Gindlesberger, 2009). But rather than traveling along and shooting this path with a camera – Gindlesberger's training and academic position are as a photographic artist – he produced a fifty-minute video by manually traversing Google Street View across its online version of the USA, removing all the photographed images, and instead only showing the interpolated movements, the computer generated animations or fades or whatever we might call them, between each photo and a point in the distant horizon. Gindlesberger edited out all the static and 'real' moments shot by Google's cameras to make visible the blurry, virtual, and potently actualizing movements of a digitally interpolated great migration westward. It is not real movement, but movement potential: movement that is *only* calculated, animated, and seen, but voluminous nonetheless. Here the artist conflates his family's history, the broader American history, and now Google's version of present, past, and future, as always potentialized and in relation to each other. *Westering* is a performative memorial that defies nostalgia by exploring complex ideas of space, our place within it, and how it is mediated and formed through continuous encounters, human and otherwise.

Scott Kildall and Victoria Scott's *No Matter* (Figure 40), another *Turbulence.org* commission, plays with irony and materiality via the network; but rather than stripping bodies from all sides of our telecommunications wires, or showing simulated movement, they give flesh to conceptual and data-based online artworks. Here they take what they call imagined objects – things created and maintained only in myths and stories – produce them in the virtual space of the Internet, and remake these 'soft' objects with physical materials.

More broadly in his work, Kildall attempts to collapse relationships between 'producer and consumer, viewer and viewed and simulated and real' (Kildall, 2008). Some of his most well-known artworks take place in the virtual, networked, 3D environment and community, *Second Life*. This is a fairly open software and population, where anyone can join for free, then log in to construct personal avatars, landscapes and buildings. *Second Life* members (called 'residents') engage in online correspondence based on real-life, ranging from sexual or platonic relationships to academic lectures or panel discussions. Residents – there are more than 20 million registered users and one million active users, with more than 50,000 logged in and 'in-world' at any given moment – go clubbing, purchase land and homes and art, and can convert money from real-world currency to *Second Life*'s 'Linden dollars,' and back again.

Despite their attempts to ape reality, Kildall claims an interest in simulated worlds because of where they fail. He is interested in the layers of socialization and materialization that both converge with and diverge from our real-world experiences. He wants us to examine how we 'relate to the dissonances in the simulated – whether it is as a viewer, performer or active participant' (Kildall and Quaranta, 2007). *Second Life* is a simulated physical space, but a very real social one, where you can engage as a semi-anonymous individual – and Kildall finds this to be fertile artistic ground. Kildall's interests contain echoes of socially participatory work akin to relational aesthetics, but his concentration on technology, especially the putatively immaterial and avatar-based world of *Second Life*, make him a fascinating case study with the implicit body approach.

Kildall is, for example, a founding member of *Second Front* (2006 and ongoing), an avatar-based performance art group in *Second Life*. *Second Front*'s various members have taken on a platform whose medium is traditionally the body (performance art), and instead use supposedly disembodied and conceptual code to explore meaning and performance in the datascape. They ironically ask where and how per-formed meaning might be found *without* a body. Kildall's *Paradise Ahead* (2006–7) contains echoes of MTAA's work, but rather than resounding *Updates* where the *work* is done by technology, he 'remediate[s] iconic performances' with computer avatars, blurring 'the line between document and event,' creating art that is virtual and virtualized in both senses of the word (Kildall, 2007).[9] These works intervene in the original performances they recreate – the embodied artists' works – *and* the iconic images such performances have become for the art world. Even most scholars and lifetime appreciators of performance art never saw the first instantiation of Bueys and his coyote, and certainly not Klein's staged *Leap into the Void*. We only know them through their famous photographs, which Kildall recreates in *Second Life*.

Victoria Scott's work concentrates on visualizing 'social and psychological states' through 'large-scale installations, objects, prints and audio works' (Scott, 2007), though her recent art with Kildall has brought such pieces into, or through, digital environments. *No Matter* is Scott's first foray into *Second Life*, and potentialized art. She and Kildall basically produce an installation of 'imaginary objects,' for display in both *Second Life* and a real world gallery. First, the pair publicly invited proposals for commissioned fairytale sculptures to be constructed in *Second Life*. They asked for *Second Life* builders, architects, and coders to create 3D works that 'appear repeatedly in myth [and] literature, in thought experiments, popular culture and as placeholder objects in language' (Kildall and Scott, 2008). In this call, they listed items like the 'Holy Grail, Time Machine or Schrödinger's Cat,' none of which exist in the material world, except as replicas with no original. The objects, Kildall and Scott maintain, 'embody the tension between the ideal and real' (Kildall and Scott, 2008).

Their commissioned constructs are displayed in a virtual gallery in *Second Life* so that resident avatars 'can climb inside the Trojan Horse, open Pandora's Box and teleport through a Portable Hole' (Kildall and Scott, 2008). But *Second Life*, the artists say, already traffics in objects that are, to some extent, imaginary. Although many of them are based on real-life (to *Second Life* residents, 'RL') counterparts, they exist exclusively in that virtual space, and cannot be exported. In the second phase of *No Matter*, Kildall and Scott 'smuggle' out the *Second Life* objects 'as digital plunder, amassing them into a real life trophy room of ontological treasures' (Kildall and Scott, 2008). This 'smuggling' was accomplished by running software on the *Second Life* primitive three-dimensional forms to turn them into flat paper patterns, which were printed and folded into models for display on fake wooden plinths in a traditional gallery space in the physical world. Their virtual re-

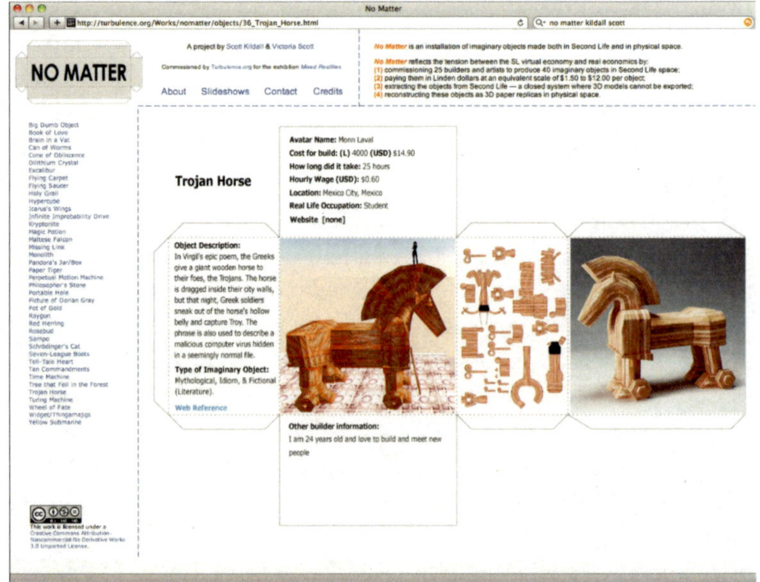


Figure 40. Scott Kildall and Victoria Scott | *No Matter*, 2008 | commissioned by *Turbulence.org*

making of objects that were never really there, and the opportunity to view them in both real and virtual space, is yet another gesture towards rethinking materiality and relationality. In phase three, a website 'ties these two worlds together as a catalog of economic relations and study of value' (Kildall and Scott, 2008). Here the commissioned *Second Life* builders are listed alongside documentation of their *Second Life* objects, paper patterns, and RL counterparts, as well as what Kildall and Scott paid the workers for their labor.

These potentialized 'objects,' which are never exactly objects, emerge from both the real and the virtual, through an active and relational engagement with each. The *Second Life* builders perform their virtual matters and materializings from in front of their computer screens, which are then purchased by Kildall and Scott, and performed again through software, printing, and literally folded formations. Bodies and avatars, real and virtual flesh and material and data, are all wrapped up in a series of networked and imaginary 'things,' and then exhibited as all that potential, always, across the three spaces of *Second Life*, real life, and a website. The seemingly arbitrary monetary values attributed to these imaginary objects online are contrasted with the amount of work-time contributed by their participant builders, and with what that work translates into when it is itself translated from the imagined to the real world. Just like financial currency, the imaginary 'stuff' of *No Matter*, really does matter. These 'objects' act 'as symbolic containers with little inherent worth embedded in the material itself' (Kildall and Scott, 2008), and so intervene in and challenge the sociopolitical spaces substantiated through our supposedly insubstantial online relations. Here construction and constitution are virtually valued and actually per-formed.

Kildall and I have also produced a collaborative virtual-performance, where we intervene in *Wikipedia*, the 'free encyclopedia that anyone can edit,' to challenge knowledge and power in the Information Age. Our goal was to highlight and suspend the continuous yet questionable relationships between 'virtual' epistemology and / with 'actual' empiricism. *Wikipedia Art* is a text-based artwork composed on *Wikipedia*, and is thus art that anyone can edit. It manifests as a standard page on *Wikipedia* – entitled *Wikipedia Art* – and like all

*Wikipedia* entries, anyone can alter this page as long as their alterations meet *Wikipedia*'s standards of quality and verifiability: the modifications must reference information from other 'credible' sources. Here a feedback loop between the necessary external blog articles, interviews, and press, and internal, *Wikipedia*-based, discussions and citations, ontogenetically make and remake a work of art. As a consequence of outsider writings and insider agreed-upon edits to the page, *Wikipedia Art*, itself, is collaboratively transformed. We playfully call this ongoing social inter-activity 'performative citations.'

On 14 February 2009, Kildall and I published a two-way interview about *Wikipedia Art* on the once popular emerging artist website, *MyArtSpace.com* – with the help of their editor, Brian Sherwin. Five seconds later, we birthed an entry by the same name on *Wikipedia*, citing that very interview as a credible and verifiable source of knowledge / information. The aforementioned interview avows that our work 'intervenes in Wikipedia as a venue in the contemporary construction of knowledge and information, and simultaneously intervenes in our understandings of art and the art object' (Sherwin et al., 2009). Kildall and I request writers and editors to join in the 'collaboration and construction, the transformation, the destruction and the resurrection' of the work; we want our 'intervention to be intervened in' (Sherwin et al., 2009). Like 'knowledge and like art, *Wikipedia Art* is always already variable' (Sherwin et al., 2009).

As suspected, the *Wikipedia Art* entry on *Wikipedia* did not survive; it lasted only 15 hours (and the Wikimedia Foundation, owners of the Wikipedia trademark, later threatened litigation in an attempt to shut down the archive of the project at wikipediaart.org). But during and after that time, there has been extensive writing about the work, making it a continuous performance after all. According to new media arts professor Shane Mecklenburger:

> The *Wikipedia Art* page is a self-aware exploration of Wikipedia's mission of collective epistemology. It enacts and describes Wikipedia's strengths, weaknesses, potential, and limits as both a system of understanding and as a contemplative object of beauty. It demonstrates how a Wikipedia page can transcend the medium of Wikipedia while

> retaining its basic utilitarian Wikipedia function. The page is similarly a self-aware example of the strengths, weaknesses, potential, and limits of new media art. (Mecklenberger, 2009)

At their limits or boundaries, *Wikipedia* and *Wikipedia Art* are self-referential topological figures that feed back between everyday and philosophical notions of actual and virtual, fact and fiction, narrative and knowledge.

Interestingly and as alluded to by Mecklenburger, it is in the new media art blogosphere, and later in the mainstream press – and not on *Wikipedia* – where most of the piece's transformation takes place. While the multi-paged 'deletion debates' on *Wikipedia,* between 14–16 February 2009 (and again when a third party added it back to the site in March), discussed the merits and flaws of the project as an encyclopedic entry,[10] the art world moreover discusses what the project is, how it forms, what that means, and who says so. According to digital artist and theorist Curt Cloninger, such debates were '"policing" the "art-worthiness" of the piece ... the same way the wikipedians were policing its "encyclopedia-worthiness"' (Rhizome Discussion Thread, 2009a). And *Wikipedia Art,* he goes on, is 'conceptually porous enough' to 'absorb' these 'unexpected propagations' as a 'life' (Rhizome Discussion Thread, 2009a). It is through these very discussions that the piece forms, changes, and matters.

Paul Wehage's description of *Wikipedia Art* on *Akahele.org* explains that Kildall and I are 'reflecting the bureaucratic structure and highly ritualized practices' of *Wikipedia* 'back to the very society that has created them' (Wehage, 2009). Here interrelated social practices per-form systems, which per-form practices (a social-anatomy). On *Furtherfield.org,* maker and scholar Patrick Lichty states that the 'work is open to repetitive writing and re-writing to the point where it is possible that the only remnant is the gesture' and practice of writing itself (Lichty, 2009). While Kildall and I are the progenitors of the form, he goes on, 'the destination of the vector is by no means assured.' *Wikipedia Art*'s 'indeterminacy makes it largely conceptual, and slippery at best, making it a strong relative of networked conceptualism or highly formal online media art' (Lichty, 2009). He highlights the piece's collaborative *and* generative mattering.

Cloninger furthers Lichty's argument in another post by claiming that *Wikipedia Art* utilizes / is:

> a form of resistant / tactical media, but one not afraid to co-opt and implement corporate consumer strategies. It is simultaneously subversive and overt. It is fluid enough to have discrete manifestations in offline galleries, to take on non-'new media' forms, to assume the form of critical essays, books, and talks. It is basically a project of ongoing, widely-dispersed, inflected language. (Rhizome Discussion Thread, 2009b)

Cloninger was very forward thinking here. Since this post, the piece has appeared, virtually and physically, as every one of these forms and more: as essays, articles, lectures, and chapters across academic and popular literature, as performances, prints, videos, and installations in galleries, museums, and festivals across Europe, Africa, and the Americas. While it began as inflected language, its wide dispersion and ongoing movements make it a topological and socially networked formation. It performs and transforms, continuously becomes (a) material, through its relation to people and ideas and forces on- and offline.

Artist Pall Thayer gives a temporal context for *Wikipedia Art,* and thinks of it as permanently virtualized through its deletion. He argues that 'Art is always strictly tied to the time and culture from whence it came' (Rhizome Discussion Thread, 2009b). Perhaps for this very reason, 'it was best that *Wikipedia Art* was deleted.' Rather than forever being changed, and perhaps diluted, in its ongoing-ness, *Wikipedia Art* 'gets to live on as a reference point to the time and culture that created it' (Rhizome Discussion Thread, 2009b). In other words, *Wikipedia Art* lives on because of its death; it is permanently inscribed in collective memory precisely because its incorporation, as with all incorporating practices, was *contextually per-formed.* It was made, and re-made, and continues to live through its death, as a potentialized, re-iterated, re-written, and re-made work of art. Like Jean-Luc Nancy says of the body in writing, English artist Helen Jamieson believes 'the ghost of *Wikipedia Art* is bound to haunt the web for some time yet' (Rhizome Discussion Thread, 2009b).

MTAA, Gindlesberger, Kildall and Scott, and Kildall and I all use the network to intervene in, birth, or transform relations, ideas, and materiality both online and in the physical world. The artworks discussed here have been shown to re-present and make sense of Internet-based relationships, amplifying virtual bodies, and suspending matter's virtuality. And the implicit / potentialized art readings throughout this chapter accent and extend how we might encounter emergence and relationality, with materialization and embodiment, more generally. They bring to light how art can play with the tensions between the per-formed and pre-formed, and help us to experience, practice, question, and understand media and the bodies that make them, bodies and the media that make them.

## In Closing: Given Time

The theorization of potentialized art, works that are doubly performed through mediation / production and experience / practice, offers 'other' conceptual and material possibilities for understanding more traditional art forms. Overall, these studies – in fact all the case studies written for this book – only begin to address the vast academic and artistic possibilities for encountering, rehearsing, and understanding affection and reflection in the gallery space. But in doing so, they both propose and model an approach for continuing such research into the future.

This future lies across many applications; I will put forward three possibilities. First and foremost, as is its intention, the framework can be utilized in more case studies of artwork. Each study would serve towards a better understanding of what is at stake in interactive and potentialized art (both at large and in any individual work), as well as refining the framework itself. I foresee possibilities, for example, in art exhibitions and catalogs, themed conference panels and journals, that aim to incorporate and unpack an implicit body approach into their works and texts. Some well-known interactive artists worthy of examination but not mentioned in this book include Lynn Hershman Leeson, Liz Phillips, Yael Kanarek, and Ken Rinaldo to name four. In the field of potentialized art, the works of Olafur Eliasson, Anne Hamilton, Bill Viola, and Miranda July could provide exemplary studies. And perhaps most importantly, there are a large number of extremely talented emerging artists, theorists, writers, and curators, working across different spaces of resistance and new genres, who could be studied and engaged with. They participate in cutting edge online and worldwide communities, such as *Turbulence.org, CRUMB* (the Curatorial Resource for Upstart Media Bliss), *Rhizome,* and *Furtherfield*. These communities have much to offer to, and to gain from, an ongoing corpus of implications.

Second, although perhaps not completely separate, I foresee a growing number of thematics offered for the framework at large. While this book has put forward body-language, social-anatomies, flesh-space, vestigial-vision, tangible-temporality, and virtual-performance, I doubt the list could ever be exhausted. Vestigial-vision, for example, addresses only one mode of perception as emergent in relation with the process of embodiment. In addition to listing the other four exteroceptive modes (touch, taste, smell, sound), there are possibilities for reading an emergent and affective proprioception, as well as interoception. Here the process of embodiment, and its perceptual and constitutional activities with its own insides and outsides, could make for a fascinating study. Or, rather than being limited to broad notions of an emergent 'technology' with the body (Ihde, Hayles) or even technology's 'evolution' with the body (Hansen), one could be more precise: biology, chemistry, analog electronics, or digital media, for instance, could *each* be examined (or broken down further still) as incipient sensible concepts that emerge with the body. As is the case with all previous thematics, the specificity of the inter-action and relation is key to its experience and rehearsal.

And third is the possibility – and need – for all of the above to feed into artistic inquiry and practice. As an example, I conclude this book in a very non-traditional way – with my own artist statement for a new work, completed just as I finished the first draft of the manuscript in 2010. My piece, entitled *Given Time* (Figure 41), amplifies most of

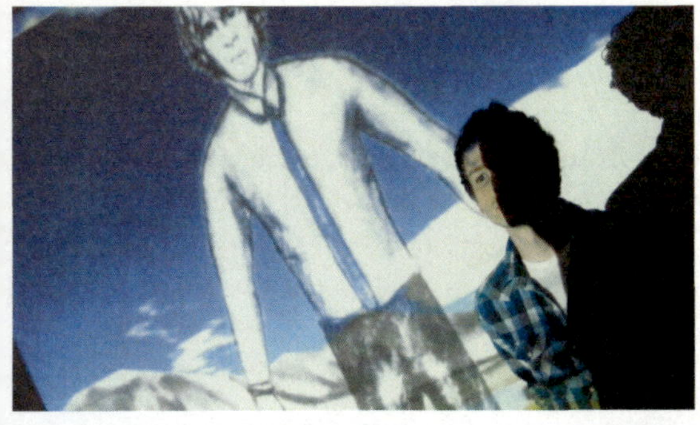
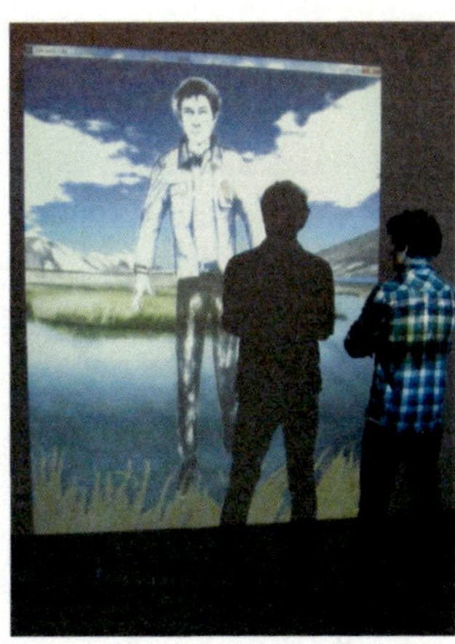
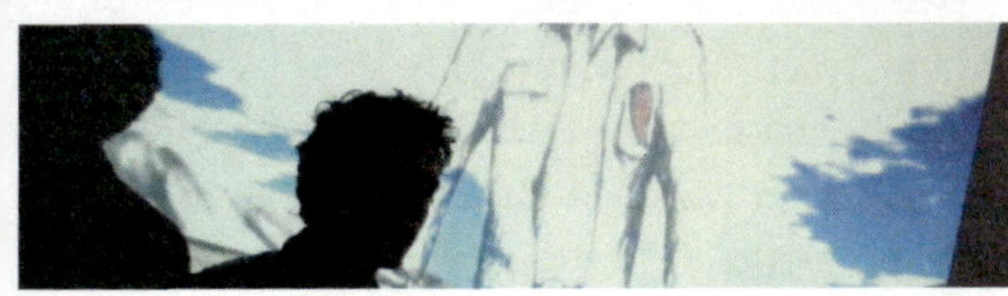
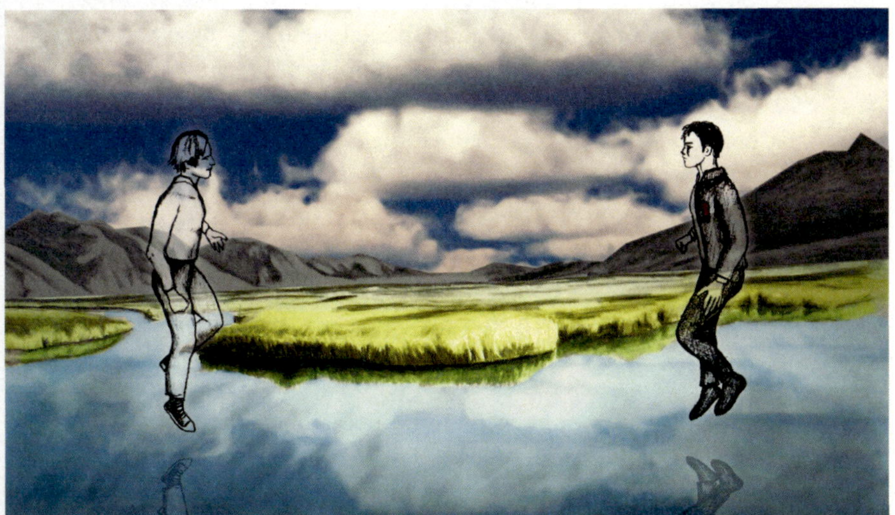
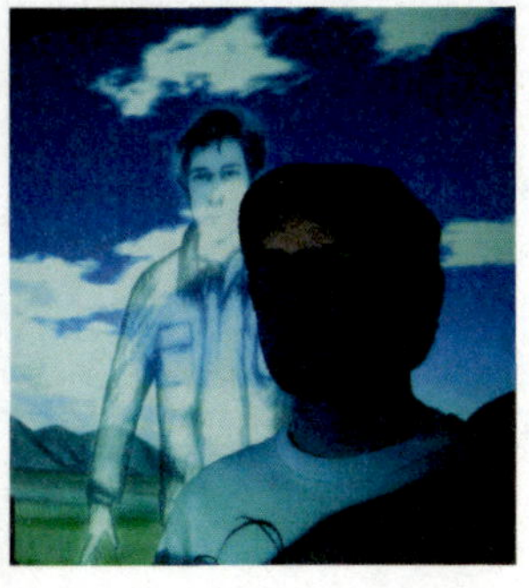
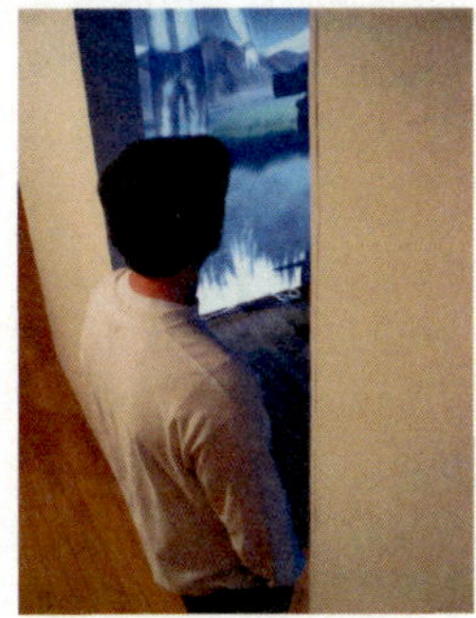
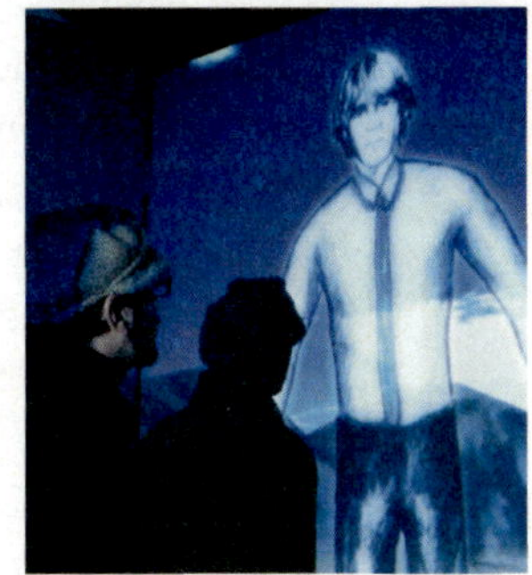

Figure 41. Nathaniel Stern | *Given Time*, 2010

the sensible concepts discussed in this book (and more); it speaks back to the discourses surrounding embodiment and relationality; and it is a performed and potentialized artwork that lives both on the network and in physical space.

*****

*Given Time* simultaneously activates and performs two permanently logged-in *Second Life* avatars, each forever and only seen by and through the other. They hover in mid-air, almost completely still, gazing into one another's interface. Viewers encounter this networked partnership as a diptych of large-scale and facing video projections in a real world gallery, both exhibiting a live view of one avatar, as perceived by the other. To create a visceral aesthetic, these custom-designed and life-sized 'bodies' are hand-drawn in subtly animated charcoal, graphite, and pastel. The audience is invited to physically walk between them; they are able to hear and see them breathing, witness their hair blowing in the wind, pick up faint sounds such as rushing water or birds crying out from the surrounding simulated environment. Here, an intimate exchange between dual, virtual bodies is transformed into a public meditation on human relationships, bodily mortality, and time's inevitable flow.

*Second Life* is a 3D social network accessed exclusively by logging in as a representational character. Real life 'residents' experience *Second Life* through a computer game-like first-person interface, and are seen by others as human-like forms. Every avatar in *Second Life*'s virtual buildings and streets has a corresponding person somewhere in the physical world. There is no entry to *Second Life* without a user, computer, and avatar; we perceive, act, activate, and are activated through our virtual interactions with its residents. In *Given Time,* however, there are no users, and the *Second Life* 'in-world' location is not made available. These avatars are realized only through each other and their publicly shared installation and engagement, incarnated through a feedback loop across virtual and actual space.

Although *Given Time* invests in and points to relationships, embodiment, and time, it attempts to render them all 'im-material.' While

*Second Life* suggests people behind every avatar, these performers are precisely no one and no-body; the time and space in which they unfold does not actually exist, except as part of a networked computer software held loosely together by intangible encounters. While the computers and projections sit side by side in the real world, and the avatars face one another in *Second Life*'s imagined world, they are only 'there' as electrical pulses sent through, potentially, thousands of miles of telecommunications wires that circle the globe. It is a meeting between ever-present entities that are also not-there until we give them our eyes and our flesh. We, the viewers, act as their real-world and material avatars, giving life to the space between them.

*Given Time*'s minimal aesthetic and avatar-driven partnership is not dissimilar to Felix Gonzales-Torres' slowly dying battery-operated clocks in *Untitled (Perfect Lovers)* (1991). But this piece does not ask us to reflect on private grief or public yearning, on loss, death, or desire. Instead, it asks, 'When we have already given everything – our desires, bodies, and time – what, then, is left to give?' It is a tension, hovering in the air, tracing the invisible and untouchable connection that is no-thing and every-thing. All it can give is the reciprocity between its actors.

*****

A vital part of *Given Time*, which premiered at Greylock Arts in Massachusetts (curated by Jo-Anne Green of *Turbulence.org*) and has since been shown at Furtherfield Gallery in London, is that the avatars each have identical, dedicated computers, logged in as permanently as possible. They are forced to log out when *Second Life* or the Internet are down, or when the installation is moved, and I, the gallerist, curator, or someone at the exhibition space needs to log them each back in. Although it is a rare occurrence, here the element of time, the limits of technology, and the much-needed performance of those who are invested in and will take care of the avatars – both in Real Life and *Second Life* – are very much a part of the ongoing performance and installation. Bodies and network, space and time, society and structure, person and people, all conceptually sense, experience, and practice their continuous and mutually implicated relation. Given time, art viewers can see and feel this. It is an art philosophy, in practice.

I would like to close by unequivocally stating that the stakes for digital and interactive art are paramount. We per-form our bodies and media, our material and conceptual frames and selves. We continuously trans-form what we are through what we do and how we move–think–feel – intensively and extensively, virtually and actually, and always in relation. Exterior and interior forces perpetually fold in on each other, all moving and thinking and feeling, constituting both us, and the materials, ideas, and habitats around us. We must therefore affect a doubled agency in how we take account of and engage with our surroundings, both human and non-human. New media art, at its very best, sets a stage for the experience and practice of that performance, transformation, and agency.

## Notes

1 A more in-depth reading of my (interactive) work is in the companion chapter at http://stern.networkedbook.org

2 Also see Volker Morawe and Tilman Reiff's *Pain Station* (2002–3; http://www.painstation.de). This is a pong-like two-player (interactive) game that electrocutes its players in real-time when they do poorly.

3 Another interesting (and participatory) work that uses scanners to create dynamic images is Joachim Blank and Karl Heinz Jeron's *Scanner++*, a real-time installation that scans from below a glass bottom room (Blank and Jeron, 2007). Leanne Eisen (http://leanneeisen.com/) has also done some beautiful abstract prints from performances around or in front of scanners, a not uncommon practice found on sites like *Flickr* when searching for scanner art. In most cases of such work, the artist will move an object, screen, or themselves in front of his or her capture device. *Compressionism*, on the other hand, places emphasis on the dynamism of the continuously moving relations between body, technology, and landscape: each has agency in its production. *Compressionism*, like Camille Utterback's *Liquid Time*, has sometimes been called a slit-scan art project. Golan Levin's catalogue of such work mentions several pieces that have similarities to it: Bryan Mumford's *Streak Photography* (ongoing), where he spins his object matter in front of his scanner; Romy Achituv's numerous time- and space-based interactive slit scan projects from 1997–8;

David Tinapple's hi-res scanner *Portraits* (2001–5); Michael Cohen's *Image Stacks* (2003) that process temporal motion as slit-scan images over a background; Kurt Ralske's *Amstel* (2003) and *Electro* (2004), which sequentialize video frames through slits; and Daniel Rozin's *Time Scan Mirror* (2004) that logs 30 seconds of slit-scanning in front of/as one of his mirrors (Levin, 2008). For more art that explores digital gestures as a mode of production, see curator Kristin Trethewey's *Frame Work*, an exhibition with Node Center for Curatorial Studies and Grimmuseum in Berlin (December 2011), featuring art by Malcolm Levy, Jeremy Rotsztain, Nathaniel Stern, and Santiago Taccetti, https://frameworkexhibition.wordpress.com

4 It is interesting to note that Nicolas Bourriaud, too, writes on the image in *Relational Aesthetics*. His glossary definition for images states, 'Making a work involves the invention of a process of presentation. In this kind of process, the image is an act' (Bourriaud, 1998: 111). And he more generally writes, 'The contemporary image is typified precisely by its generative power; it is no longer a trace (retroactive), but a programme (active)' (Bourriaud, 1998: 69–70). On relational works that involve objects (paraphrasing Philip Parreno): 'They display and explore the process that leads to objects and meanings. The object is just a "happy ending" to the exhibition process' (Bourriaud, 1998: 54).

5 Up to this point, I have used the word 'topology' to mean the study of topological figures and features, and then used the words topological or topographical to describe such figures and features. Here, Hansen might be using this word as a noun that explains either a 'study' of, or a 'formation' in, topology – or both.

6 A similar work of the same title was installed at the Gairloch Gallery, Oakville, Canada from 2001–4. Rokeby's parentheses in the title here mark Boul. St-Laurent's site-specificity in this updated, permanent installation.

7 Machinima is the use of real-time 3D rendering tools as a method for video production. Authors play computer games or explore virtual worlds on their desktop, capture real-time video of their digital interactions on screen, and then creatively edit this footage together. Chinese, Art 21-featured artist Cao Fei, for example, has made an entire documentary about her *Second Life* avatar and its love affair with a political prisoner (Art 21, 2009). And a web company named, simply, Machinima, makes, promotes, and distributes MTV-like re-mix videos of gamers playing popular video

games (Bulkley, 2012). In the case of *Distill Life*, Meuninck-Ganger and I use the virtual world of *Second Life* as the material in our video footage.

8 'Networked performance,' a common phrase that is most used and promoted by the public Internet art commissioners and writers / bloggers behind *Turbulence.org*, advances a much broader meaning of the word 'network' than the one put forward in the virtual-performance thematic. Several works featured on their site do not use the Internet at all, and instead intervene in, for example, 'real world' social, material, or spatial networks. They also use a more everyday understanding of 'performance': performance art, theatre or interactive installation, rather than my per-formed emergence. *Turbulence.org*'s co-directors, Jo-Anne Green and Helen Thorington, would likely place the entirety of interactive and potentialized art within their networked performance label, and likewise, many of the works they write about in their extensive, ongoing blog / catalogue could benefit from readings within various implicit body thematics. The name virtual-performance was chosen partially in homage to, as well as to differentiate it from, *Turbulence.org's* contributions to the fields of interactive and networked art. (See http://turbulence.org and http://turbulence.org/blog). Also worthy of note here is Furtherfield Gallery's internationally collaborative, networked performances that incorporate their web-based VisitorsStudio software; see http://blog.visitorsstudio.org (Furtherfield, 2008).

9 Eva and Franco Mattes (aka 0100101110101101.org) also made a series of 'synthetic performances' in *Second Life* (2009–2010), and 'performance reenactments in videogames' (2007–2010). See http://0100101110101101.org/works.html

10 See, for example, http://en.wikipedia.org/w/index.php?title=Wikipedia:Articles_for_deletion/Wikipedia_Art&oldid=270889994 and http://en.wikipedia.org/w/index.php?title=Wikipedia:Village_pump_(miscellaneous)&oldid=271199202#Help._I_have_created_a_monster.21 and http://en.wikipedia.org/wiki/Wikipedia:Deletion_review/Log/2009_February_15

# In Production

A very different kind of case study, 'In Production (A Narrative Inquiry on Interactive Art),' is a somewhat fictionalized story that folds the anxieties and emotions of an artist / PhD student into the making and thinking, moving and feeling, of digital art. The chapter is freely available in its entirety as part of *networked: a networked book about networked art* (2013), in a collaborative publication between Gylphi, Arts Future Book, and *Turbulence.org*. You can view it in any browser, or download it as a Creative Commons-Licensed and DRM-free PDF for your computer, printer, e-reader, or mobile device. The online version accepts new contributions, and I invite practicing artists, curators, and scholars to make their own additions – whether as artist writings /narrative inquiries, curatorial or critical case studies, or broad theoretical texts – to continue to expand and explore *Interactive Art and Embodiment: The Implicit Body as Performance*. http://stern.networkedbook.org

## Introduction to an Experiment

On the balls of my feet, I involuntarily hover in the doorway to my supervisor's office.

'Was there something else you needed?' Linda asks me, not even turning to face me from her computer. I want there to be. I rack my brain for a second, trying to think through how to voice my anxieties, before I finally summarize them with two simple words.

'I'm... scared?' My tone is surprised; the words come out along with a laugh. And it isn't a nervous laugh; I find my fear funny. And it isn't even real fear; it's academic fear. In both my personal and professional lives, I've done and endured far worse than simply exiting my comfort zone whilst researching and writing a paper. Still, 'I don't know if I can do this.'

Linda turns around to face me. It's hard to read her expression. I had only left the office 15 minutes ago, after convincing her that what I had been calling an autoethnographic experiment is the best way forward for the chapter on my own art, to bring in another aspect of my work and research that is itself material process. I want to find a way to show the moving–thinking–feeling of experience and practice, what I say interactive art *is*, via studio production. I want to narrativize the performed connections of making art that led to my PhD research in the first place. I arrived with a stack of books and articles and notes, and outlined an argument for her, tying together institutionally recognized artistic work, action research, self-reflective design, feminist epistemology, with dashes of performance studies and embodied praxis here and there for good measure. I then looped it all together into how I might make the most dialogical text around my arts and research methodology – through something which has its own creative writing methodology. 'I need,' I'd concluded, 'to be completely present if I'm going to show how this kind of critical thinking can be applied to critique, affection, reflection, and production. And I don't mean that I will simply be writing as a subjective I,' I had asserted – that wasn't enough. 'The art-making process needs to be detailed, on a personal and evocative level, so that readers can extrapolate and imagine their own potential implementation, and implications.' The finale to my monologue was my handing over a copy of *The Ethnographic I: A Methodological Novel about Autoethnography* (Ellis, 2004).

'Oh my god,' was Linda's initial utterance after skimming the first two pages. The book begins in a completely casual and autobiographical literary style, with Carolyn Ellis emphatically, and empathetically, telling a potential graduate student and cancer survivor that of course she *must* let her experiences not only 'get in the way' of her research on the disease, but inform and guide it at its core. It will anyway, Ellis says in so many words, so why not be honest and transparent about it? The text will be far stronger for it. This is diametrically opposed to what most students in Linda's department are told.

Professor Linda Doyle is a telecommunications engineer, who occasionally takes on artists for PhDs. She likes to shake things up a bit, and sees inherent value to bringing artistic and design practices – not to mention creativity – into usually rigid scientific fields. And she also likes artists that are fearless when it comes to taking on new technologies, and I (mostly) fit into this category. Sometimes her engineering background means she is wholly pragmatic about getting from point A to point B, and that's been extremely helpful in my learning how to write more like a traditional academic (when I decide to do so). An added and unexpected bonus, I learned only after enrolling at Trinity College, is that Linda has little to prove when it comes to the validity of what she does within the academy – as many in the arts, in all fields really, do – and so is herself fearless when it comes to going out on a limb and pushing, sometimes obliterating, boundaries.

From the first time I met Linda, we agreed that my role as an artist is, will, must be, present in my research; by the time I arrived at Trinity, I clearly saw artistic practice *as* research and my writing as inseparable from said research.[1] But I never imagined I would write about my own work in the final text. That idea, not without its own heartaches, was all Linda's; her engineering students are required to write about what they make, why wouldn't I be? Colleagues and supervisors in arts departments at our and other local institutions in Dublin called this idea a 'huge mistake,' 'unacceptable,' and 'implicitly lacking rigor.' I imagine they'd cringe further at the format we finally agreed on.

I honestly never expected Linda to go along with it, never thought it *would* be agreed upon. Write about my work, sure, but write about it creatively, autobiographically, with unfolding tensions as opposed to academic assertions? Sounds great to me, I admit, but I didn't actually think my supervisor, the *engineer*, would think so, too. And now that Linda *has* agreed, rather than feeling elated, I feel uneasy, exposed, up the creek.

Am I even capable of this? What's the narrative arc? Why should people care? How far do I go back – to when I first started making art? Do I begin with my personal motivations or my academic curiosities? These are inseparable, really, but I hadn't always understood them as such. And, perhaps most importantly, aren't the criteria that are meant to help us judge if an autoethnographic text is 'working' pretty vague? Ironically, all the arguments *against* autoethnography, all the points refuted so eloquently – and practically, using the autoethnographic style itself – by Ellis and Bochner and Denzin and countless others I have been reading over the preceding weeks, come flooding into my mind. And Linda sees it in my eyes, in my precarious doorway hovering.

Her response is twofold. She points at a chair for me to sit down, and while I oblige, she starts with the academic and pragmatic side of things.

'You're really far along here, Nat.' Her voice is just above a whisper, as if she doesn't want the neighbors – office neighbors that is – to hear. And she also purposefully calls me 'Nat'; only my family and other people who have known me for ages – as a teenager – call me Nat, rather than Nathaniel. Linda doesn't fall into this small crowd, but has met my family, seen 'Nat' in action, and is probably trying to make me feel more at ease. 'You could always edit, re-write, or cut this if we agree you have to. You have more than enough traditionally rigorous academic text in the rest of your dissertation, and certainly enough time for changes. Yes, you are walking through a minefield of controversy in several different disciplines. No, it may not be worth it, given how small a percentage of the writing is about your own work. But it may very well wind up being one of the major contributions your research and text have to offer.'

This takes a few moments to sink in. When it does, I'm not sure I want it. This is way bigger than me and my practice. If I didn't believe that I had something to offer in a comprehensive text, if I thought that my 'biggest contributions' were available only through my art – even if that included practice as well as the fruits of my labor – I wouldn't be doing all this writing. Linda pauses briefly, then goes on as if reading my mind, with the more personal and second – but not secondary – response.

'This is so *you*, Nathaniel,' she starts. 'You are an artist and a writer. That is your practice and your research, and the two are one and the same. You're a storyteller and interrogator who works in and with many forms. Although the engineer in me wants to find a way, you simply can't have the results of your multimodal explorations only represented in and as argumentative writing.[2] All your hand-waving and excitement are themselves embodied through narrative voice and activity. This is exactly the place where your ideas come from. This is why your critical methodology includes looking at movement itself: "body-language,"' she laughs with the last four syllables – a chapter title – but then goes on after a half-second pause, and with a more serious tone.

'I'm not that comfortable with this style of writing either. I think you have amazing courage for trying. I don't know how it'll fit, how it'll work, if the University high-ups will be OK with –' Linda shakes her head and waves her hand as if swatting that idea away. My mind wanders to a paper I read recently, where the author notes the accepted practice of 'experimental discourse' and writing for 'respectable, established' academics, but never for 'graduate students writing dissertations' (Spigelman, 2001: 68).[3] I already know Linda and I both agree this is worth trying.

We both keep quiet for what seems a long minute, and then I get an unexpected rush of energy, picking up where I left off. 'It's really just a chapter on one of the many avenues of my research practice, and how it feeds back into itself. That's it. I have to make two concrete arguments.' I loosely hold my right thumb up in front of me,

'One, *why it's there*: to show the ongoing development and understanding of interactive art through embodiment, and vice versa, but in arts production and *that* experience, in addition to historical criticism and the museum space. My approach to, and practice of, viewing and criticizing art continues to be per-formed, as in birthed and changed, along with my experience and practice of *making* art. I am trying to engage with incipient materials and ideas, and their emergent relations, and then attempting to carry that framework of engagement over from my studio to the gallery, and back again.' I pause, reflecting on what I just said, and nodding to myself (I hope I don't look smug), before I go on. 'And,' I flip out my second, pointer finger along with the first, 'Two, *why a narrative inquiry* is most befitting: because everything here,' I wave my hand around as if my computer and notes and ideas are in the air, 'is about material process *along with* critical inquiry: moving and thinking and feeling provoked through affective evocation. It's about how they are all mutually emergent and, you know, *with*,' I criss-cross my two extended fingers to illustrate that last word. I stop again for a moment, this time keeping still and nodding only in my mind. 'Those two points are a good foundation, whether my readers – or whomever – like and agree with the style I've chosen or not'.

We both breathe in, purse our lips, then breathe out at the same time. We look at each other and laugh-snort awkwardly. I close my eyes for a moment to think: this is going to be really difficult. I open my eyes and continue, more slowly.

'I just have to get across that while my writing and making, and my moving–thinking–feeling between them, are entwined *practically*, the best way to re-present them and what they each accomplish *in text* is by very different – and thus also obviously separate – means. We can be blunt about it: narrative is affective.'

I'm silent for a few seconds, then add, 'I should also make clear that this chapter can be read as staging an implicit body as performance. It situates bodies and matter as always per-formed (emergent and relational, etc), and it implicates other conceptual and material forms and agencies in that ongoing formation.' I look at the ceiling as if it will tell me what comes next, then go on. 'It performs art and philosophy as potential practices of one another. It simply,' I shake my hands at the air a bit 'starts earlier, whilst the work is in production in the studio. It keeps going as it carries on through situations in the gallery, then back to the studio again – feeding into the next work, and so on. I'm… *amplifying* that experience, creating a kind of semblance of it. Potentializing it.'

I take a long breath and look at Linda again. 'I'll make a story about how each question leads to the following piece, in that quirky way you keep telling me I do, but stress that this is examining production, affection, and reflection with the same method, or at least the same theoretical and creative approach, as the rest of my text and work.'

Another pause. I sigh, and my supervisor half smiles / half grins.

'I think you can write this,' Linda answers firmly. 'I think you can make this interesting, and make all your points within the narrative.' She nods, almost to herself. 'But I also think you have to convince Nicole that it's the right way to proceed.' I raise my eyebrows. 'If you can convince her, you'll have convinced yourself,' she wisely finishes. 'And also me,' she attaches to the end a moment later.

I get up to leave. 'I don't think Nicole will go for it,' I say as I walk out, but I'm happy we've agreed on a threshold test for our unfolding plan. My wife will give me a run for my money on this. She'll save me from myself – and not for the first time, I laugh internally. Like I always say: Nicole is the smart one; I'm the loud one.

**The rest of this chapter is available for viewing or download from http://stern.networkedbook.org.**

## Notes

1 Here I'm reminded of Elaine Bass Jenks. When studying a group of visually impaired children, including her own, Jenks continuously reminds herself and the reader that 'My mom role was always present … My self image as a mom affected my study as well … And as a researcher who is a mom, I believe I expend more energy researching a topic that affects my child than I would if I studied a more distant "other"' (Jenks, 2002: 180–1). Similarly – though certainly *not* as intensely – my own role as an artist relates to my roles as writer and researcher of the arts, and as husband and father and teacher and collaborator (and friend and, and, and… ). I am always playing all of these roles at once, but I expend more energy on given texts and their analyses if they affect my other practices.

2 As Ellis asserts in a collaborative paper with her partner, 'I don't want to write in an argumentative style – you know, the "here's what's wrong with what you say, you don't understand my position, mine is better than yours" kind of writing ... Point-to-point refutation has never changed my mind; it certainly has never changed what I feel in my heart' (Ellis and Bochner, 2006: 434). Also see 'Being real: moving inward toward social change' (Ellis, 2002).

3 There are, despite this, a number of autoethnographic PhDs – or sections of PhDs – that have indeed been written, and more every year. Up until very recently, these have been mostly by students of the aforementioned scholars – and other advocates of the form – but also include professional and managerial practices, as well as researchers in the field of art education. See, for example, 'Up Close and Personal: Reflections on our Experience of Supervising Research Candidates who are Using Personal Reflective Techniques' (Boucher and Smyth, 2004).

# Bibliography

Anders, P. (2001) 'Anthropic Cyberspace: Defining Electronic Space from First Principles', *Leonardo Journal of Art, Science and Technology* 34(5): 409-16.

Arnaud, J. (2005) 'Touching to See', *October* (114): 5-16.

Arns, I. (2002) 'Metonymical Mov(i)es: Review of The Language of New Media (Lev Manovich), 2001', *ArtMargins,* accessed 20 March 2007, http://www.projects.v2.nl/~arns/Texts/Media/manovich-review.html.

Art 21 (2009) 'Cao Fei', *Art 21,* accessed 12 August 2012, http://www.art21.org/artists/cao-fei

Art Review (2005) 'Mathieu Briand', *Art Review,* December.

Austin, J. (1962) *How to do Things with Words: The William James Lectures Delivered at Harvard University in 1955*. Oxford: Clarendon.

Austin, J. (1962) *How to do Things with Words: The William James Lectures Delivered at Harvard University in 1955*. Oxford: Clarendon.

Bal, M. (1997) *Narratology: Introduction to the Theory of Narrative.* Toronto: University of Toronto Press.

Banksy (2010) *Exit Through the Gift Shop*. London: Paranoid Pictures.

Barad, K. (2003) 'Posthumanist Performativity: Toward an Understanding of How Matter Comes to Matter', *Signs: Journal of Women in Culture and Society* 8(3): 801-30.

Barlow, J.P. (1996) 'A declaration of the independence of cyberspace', *Electronic Frontier Foundation*, accessed 1 August 2012, https://homes.eff.org/~barlow/Declaration-Final.html

Baross, Z. (2000) 'The (False) Gifts of Writing', *New Literary History* 31(3): 435-58.

Baumgaertel, T. and Simon, J.F. (1999) 'Interview with John F. Simon', *nettime*, accessed 18 June 2008, http://www.nettime.org/Lists-Archives/nettime-l-9907/msg00067.html

Benjamin, A. (1997) *Present Hope: Philosophy, Architecture, Judaism*. London: Routledge.

Bennett, J. (2010) *Vibrant Matter: A Political Ecology of Things*. Durham, NC: Duke University Press.

Bergson, H. (2004) *Matter and Memory*. New York: Dover Philosophical Classics.

Bishop, C. (2004) 'Antagonism and Relational Aesthetics', *October* 110: 51-79.

Bishop, C. (2005) *Installation Art: A Critical History*. New York: Routledge.

Bishop, C. (2006) 'Viewers as Producers', in C. Bishop (ed.) *Participation*. Cambridge, MA: MIT Press.

Blake, N. (2006) 'Text Rain', *Transliteracies*, accessed 20 January 2008): http://transliteracies.english.ucsb.edu/post/research-project/research-clearinghouse-individual/research-reports/text-rain-2

Blank, J. and Jeron, K.H. (2007) 'Take Part in Our Happiness!', *A Minima*, accessed 3 April 2009, http://aminima.net/wp/?language=en&p=754

Blume, H. (1998) 'Subtle Mechanisms', *The Atlantic Online*, accessed 17 June 2008, http://www.theatlantic.com/unbound/criticaleye/ce980813.htm

Bogost, I. (2011) 'Object-Oriented Answers: Responses to Parikka', *Ian Bogost: Videogame Theory, Criticism, Design*, URL (30 December 2012): http://www.bogost.com/blog/object-oriented_answers.shtml

Bohm, D. (1980) *Wholeness and the Implicate Order*. London: Routledge.

Bolivar, M. (2011) 'Artist Statement: Within and Between', *Maria Bolivar*, accessed 9 January 2012, http://www.mariabolivar.com/PDF/MFA_AS.pdf

Bolt, B. (2004) *Art Beyond Representation: The Performative Power of the Image*. London: I.B. Tauris.

Bolter, D.J. and Gromala, D. (2003) *Windows and Mirrors: Interaction Design, Digital Art, and the Myth of Transparency*. Cambridge, MA: MIT Press.

Borland, R. (2000) 'Front', *ralphborland.net*, accessed 26 April 2007, http://ralphborland.net/front/index.html.

Borland, R. (2002) 'Suited for Subversion', *ralphborland.net,* accessed 26 April 2007, http://ralphborland.net/s4s/index.html.

Borland, R. (2007) 'DDT', *ralphborland.net,* accessed 19 January 2008, http://ralphborland.net/ddt/index.html.

Boucher, C. and Smyth, A. (2004) 'Up Close and Personal: Reflections on our Experience of Supervising Research Candidates who are Using Personal Reflective Techniques', *Reflective Practice* 5(3): 345—56.

Bourriaud, N. (1998) *Relational Aesthetics.* Dijon: Les Presses du reel Dijon.

Bourriaud, N. (2005) *Postproduction: Culture as Screenplay: How Art Reprograms the World.* New York: Lukas & Sternberg.

Braidotti, R. (1994) *Nomadic Subjects: Embodiment and Sexual Difference in Contemporary Feminist Theory.* New York: Columbia University Press.

Briand, M. (2006) 'Mathieu Briand', in Jones, C. A. (ed.) *Sensorium: Embodied Experience, Technology, and Contemporary Art.* Boston: MIT Press.

Briand, M. (2007) 'SYS*011. MIE>ABE/SOS\ SYS*010', *Mathieu Briand,* accessed 18 April 2008, http://www.mathieubriand.com/index.php?b=installations/systemes/sys11

Bristow, T. (2011) 'Chalk Vision Project', *Tegan Bristow,* accessed August 13 2012, http://teganbristow.co.za/?p=29

Bristow, T. (12 August 2012) *personal communication.*

Broadhurst, S. (2006) *Performance and Technology: Practices of Virtual Embodiment and Interactivity.* New York: Palgrave Macmillan.

Brodsky, J. (2010) 'New Media: Culture and Image', *Journal of Communication* E22-3.

Broeckmann, A. (2007) 'Process, Performance, Machine: Aspects of an Aesthetics of the Machinic', in Grau, O. (ed.) *MediaArtHistories,* Cambridge: MIT Press.

Brouwer, J. and Mulder, A. (ed.) (2007) *Interact or Die!: There is Drama in the Networks.* Rotterdam: NAi Publishers.

Bulkley, K. (2012) 'Machinima: Monetising the Gaming Industry's "Lost Boys"', *Guardian,* 12 August 2012, http://www.guardian.co.uk/media-network/media-network-blog/2012/jul/31/machinima-monetising-gaming-industry-lost-boys?newsfeed=true

Butler, J. (1990) *Gender Trouble: Feminism and the Subversion of Identity.* New York: Routledge.

Butler, J. (1993) *Bodies That Matter: On the Discursive Limits of 'Sex'.* New York: Routledge.

Candy, L. (5 March 2006) *Creativity & Cognition Studios: Practice-Based Research: A Guide.* Sydney: University of Technology.

Candy, L. (2008a) 'Practice-Based Research', *Creativity & Cognition Studios,* accessed 10 July 2008, http://www.creativityandcognition.com/content/category/10/56/131/

Candy, L. (2008b) 'Practice-Related Research', *Creativity & Cognition Studios,* accessed 28 July 2008, http://www.creativityandcognition.com/content/view/122/131/

Canonico, T. (2007) 'Constraint City, Body as a Living Map', *neural,* accessed 12 June 2008, http://www.neural.it/art/2007/11/constraint_city_body_as_a_livi.phtml

Celant, G. (1977) *Ambiente/Arte: dal Futurismo alla Body Art.* Venice: Edizioni La Biennale di Venezia.

Chase, S.E. (2005) 'Narrative Inquiry: Multiple Lenses, Approaches, Voices', in N. K. Denzin (ed.) *Handbook of Qualitative Research, 3rd edn.* Thousand Oaks: Sage.

Cohen, T. (1998) *Ideology and Inscription: Cultural Studies after Benjamin, de Man and Bakhtin.* Cambridge: Cambridge University Press.

Connor, J. (2012) 'ITP Launches Entrepreneurs, Dreamers', *The Village Voice,* accessed 10 August 2012, http://www.villagevoice.com/2012-08-08/news/itp-launches-entrepreneurs-dreamers/

Cook, S. and Graham, B. (2010) *Rethinking Curating: Art after New Media.* Cambridge: Leonardo Books/MIT Press.

Cooper, D. and Rokeby, D. (2003) 'Very Nervous System: Artist David Rokeby Adds New Meaning to the Term Interactive', *Wired Magazine,* accessed 11 June 2008, http://www.wired.com/wired/archive/3.03/rokeby_pr.html

Corrigall, M. (2011) 'Creating new Impressions', *Sunday Independent,* 21 August, p. 3.

Craig, M. (2010) 'BOOK REVIEW, Susan Kozel: Closer: Performance, Technologies, Phenomenology', *Human Studies* 33(1): 103-8.

Crary, J. (1992) *Techniques of the Observer: On Vision and Modernity in the 19th Century.* Cambridge, MA: MIT Press.

Crossley, N. (1995) 'Body Techniques, Agency and Intercorporeality: On Goffman's Relations in Public', *Sociology* 29(1): 133-49.

Darke, C. (2003) *Tall Ships (Slight Return): Gary Hill: Tall Ships.* Liverpool: FACT.

Davies, C. (1995) 'Osmose', *immersence,* accessed November 2007, http://www.immersence.com/osmose/

Dea, C. (2006) 'The Viewer Becomes the Art. Mathieu Briand's 'Ubiq' Invites the Spectator to Nab a Bit of Fame', *Los Angeles Times,* 27 April.

Debatty, R. (2010) 'Book Review - Chroma: Design, Architecture and Art in Color', *we make money not art*, accessed 29 November 2011, http://www.we-make-money-not-art.com/archives/2010/01/book-review-chroma-design-arch.php

Debatty, R. and Findley, J. (2007) 'Interview with Jessica Findley', *we make money not art*, accessed 12 December 2007, http://www.we-make-money-not-art.com/archives/009675.php

deLahunta, S. and Zuniga Shaw, N. (2006) 'Constructing Memories: Creation of the Choreographic Resource', *Performance Research* 11(4): 53-62.

Deleuze, G. (1988) *Bergsonism*. New York: Zone Books.

Deleuze, G. (1989) *Cinema 2: The Time-Image*. Minnesota: University of Minnesota Press.

Deleuze, G. and Guattari, F. (1987) *A Thousand Plateaus: Capitalism and Schizophrenia*. Minneapolis: University of Minnesota Press.

Denzin, N. K. (ed.) (2005) *Handbook of Qualitative Research, 3rd edn*. Thousand Oaks, CA: Sage.

Denzin, N. K. (2006) 'Analytic Autoethnography, or Deja Vu all Over Again', *Journal of Contemporary Ethnography* 35: 419-28.

Derrida, J. (2005) *On Touching: Jean-Luc Nancy*. Stanford: Stanford University Press.

Devisch, I. (2000) 'A Trembling Voice in the Desert: Jean-Luc Nancy's Rethinking of the Space of the Political', *Cultural Values* 4(2): 239–56.

Diamond, E. (1989) 'Mimesis, Mimicry, and the True Real', *Modern Drama* 32(1): 58-72.

Diamond, E. (1995) 'The Shudder of Catharsis in 20th Century Performance', in Parker, A. and Sedgwick, E. K. (ed.) *Performance and Performativity*. London: Routledge.

Dolan, J. (1989) 'Bending Gender to Fit the Canon: The Politics of Production', in L. Hart (ed.) *Making a Spectacle: Feminist Essays on Contemporary Women's Theatre*. Ann Arbor, MI: University of Michigan Press.

Drewal, H. J. and Drewal, M. T. (1983) *Gelede: Art and Female Power among the Yoruba: Traditional Arts of Africa Series*. Bloomington: Indiana University Press.

Driessens, E. and Verstappen, M. (2002) 'Introduction: Generative Art and Present Day Experience of Nature', *Driessens & Verstappen*, accessed 17 June 2008, http://www.xs4all.nl/~notnot/text/introduction.html

Driessens, E. and Verstappen, M. (2004) 'Emerging Technologies: Tickle Salon', *SIGGRAPH 2004*, accessed 19 June 2008, http://www.siggraph.org/s2004/conference/etech/tickle.php?=conference

Ellis, C. S. (2002) 'Being Real: Moving Inward Toward Social Change', *International Journal of Qualitative Studies in Education* 15(4): 399–406.

Ellis, C. S. (2004) *The Ethnographic I: A Methodological Novel About Autoethnography.* Lanham: Rowman Altamira.

Ellis, C. S. and Bochner, A.P. (2006) 'Analyzing Analytic Autoethnography: An Autopsy', *Journal of Contemporary Ethnography* 35(4): 429-48.

Feingold, K. (2002) 'The Interactive Art Gambit', in M. Rieser and A. Zapp (ed.) *The New Screen Media: Cinema/Art/Narrative.* LDN: BFI Publishing.

Findley, J. (2011) 'Aeolian Ride Information', *Aeolian Ride,* accessed 25 July 2012, http://aeolian-ride.info/info.html

Forsythe, W. (2011) 'Choreographic Objects', *William Forsythe,* accessed 4 January 2012, http://www.williamforsythe.de/essay.html

Frohne, U. and Katti, C. (2000) 'Crossing Boundaries in Cyberspace? The Politics of "Body" and "Language" after the Emergence of New Media', *Art Journal* 59(4): 9-13.

Fuchs, E. (1989) 'Staging the Obscene Body', *TDR* 33(1): 33-58.

Fuery, K. (2009) *New Media: Culture and Image.* New York: Palgrave Macmillan.

Furtherfield (2008) 'VisitorsStudio', *VisitorsStudio,* accessed 20 March 2008, http://blog.visitorsstudio.org/

Gagnon, J. (2007) 'David Rokeby, Machine for Taking Time', *E-Art at the Daniel Langlois Foundation,* accessed 17 June 2008, http://www.fondation-langlois.org/e-art/e/index.php

Gallagher, S. and Cole, J. (1995) 'Body Image and Body Schema in a Deafferented Subject', *Journal of Mind and Behavior* 16: 369-90.

Gil, J. (1998) *Metamorphoses of the Body.* Minneapolis: University of Minnesota Press.

Gil, J. (2006) 'Paradoxical Body', *The Drama Review* 50(4): 21-35.

Gillick, L. (2006) 'Contingent Factors: A Response to Claire Bishop's "Antagonism and Relational Aesthetics"', *October* 115: 95–107.

Gindlesberger, H. (2009) 'Westering', *Hans Gindlesberger,* accessed 9 January 2012, http://www.gindlesberger.com/westering/index.html.

Glasner, B. and Schmidt, P. (2010) *Chroma: Design, Architecture and Art in Color.* Basel: Birkhauser Basel.

Gleick, J. (2007) 'Is the Universe Actually Made of Information?', *Wired* 15(02).

Goffman, E. (1959) *The Presentation of Self in Everyday Life.* Garden City, NY: Doubleday.

Goffman, E. (1971) *Relations in Public: Microstudies of the Public Order.* New York: Basic Books.

Graham, J. and Zuniga Shaw, N. (2011) 'Synchronous Objects: What Else Might Dance Look Like?: An Interview with Professor Norah Zuniga Shaw', accessed 4 January 2012, http://www.dancersgroup.org/content/programs/articles/2011/2011July_389.html

Grau, O. (2003) *Virtual Art: From Illusion to Immersion.* Cambridge: MIT Press.

Gray, L. (2007) 'Cross Platform: Sound in Other Media', *The Wire*, July, pp. 16-17.

Gray, B. (2007) 'Meditations on the Doubting, Playing Animal', *Art South Africa*, August, pp. 61-3.

Grosz, E. (1994) *Volatile Bodies: Toward a Corporeal Feminism.* St Leonards, NSW: Allen & Unwin.

Grosz, E. (1999) 'Thinking the New: Of Futures Yet Unthought', in E. Grosz (ed.) *Becomings: Explorations in Time, Memory and Futures.* Ithaca, NY: Cornell University Press.

Grosz, E. (2006) 'Chaos, Territory, Art. Deleuze and the Framing of the Earth', *IDEA (Interior Design / Interior Architecture Educator's Association)*: 15-29.

Grusin, R. (2010) *Premediation: Affect and Mediality After 9/11.* New York: Palgrave Macmillan.

Grusin, R. (13 December 2011) *personal communication.*

Grusin, R. (2012) 'Reading Semblance and Event', *Postmodern Culture.*

Guerrilla Girls (2007) 'Fighting Discrimination with Facts, Humor and Fake Fur', *Guerrilla Girls*, 10 December 2007, http://www.guerrillagirls.com/

Hansen, M. B. N. (2000) *Embodying Technesis: Technology Beyond Writing.* Ann Arbor: University of Michigan Press.

Hansen, M. B. N. (2001a) 'Embodying Virtual Reality: Touch and Self-Movement in the Work of Char Davies', *Critical Matrix* 112-47.

Hansen, M. B. N. (2001b) 'Seeing With the Body: The Digital Image in Post-photography', *Diacritics* 31(4): 54-82.

Hansen, M. B. N. (2004) *New Philosophy for New Media.* Cambridge: MIT Press.

Hansen, M. B. N. (2006) *Bodies in Code: Interfaces with Digital Media.* New York: Routledge.

Harman, G. (2010) *The Quadruple Object.* Alresford: John Hunt Publishing.

Hasegawa, Y. (2006) 'Mathieu Briand', in C. A. Jones (ed.) *Sensorium: Embodied Experience, Technology, and Contemporary Art.* Boston: MIT Press.

Hayles, N.K. (1999) *How We Became Posthuman: Virtual Bodies in Cybernetics, Literature, and Informatics.* Chicago, IL: University of Chicago Press.

Hayles, N.K. (2002) 'Flesh and Metal: Reconfiguring the Mindbody in Virtual Environments', *Configurations* 10: 297–320.

Heidegger, M. (1962) *Being and Time.* Albany: State University of New York Press.

Herst, D. and Watson, T. (2008) 'Audio Space: An Interview with Theo Watson', *TAGMAG* 6: 12–14.

Huff, J. (2011) 'Technology is Not Enough: The Story of NYU's Interactive Telecommunications Program', *Rhizome,* accessed 16 December 2011, http://rhizome.org/editorial/2011/dec/15/technology-not-enough-story-nyus-interactive-telec/

Huhtamo, E. (2007) 'Twin-Touch-Test-Redux: Media Archaeological Approach to Art, Interactivity, and Tactility', in O. Grau (ed.) *MediaArtHistories.* Cambridge, MA: MIT Press.

Ihde, D. (1990) *Technology and the Lifeworld: From Garden to Eden.* Bloomington: Indiana University Press.

Jacobs, M. (2006) 'Margot Jacobs', *Design Gotenburg,* accessed 19 January 2008, http://www.tii.se/reform/people/jacobs_margot.html

Jenks, E. B. (2002) 'Searching for Autoethnographic Credibility: Reflections from a Mom wth a Notepad', in A. Bochner and C. Ellis (eds) *Ethnographically Speaking: Autoethnography, Literature, and Aesthetics.* Walnut Creek, CA: Alta Mira Press.

Johnson, S. (2002) *Emergence: The Connected Lives of Ants, Brains, Cities and Software.* New York: Touchstone.

Jones, C. A. (2006) 'Introduction', in C. A. Jones (ed.) *Sensorium: New Media Complexities for Embodied Experience.* Cambridge, MA: MIT Press.

Jones, M. J. (1995) 'Stelarc'(1.2), 20 June 2008, http://www.cyberstage.org/archive/cstage12/stelrc.htm

Jouanno, E. and Briand, M. (2004) 'Mathieu Briand. Hacking Contemporary Reality (Interview)', *Flash Art,* October, pp. 114–16.

Kapferer, B. (1983) *A Celebration of Demons: Exorcism and the Aesthetics of Healing in Sri Lanka.* Bloomington: Indiana University Press.

Kellner, C. (January 2007) *The Compressionist.* Johannesburg: Nathaniel Stern and Art on Paper Gallery.

Kildall, S. (2007) 'Paradise Ahead', *Scott Kildall,* accessed 23 June 2008, http://www.kildall.com/artwork/2007/paradise_ahead/paradise_ahead.html

Kildall, S. (2008) 'Artist Statement', *Scott Kildall*, accessed 21 June 2008, http://www.kildall.com/statement/statement.html

Kildall, S. and Quaranta, D. (2007) 'Displaced Familiarity: Interview with Scott Kildall', *Networked_Performance*, accessed 23 June 2008, http://transition.turbulence.org/blog/2007/08/31/displaced-familiarity-interview-with-scott-kildall/

Kildall, S. and Scott, V. (2008) 'No Matter', *Scott Kildall*, accessed 21 June 2008, http://www.kildall.com/artwork/2008/no_matter/no_matter.html

Kirshenblatt-Gimblett, B. (1999) 'Performance Studies', *NYU*, accessed June 2001, http://www.nyu.edu/classes/bkg/ps.htm

Kittler, F. (1999) *Gramophone, Film, Typewriter.* Palo Alto, CA: Stanford University Press.

Kozel, S. (2008) *Closer: Performance, Technologies, Phenomenology.* Cambridge: MIT Press.

Krueger, M. (1991) *Artificial Reality II.* Boston: Addison-Wesley Reading.

Labelle, B. (2005) 'Sonographic Stele', *Aux*, accessed 13 June 2008, http://aux.dk/technicalbreakdown/cinemateket/brandon-labelle-death-of-the-composer-or-all-tongues-are-mothers-(729)

Labelle, B. (2007a) 'Brandon Labelle', *Errant Bodies*, accessed 12 June 2008, http://www.errantbodies.org/labelle.html

Labelle, B. (2007b) 'Social Radio', *Errant Bodies*, accessed 16 June 2008, http://www.errantbodies.org/socialradio.html

Lacan, J. (1949/2006) 'The Mirror Stage as Formative of the Function of the I as Revealed in Psychoanalytic Experience', in J. Storey (ed.) *Cultural Theory and Popular Culture: A Reader.* Atlanta: University of Georgia Press.

Lakoff, G. and Johnson, M. (2003) *Metaphors we live by.* Chicago, IL: University of Chicago Press.

Laster, P. (2008) 'Tehching Hsieh: The Art of Survival', *Art Asia Pacific*, accessed 23 June 2008, http://www.aapmag.com/56features4.htm

Lazzarato, M. (2002) 'From biopower to biopolitics', *PLI: Warwick Journal of Philosophy* 13(2): 100-11.

Lenoir, T. (2004) 'Foreword', in M. B. N Hansen, *New Philosophy for New Media.* Cambridge, MA: MIT Press.

Levin, G. (2008) 'An Informal Catalogue of Slit-Scan Video Artworks and Research', *Flong*, accessed 20 June 2008, http://www.flong.com/texts/lists/slit_scan/

Levin, G. and Lieberman, Z. (2003a) 'Messa di Voce', *Tmema*, accessed 16 June 2008, http://www.tmema.org/messa/messa.html

Levin, G. and Lieberman, Z. (2003b) 'Messa di Voce Report', *Tmema,* accessed 16 June 2008, http://www.tmema.org/messa/report/messa_report_600.pdf

Levin, G. and Lieberman, Z. (2004) 'In-situ Speech Visualization in Real-time Interactive Installation and Performance', *Proceedings of the 3rd International Symposium on Non-photorealistic Animation and Rendering,* Annecy, France, 7-14.

Levy, P. (1996) 'The Art of Cyberspace', in T. Drucker (ed.) *Electronic Culture: Technology and Visual Representation.* London: Aperture.

Leys, R. (2011) 'The Turn to Affect: A Critique', *Critical Inquiry* 37(3): 434-72.

Lichty, P. (2009) 'WikiPedia Art?', *Furtherfield,* accessed 4 April 2009, http://blog.furtherfield.org/?q=node/267

Lozano-Hemmer, R. (2001a) 'Body Movies: Relational Architecture 6', *Absolute Arts,* accessed 8 July 2005, http://www.absolutearts.com/artsnews/2001/08/31/29058.html

Lozano-Hemmer, R. (2001b) 'Relational Architecture', *Rhizome.org,* accessed 5 July 2005, http://rhizome.org/artbase/2398/fear/relarc.html

Lozano-Hemmer, R. (6 December 2001c) *Too Interactive (Belated).* Montreal: CRUMBweb.

Lozano-Hemmer, R. (2003) 'Relational Architectures: Rafael Lozano-Hemmer', *Absolute Arts,* accessed 8 July 2005, http://www.absolutearts.com/artsnews/2003/05/28/31074.html

Lozano-Hemmer, R. (2006) 'Information', *Rafael Lozano-Hemmer,* accessed 17 January 2008, http://www.lozano-hemmer.com/einfo.html

Lozano-Hemmer, R. (2007) 'Projects', *Rafael Lozano-Hemmer,* accessed 11 June 2008, http://www.lozano-hemmer.com/eproyecto.html

Lyotard, J.-F. (1988) *The Differend: Phrases in Dispute.* Minneapolis: University of Minnesota Press.

Maart, B. (2006) 'Nathaniel Stern at Outlet', *Art South Africa* 5(1): 68.

McQuaid, C. (2005) 'Interactive Works Capture Interplay of Shadows, Light', *The Boston Globe,* 24 June.

Manning, E. (2009) *Relationscapes: Movement, Art, Philosophy.* Cambridge: MIT Press.

Manning, E. (16 December 2010a) *personal communication.*

Manning, E. (2010b) 'When Tables Dance: Technicity in Motion', *In Medias Res,* accessed 3 January 2012, http://mediacommons.futureofthebook.org/imr/2010/04/26/when-tables-dance-technicity-motion

Manning, E. and Massumi, B. (2009) 'SenseLab', *SenseLab: A Laboratory for Thought in Motion*, accessed 9 December 2011, http://senselab.ca/.

Manning, E. and Massumi, B. (2011) 'Into the Diagram', *ArtSpace*, accessed 5 January 2012, http://artspace.org.au/content/public/lectures/20/pdf/Artspace_Into_the_Diagram.pdf

Manovich, L. (2001) *The Language of New Media.* Cambridge, MA: MIT Press.

Manovich, L. (2002) 'Ten Key Texts on Digital Art: 1970-2000', *Leonardo* 35(5): 567–75.

Marks, L. U. (2006) *Touch: Sensuous Theory and Multisensory Media.* Minneapolis: University of Minnesota Press.

Massumi, B. (2002) *Parables for the Virtual: Movement, Affect, Sensation.* Durham, NC: Duke University Press.

Massumi, B. (2007) 'The Thinking-Feeling of What Happens: An Interview with Brian Massumi', in B. Joke and M. Arjen (ed.) *Interact or Die: There is Drama in the Networks.* Rotterdam: NAi Publishers.

Massumi, B. (2011) *Semblance and Event: Activist Philosophy and the Occurrent Arts.* Cambridge, MA: MIT Press.

Mecklenberger, S. (2009) 'Hello Wikipedia, it's the blogosphere calling', *Two Coats of Paint,* accessed 27 July 2012, http://www.twocoatsofpaint.com/2009/02/hello-wikipedia-its-blogosphere-calling.html

Merleau-Ponty, M. (1962) *The Phenomenology of Perception.* New York: Humanities Press.

Meuninck-Ganger, J. (December 2011) *personal communication.*

Milon, A. (2005) *La Réalité Virtuelle: Avec ou Sans le Corps?* Paris: Autrement.

Mitchell, W. (1992) *The Reconfigured Eye: Visual Truth in the Post-Photographic Age.* Cambridge: MIT Press.

Mondloch, K. (2010) *Screens: Viewing Media Installation Art.* Minneapolis: University of Minnesota Press, http://dx.doi.org/10.3202/caa.reviews.2001.10 [5 November 2007].

Morse, M. (1991) 'Video Installation Art: The Body, the Image, and the Space-in-Between', in D. Hall and S. J. Fifer (ed.) *Illuminating Video.* New York: Aperture.

Morse, M. (1998) *Virtualities: Television, Media Art, and Cyberculture.* Bloomington: Indiana University Press.

MTAA (2004) 'Background', *1 Year Performance Video (AKA SamHsiehUpdate),* accessed 21 June 2008, http://turbulence.org/Works/1year/info.php?page=bg

MTAA (2006) 'Long Bio', *MTAA*, accessed 21 June 2008, http://www.mtaa.net/mtaaRR/bio/long.html

Mulvey, L. (1989) 'Visual Pleasure and Narrative Cinema', in L. Mulvey (ed.) *Visual and Other Pleasures*. Basingstoke: Macmillan.

Munster, A. (2006) *Materializing New Media: Embodiment in Information Aesthetics*. New Hampshire: Dartmouth.

Murphie, A. (2008) 'Clone Your Technics: Research creation, radical empiricism and the constraints of models', *Inflexions 1.1*, accessed 10 January 2012, http://www.senselab.ca/inflexions/pdf/Murphie.pdf

Murphie, A. (2010a) 'Affect - a basic summary of approaches', *Adventures in Jutland*, accessed 14 December 2011, http://www.andrewmurphie.org/blog/?p=93

Murphie, A. (2010b) 'blog comment on "Richard Grusin on affect, premediation and security -- Anglia Ruskin ArcDigital talk", *Machinology (Jussi Parikka)*, accessed 8 January 2012, http://machinology.blogspot.com/2010/01/richard-grusin-on-affect-premediation.html.

Murphie, A. and Potts, J. (2003) *Culture and Technology*. New York: Palgrave Macmillan.

Nancy, J.-L. (1990) 'Exscription', *Yale French Studies* 78: 47-65.

Nancy, J.-L. (1992) *Corpus, Corpus edition*. Paris: Editionsié.

Nancy, J.-L. (1993) *The Experience of Freedom*. Stanford, CA: Stanford University Press.

Nancy, J.-L. (1994) *The Birth to Presence*. Stanford, CA: Stanford University Press.

Nancy, J.-L. (2000) *Being Singular Plural*. Stanford, CA: Stanford University Press.

Nancy, J.-L. (2007) *The Ground of the Image*. New York: Fordham University Press.

Navas, E. (2005) 'Review of MTAA's 1 Year Performance Video (SamHsiehUpdate)', *netartreview.net*, accessed 21 June 2008, http://www.netartreview.net/logs/2005_01_02_backlog.html

Nicolai, C. (2007) 'Static Balance', *Carsten Nicolai*, accessed 12 June 2008, http://www.carstennicolai.com/?c=works&w=static_balance

Oliviera, N.d. (2003) *Installation Art in the New Millennium*. London: Thames and Hudson.

Pacific Northwest Ballet (2008) 'One Flat Thing, Reproduced', 5 January 2012, http://www.pnb.org/AboutPNB/Repertory/OneFlatThing.aspx

Parikka, J. (2010) 'What is New Materialism – Opening words from the event', *Machinology*, accessed 6 December 2011, http://machinology.blogspot.com/2010/06/what-is-new-materialism-opening-words.html

Parikka, J. (2011a) 'OOQ: Object-Oriented-Questions', *Machinology*, 28 December 2011, http://jussiparikka.net/2011/12/21/ooq-object-oriented-questions/

Parikka, J. (2011b) 'Ooops', *Machinology*, accessed 29 December 2011, http://jussiparikka.net/2011/12/23/ooops/

Parikka, J. and Tiainen, M. (2012) 'The Primacy of Movement: Variation, Intermediality and Biopolitics in Tero Saarinen's Hunt', in B. Bolt and E. Barrett (eds) *Carnal Knowledge: New materialism through the Arts*. London: I.B.Tauris.

Paul, C. (2002) 'Renderings of Digital Art', *Leonardo* 35(5): 471-2.

Paul, C. (2003) *Digital Art (World of Art)*. New York: Thames & Hudson.

Pearson, M. (2011) *Generative Art*. New York: Manning Publications.

Penny, S. (1995a) 'Consumer Culture and Technological Imperative: The Artist in Dataspace', in Penny, S. (ed.) *Critical Issues in Electronic Media*. Albany, NY: State University of New York Press.

Penny, S. (1995b) 'Introduction', in S. Penny (ed.) *Critical Issues in Electronic Media*. Albany: State University of New York Press.

Penny, S. (1999) 'Traces', *Simon Penny*, accessed 20 May 2008, http://ace.uci.edu/penny/works/traces.html

Penny, S. (2003) 'Telepanoscope/Vivatars', *Simon Penny*, accessed 27 May 2008, http://ace.uci.edu/penny/works/vivitars.html

Penny, S. (2004) 'Fugitive 2', *Simon Penny*, 20 May 2008, http://ace.uci.edu/penny/works/fugitive2.html

Penny, S. (2005) 'Representation, Enaction, and the Ethics of Simulation', *Electronic Book Review*, 20 May 2008, http://www.electronicbookreview.com/thread/firstperson/machanimate.

Penny, S. (21 May 2008) *personal communication*.

Penny, S., Bernhardt, A., Schulte, J., Sengers, P. and Smith, J. (2001) 'Traces: Embodied Immersive Interaction with Semi-Autonomous Avatars', *Convergence: The International Journal of Research into New Media Technologies* 7(2): 47-65.

Penny, S., Sengers, P. and Smith, J. (2000) 'Traces: Semi-Autonomous Avatars', *infosci.cornell.edu*, accessed 2008 May 2008, http://www.infosci.cornell.edu/cemcom/papers/traces--semi-autonomous-avatars.pdf

Perpich, D. (2005) 'Corpus Meum: Disintegrating Bodies and the Ideal of Integrity', *Hypatia* 20(3): 75-91.

Perron, J. (2004) 'Rafael Lozano-Hemmer: Standards and Double Standards', *La fondation Daniel Langlois,* accessed 11 June 2008, http://www.fondation-langlois.org/html/e/page.php?NumPage=360

Petersson, D. (2003) 'On the Aesthetics of Digitization', *Nmediac: The Journal of New Media and Culture,* accessed 18 March 2009, http://www.ibiblio.org/nmediac/summer2003/digitization_files/index.html

Plohman, A. (2001) 'Simon Penny', *La Fondation Daniel Langlois,* accessed 20 May 2008, http://www.fondation-langlois.org/html/e/page.php?NumPage=262

Polk, M. (2005) *Shadow Play.* Cambridge: Art Interactive.

Rajah, N. (1999) 'The Representation Of A New Cosmology: Immersive Virtual Reality and the Integration of Epistemologies', *Invenção: thinking the Next Millennium.*

Reas, C. and McWilliams, C. (2010) *Form+Code in Design, Art, and Architecture.* New York: Princeton Architectural Press.

Rhizome Discussion Thread (2009a) 'Wikipedia Art', *Rhizome,* accessed 4 April 2009, http://rhizome.org/editorial/2360

Rhizome Discussion Thread (2009b) 'WikiPedia as Art?', *Rhizome,* accessed 4 April 2009, http://rhizome.org/discuss/view/41713

Rhoades, T. (2011) 'From Representation to Sensation: The Transduction of Images in John F. Simon Jr.'s "Every Icon"', *The Fibreculture Journal,* accessed 9 January 2012, http://eighteen.fibreculturejournal.org/2011/10/09/fcj-125-from-representation-to-sensation-the-transduction-of-images-in-john-f-simon-jr-%E2%80%99s-%E2%80%98every-icon%E2%80%99/.

Richardson, I. (2003) 'Telebodies & Televisions: Corporeality and Agency in Technoculture', *University of Western Sydney,* accessed 5 April 2008, http://library.uws.edu.au/adt-NUWS/public/adt-NUWS20041101.172222/

Ridgway, N. (2008) 'Of the Between (Thinking the Im-mediate)', in D. Meyer-Dinkgräfe (ed.) *Consciousness, Theatre, Literature and the Arts 2007.* Newcastle: Cambridge Scholars Publishing.

Ridgway, N. (2009) 'In Excess of the Already Constituted: Interaction as Performance', in O. Kelly (ed.) *Cybercultures and New Media.* Amsterdam: Rodopi Press.

Ridgway, N. (2010) *Passing Between: Thinking With Passing Between.* Johannesburg: GALLERY AOP.

Rodemeyer, L. (2008) 'From the Diaries of Lou Sullivan: Intersubjective Discourse and the Intersection of Embodiment', *Intercorporeality and Intersubjectivity.* Dublin.

Rodowick, D. N. (2001) *Reading the Figural, Or, Philosophy after the New Media*. Durham, NC: Duke University Press.

Rokeby, D. (1990) 'Very Nervous System', *David Rokeby*, accessed 12 July 2005, http://www.davidrokeby.com/vns.html

Rokeby, D. (1995) 'Transforming Mirrors: Subjectivity and Control in Interactive Media', in S. Penny (ed.) *Critical Issues in Electronic Media*. Albany, NY: State University of New York Press.

Rokeby, D. (1998) 'The Construction of Experience: Interface as Content', in J. Clark Dodsworth (ed.) *Digital Illusion: Entertaining the Future with High Technology*. New York: ACM.

Rokeby, D. (2004) 'San Marco Flow', *David Rokeby*, accessed 16 July 2008, http://www.davidrokeby.com/smf.html

Rokeby, D. (2007) 'Machine for Taking Time (2007)', *David Rokeby*, accessed 17 June 2008, http://www.davidrokeby.com/mftt_fdl.html

Rush, M. (2003) *Video Art*. London: Thames & Hudson.

Salter, C. (2010) *Entangled: Technology and the Transformation of Performance*. Cambridge: MIT Press.

Saltz, J. (1996) 'A Short History of Rirkrit Tiravanija. (Thai Artist who Cooks Meals as Installation Art)', *Art in America*.

Savičić, G. (2007) 'Concept', *Constraint City*, accessed 12 June 2008, http://www.yugo.at/equilibre/?cat=4

Schechner, R. (1977) *Essays on Performance Theory 1970–1976*. New York: Drama Book Specialists.

Schechner, R. (1985) *Between Theatre and Anthropology*. Philadelphia, PA: University of Pennsylvania Press.

Schechner, R. (2002) *Performance Studies: An Introduction*. New York: Routledge.

Schneider, R. (1997) *The Explicit Body in Performance*. London: Routledge.

Scholz, T. and Penny, S. (2006) '[iDC] On Interdisciplinarity. An Interview with Simon Penny', *Institute for Distributed Creativity*, 20 May 2008, https://lists.thing.net/pipermail/idc/2006-March/000270.html

Scott, V. (2007) 'Bio', *Victoria Scott*, accessed 20 June 2008, http://www.redhotcoil.com/Bio_page/bio.html

Shanken, E. (2009) *Art and Electronic Media*. London: Phaidon Press.

Shannon, C.E. (1940) *A Symbolic Analysis of Relay and Switching Circuits*. Cambridge: MIT.

Shannon, C.E. (1948) 'A Mathematical Theory of Communication', *Bell System Technical Journal* 27: 379–423 and 623–56.

Sherwin, B., Kildall, S. and Stern, N. (2009) 'Wikipedia Art: A Virtual Fireside Chat Between Scott Kildall and Nathaniel Stern', *MyArtSpace.com*, accessed 5 April 2009, http://www.myartspace.com/blog/2009/02/wikipedia-art-virtual-fireside-chat.html

Simanowski, R. (2011) *Digital Art and Meaning: Reading Kinetic Poetry, Text Machines, Mapping Art, and Interactive Installations.* Minneapolis: University of Minnesota Press.

Simanowski, R. and Snibbe, S. (2006) 'Useless Programs, Useful Programmers, and the production of Social Interactive Artworks: Interview with Scott Snibbe', *Dichtung Digital*, accessed 20 February 2008, http://www.dichtung-digital.org/2006/1-Snibbe.htm

Simon, J. F. (1996) 'Every Icon: Artist's Statement', *Stadium @ Dia Center for the Arts*, accessed 18 June 2008, http://www.stadiumweb.com/everyicon/eicon_statement.html

Simon, J.F. (15 February 2012) *personal communication.*

Simondon, G. (1964) *L'individu et sa Genèse Physico-biologique (L'individuation à la Lumière des Notions de forme et D'information).* Paris: PUF.

Simondon, G. (2007) 'Technical Individualization', in J. Brouwer and A. Mulder (ed.) *Interact or Die!* Rotterdam: NAi.

Slayton, J. (2003) 'Foreword', in O. Grau, *Virtual Art: From Illusion to Immersion.* Cambridge, MA: MIT Press.

Sloane, N., Wyner, A. D. and Shannon, C. E. (1993) *Claude Elwood Shannon, Collected Papers.* New Jersey: IEEE, accessed 28 November 2007, http://en.wikipedia.org/w/index.php?title=Claude_Shannon&oldid=174056551

Snibbe, S. (1998) 'Boundary Functions', *Scott Snibbe*, accessed 1 April 2008, http://snibbe.com/scott/bf/index.htm.

Snibbe, S. (2003) 'Body, Screen and Shadow', *San Francisco Media Arts Council (SMAC) Journal.*

Snibbe, S. (2005) 'Compliant', *Scott Snibbe*, accessed 15 March 2008, http://snibbe.com/scott/screen/compliant/index.html

Snibbe, S. (2006a) 'Artist Statement', *Scott Snibbe*, accessed 20 February 2008, http://snibbe.com/scott/statement.html

Snibbe, S. (2006b) 'Deep Walls', *Scott Snibbe*, accessed 15 March 2008, http://snibbe.com/scott/mosaics/deep%20walls/deep_walls.html

Snibbe, S. (2006c) 'Shy', *Scott Snibbe*, accessed 15 March 2008, http://snibbe.com/scott/screen/shy/index.html

Snibbe, S. (8 October 2008) *Milwaukee Art Musem panel discussion.*

Sobchack, V. (1994) 'The Scene of the Screen: Envisioning Cinematc and Electronic "Presence"', in H. U. Gumbrecht and K. L. Pfeiffer (ed.) *Materialities of Communication.* Stanford, CA: Stanford University Press.

Sorial, S. (2004) 'Heidegger, Jean-Luc Nancy, and the Question of Dasein's Embodiment: an Ethics of Touch and Spacing', *Philosophy Today* 48(2): 216–30.

Spigelman, C. (2001) 'Argument and Evidence in the Case of the Personal', *College English* 64(1): 63-87.

Springgay, S., Irwin, R.L. and Kind, S.W. (2005) 'A/R/Tography as Living Inquiry Through Art and Text', *Qualitative Inquiry* 11: 897–912.

Stelarc (1996) 'Ping Body: A Performance by Stelarc', *Stelarc,* accessed 20 June 2008, http://www.stelarc.va.com.au/pingbody/index.html

Stelarc (2012) 'Suspensions', *Stelarc,* accessed 19 January 2012, http://stelarc.org/?catID=20316.

Stern, N. (2005) 'Compressionism, Process Documentation', *nathaniel stern,* accessed 20 June 2008, http://nathanielstern.com/2006/compressionism/

Stern, N. (2012) 'In Production', *Networked: a networked book about networked art,* accessed 15 December 2012, http://stern.networkedbook.org

Stiles, K. (1969) 'Valie Export Virtual Tour (catalog text via 1969)', *The Galleries at Moore,* accessed 10 December 2007, http://thegalleriesatmoore.org/publications/valie/valietour5.shtml

Stone, A. R. (1991) 'Will the Real Body Please Stand Up?', in M. Benedikt (ed.) *Cyberspace: First Steps.* Cambridge: MIT Press.

Sullivan, N. (2004) 'Being-Exposed: "The Poetics of Sex" and Other Matters of Tact', *Transformations Journal* 8, accessed 8 March 2005, http://www.transformationsjournal.org/journal/issue_08/article_04.shtml

Sullivan, J. and Lozano-Hemmer, R. (2002) 'Body Movies - Experimental: an Interview with Rafael Lozano-Hemmer', *I.D. online,* accessed 8 July 2005, http://www.idonline.com/imdr02/body.asp

Terranova, T. (2010) 'Another Life: social cooperation and a-organic life', *Digithum* 12: 33-58.

The Millefiore Effect (2002) 'Front', *Millefiore Presents,* accessed 12 December 2007, http://www.millefiore.info/.

Thompson, N. and Sholette, G. (ed.) (2006) *The Interventionists: Users' Manual for the Creative Disruption of Everyday Life.* Cambridge, MA: MIT Press.

Thrift, N. (2008) *Non-representational Theory: Space, Politics, Affect.* New York: Routledge.

Turbulence.org (2012) 'networked: a networked book about networked art', accessed 19 January 2012, http://networkedbook.org/

Turner, V. (1985) 'Foreword', in R. Schechner *Between Theatre and Anthropology.* Philadelphia: University of Pennsylvania Press.

Turner, B. S. and Featherstone, M. (1995) 'Body and Society: An Introduction', *Body and Society* 1(1): 1-12.

Turner, J., Kildall, S., Second_Front, Chenille, T., lizsolo, a., Michinaga, M., Spire, T. and Browne, P. L. (2008) 'Second Front: A Pioneering Avatar Performance Art Group in Second Life', *Second Front,* accessed 2008 March 2008, http://slfront.blogspot.com/

Utterback, C. (2000) 'Art Gallery 2000', *SIGGRAPH,* accessed 20 January 2008, http://www.siggraph.org/artdesign/gallery/S00/interactive/thumbnail21.html

Utterback, C. (2002a) 'Designing Systems for Human Interaction, Not Human-Computer Interaction', *Core77,* accessed 18 March 2008, http://www.core77.com/reactor/utterback.html

Utterback, C. (2002b) 'External Measures 2001', *Camille Utterback,* accessed 20 March 2008, http://www.camilleutterback.com/externalmeasures.html

Utterback, C. (2004a) 'Camille Utterback Responds in Turn', *Electronic Book Review,* accessed 20 January 2008, http://www.electronicbookreview.com/thread/firstperson/tabular

Utterback, C. (2004b) 'External Measures 2003', *Camille Utterback,* accessed 20 March 2008, http://www.camilleutterback.com/externalmeasures2003.html

Utterback, C. (2004c) 'Liquid Time Series', *Camille Utterback,* 19 March 2008, http://www.camilleutterback.com/liquidtime.html

Utterback, C. (2004d) 'Unusual Positions', *Electronic Book Review,* accessed 17 January 2008, http://www.electronicbookreview.com/thread/firstperson/multitiered

Utterback, C. (2005) 'Untitled 5', *Camille Utterback,* accessed 20 March 2008, http://www.camilleutterback.com/untitled5.html

Utterback, C. (2006) 'Artist Statement', *Camille Utterback,* URL (21 January 2008): http://www.camilleutterback.com/statement.html.

Utterback, C. (2012) 'Shifting Time - San Jose', *Camille Utterback,* accessed 30 March 2012, http://camilleutterback.com/projects/shifting-time-san-jose/

Utterback, C. and Achituv, R. (2000) 'TextRain', *A Mínima,* accessed 20 January 2008, http://aminima.net/wp/?p=542&language=en

Varela, F., Thompson, E. and Rosch, E. (1991) *The Embodied Mind: Cognitive Science and Human Experience.* Cambridge, MA: MIT Press.

Wakkary, R. (1997) 'About Every Icon', *Stadium Web,* accessed 2008, http://www.stadiumweb.com/everyicon/eicon_info.html

Watson, T. (2005) 'Thesis', *Theodore Watson Projects,* accessed 12 June 2008, http://muonics.net/school/fall04/thesis/

Watson, T. (2006) 'Audio Space', *Theodore Watson Projects,* accessed 12 June 2008, http://muonics.net/v4/?id1=15&xPos=0.

Watson, T. (16 April 2008) *personal communication.*

Wehage, P. (2009) 'In the Eye of the Beholder', *Akahele,* accessed 4 April 2009, http://akahele.org/2009/03/in-the-eye-of-the-beholder/

Wheeler, J. (1998) 'From _The End of Science_, by John Horgan', *Stanford University Web Site,* accessed November 2007, http://suif.stanford.edu/~jeffop/WWW/wheeler.txt

Whidden, T. (2008) 'Net Art 2.5 private beta', *Rhizome.org,* accessed 31 March 2012, http://rhizome.org/discuss/view/37531/.

Whitehead, A.N. (1938) *Modes of Thought.* New York: Macmillan.

Whitehead, A.N. (1970) *Nature and Life.* Westport, CT: Greenwood Publishing Group.

Wooster, A.-S. (1991) 'Reach out and Touch Someone: The Romance of Interactivity', in D. Hall and S. J. Fifer (eds) *Illuminating Video.* New York: Aperture.

Yela, M. (2011) *Position / Opposition: The Book as Relationship.* Johannesburg: GALLERY AOP.

Zanni, C. (2005) 'Average Shoveler', *Rhizome,* accessed 15 December 2011, http://rhizome.org/artbase/artwork/31867/

Zarrilli, P. B. (1986a) 'Review: Toward a Definition of Performance Studies, Part I', *Theatre Journal* 38(3): 372-6.

Zarrilli, P. B. (1986b) 'Review: Toward a Definition of Performance Studies, Part II', *Theatre Journal* 38(4): 493-6.

Zuniga Shaw, N. (2007) 'The Living Map and Other Stories of Becoming Re-enchanted with Where We Are', in Y. Hardt and K. Maar (eds) *Tanz – Metropole – Provinz: Yearbook of the Society of Dance Research.* Munster: LIT Verlag.

Zuniga Shaw, N. (2009) 'Animating Choreography (video) at TEDxColumbus', *YouTube,* accessed 4 January 2012, http://www.youtube.com/watch?v=dHqVJkgFNZY

Zuniga Shaw, N. (2010a) 'Synchronous Objects, Choreographic Objects, and the Translation of Dancing Ideas', in F. Corin and B. Andrien (eds)

*De l'un a l'autre: composer, apprendre et partarger en mouvemetns.* Brussels: Contredanse.

Zuniga Shaw, N. (2010b) 'Synchronous Objects, reproduced', *ISEA2010 RUHR,* accessed 3 January 2012, http://www.isea2010ruhr.org/programme/performances/synchronous-objects

Zuniga Shaw, N. (6 January 2012), *personal communication.*

# Index